Black Rainbow

Black Rainbow

*How words healed me: My journey
through depression*

RACHEL KELLY

First published in Great Britain in 2014 by Yellow Kite Books
An imprint of Hodder & Stoughton
An Hachette UK company

3

A CIP catalogue record for this title is available from the British Library

Hardback ISBN 978 1 444 78999 7
eBook ISBN 978 1 444 78998 0

CLACKMANNANSHIRE COUNCIL	
31513400149154	
Bertrams	16/08/2014
615.8516	£16.99
ADU	AN

Dedication

For Sebastian

Contents

Chapter One

Bless the Bed That I Lie On

MID-MAY 1997

Sunday, mid-May 1997

One day I fell ill.

It began between six and seven o'clock on a Sunday evening in May, when, as was routine, I started putting our two children to bed.

Our little trio set off up the three flights of stairs to the children's attic bedrooms, the kitchen abandoned as if an army had retreated from battle. On one hip rested three-month-old George, his plump legs slotted around me. With my free arm I held onto two-year-old Edward's hand as we slowly climbed stair by stair, talking of the day we had spent together: how he had fallen over in the park near the ducks and Daddy had given him a ride on his shoulders; how I had dropped a plate – silly Mummy! – while we were having tea but it didn't matter as we didn't want that plate anyway; and could we remember exactly how many fish fingers he had eaten? We could not.

All the busyness of the day slowed as the three of us shared a bath, my wound-up limbs softening in the hot pine-scented water with baby George on my tummy and Edward at my side. After our bath, I lined up the boys on a white towel on the chequered bathroom floor. Then, in our usual

1

post-bathtime ritual, I deposited noisy, messy kisses on each of their rounded tummies before Edward imitated me and kissed his brother.

The last few months had been exhausting but life was getting easier: George was now more or less sleeping through the night. I was beginning to think about my return to being a reporter when my maternity leave ended in three months.

I could hear the clatter of Sebastian tidying up downstairs. So far, so normal, and so lucky.

But by seven my heart was pulsing noticeably. I had a feeling of observing myself as I sat down to breastfeed George. It was as if there were two of me, and my thoughts had been diverted to someone else's head. When Sebastian stepped into the room to offer me a glass of water, I heard someone saying 'Thank you', only to realise after a few seconds that the someone was me.

By the time the two of us had supper an hour later I was sweating, though the night air that filtered in through the French windows of our little front room was cool. I felt a strange lightness in my body, despite being heavier after having another baby.

I tried to talk about our day and our children, Sebastian's forthcoming week at the office and my return to work. Already I felt as if I had lost a limb during those hours when I wasn't with the children. But I kept having to ask Sebastian to repeat what he was saying.

As he switched off the bedside light at about ten-thirty, Sebastian mumbled that it was my turn if George woke in the night. He had done a run of listening out in case George cried, for the previous four or five nights. 'Fine,' I replied, while registering a tightening of my shoulders. Sebastian rolled over towards me as if he had sensed something was wrong. 'You'll be okay with George,' he said, giving me a hug. 'You can always rest in the day if it's a busy night.'

I told myself the odd feelings would pass. It wasn't as if I hadn't listened out for George before. I knew how to settle a baby back to sleep, even if I had missed the last few nights and felt strangely out of practice. Of course I knew what to do. For goodness' sake, he was my second baby.

Soon Sebastian lay deeply asleep, like a dog after a good walk. As the clock ticked, I tossed. And turned. And stirred and turned and tossed. I went to the bathroom, opened the bedroom window more widely, closed the curtains more tightly, rearranged the pillows. A few minutes later I reshuffled the pillows, closed the window, nudged the curtains open and returned to the bathroom.

All the while I had refused to look at my alarm clock. It would be better not to know how long I had been lying awake. But eventually I looked. It was nearly one.

My shoulders tightened another notch and my breathing became shallower. I was sweating heavily. I began to hug a pillow against my chest like a shield in the face of an unknown enemy. We were used to an early-ish bedtime on Sunday nights, no later than eleven. Like everyone, I had occasional insomnia, staying awake for an hour here or there, and getting enough sleep had always been something of a preoccupation with me; but this acute sleeplessness was new. I laid the alarm clock face down on my bedside table.

Two minutes later I decided that I could at least be of some use and check the children. George seemed to be visibly absorbing sleep's nourishment, the smoothness of his even pink skin only interrupted by the surprising blackness of his thick lashes. I inhaled the sweetness of his breath and could almost hear his pulse. If only I could shrink and snuggle into George's cot and become a baby again myself.

Then I gazed at Edward's curls in the stillness of his room next door. His arms were thrown back behind his head in happy abandon; a smile seemed to play across his mouth and every now and then he twitched as though enjoying a delicious dream. I knelt over him and breathed in deeply, murmuring under my breath the prayer that I would always recite at the children's bedtime. Now I hoped its magic would work on me.

> *Matthew, Mark, Luke and John*
> *Bless the bed that I lie on.*
> *Four corners to my bed,*
> *Four angels round my head,*
> *One to watch, and one to pray,*
> *Two to bear my soul away.*

My heart was still beating just as wildly when I finished. I almost slammed the door before marching downstairs, fists clenched and eyes pricking with hot tears.

Perhaps, I thought, it was because I was hungry. I went to the kitchen and quickly ate some cereal, then a slice of toast and a banana. My hands were trembling and I managed to cut myself as I sliced the bread. My mother had always advised starch as a cure for insomnia but all that happened was that, back in bed, I felt sick as well as wide awake, as alert as if I were about to sit an exam.

The hours ticked by and my sleeplessness threatened to encompass the whole night, as did my worries. I worried about my nausea, breathlessness and palpitating heart. I worried about how I would manage tomorrow, senseless from lack of sleep: the getting up and getting dressed and making breakfast (had I used up all the milk?), the to-do lists and the play dates, the dry-cleaning and the dishwasher, the buggies and the promises I'd made, my life as mother, wife and daughter.

And, beyond those immediate worries, I worried, too, about my transition back to work. I worried that my ability to be a good mother would be compromised by being divided between the children and work. I worried that my ability to be a decent journalist would be compromised by worrying about the children. I worried about missing the job I loved if I stayed at home. I worried about missing the children if I went back to work. I worried that in my present state, I wouldn't be able to fulfil any role at all.

Such worries had been present for a while but now, lying sleepless and frightened in the middle of the night, they seemed to multiply, overwhelming me like creepers choking a ruined building. I could find no peaceful thought in my head. My mind no longer seemed to be my own. I kept trying to think of soothing subjects, happy memories, splashing with the children in the bath only a few hours earlier. But the worries wrenched me back. The spacey feeling was getting worse, my heart beat faster, all my reactions were horribly speeded up. Perhaps I was having a heart attack.

I retraced my steps, quickly this time, practically leaping upstairs to check the children once more, then swiftly back down all the way to the moonlit kitchen, the floor now slightly sticky beneath my bare feet where I had spilt some milk. I had never noticed the particular feel of the floor before, or, moments later, the touch of the sheets as I hurriedly got back into bed. Despite my racing heart, I tried to keep very, very still, like a child hiding from a monster.

The clock seemed to tick more and more loudly by my bedside as my hearing became more acute. Every second clicked past as though a gong were being struck. I was aware of each beat of my heart and my body's slightest shift, again with a sense that I was observing someone else. I kept wondering if I was better off lying on my left side. Or my right. If I was too hot. Or too cold. Or was it a case of quieting the ticking by muffling the clock under a pillow? Or the opposite, calmly facing the time again?

Maybe I should try to read. But then I might wake Sebastian by putting the light on. Was there a noise bothering me? I could use earplugs. But then I wouldn't hear George cry, should he wake up. That was my responsibility. At least I could manage that.

I went downstairs again and tried to sleep in the sitting room, fashioning a boat-like bed out of the sofa's red cushions. But the spacey buzzing in my head worsened. No sooner had I settled than I realised I wouldn't be able to hear George two floors up. Then I decamped to the spare bed in Edward's room. At least I wouldn't miss the children crying from here. But I felt even worse. An itinerant in my own house. I returned to our room, still sleepless, still hyper-alert, my heart still racing.

As dawn broke and the first inkling of sunlight began to colour the day, I imagined I could hear George crying. I was sure I had heard him. And if so, at least there had been a point to my vigil. Up I went again – only to find him sleeping like the baby he was.

In the end I stayed up all night, as vigilant as a soldier on watch, and just as lonely.

The next day the house was littered with nests where I had tried and failed to sleep.

Monday, mid-May 1997

If I acted normally, I reasoned, I would feel normal. So I told Sebastian only that I'd had a bit of a bad night. We exchanged our usual brief morning chit-chat as he rushed to get to work. Live to fight another day – it was one motto on which I had been raised as a child. We talked of our respective days ahead, my electric toothbrush whirring. He had documents to prepare for his job at Goldman Sachs, where he worked long hours and travelled a huge amount. I planned my usual trip to the park with the children. Act normal, I kept saying to myself. Refasten activity to its rightful hour: breakfast at breakfast-time; lunch at lunchtime; and sup at supper-time. Then you will sleep at bedtime.

So I washed and dressed in my favourite white cotton shirt for luck. Then I breathed deeply and went to get the children up.

Normal meant being up in the day and going to bed at night. It meant spooning porridge into Edward and strapping George into his pram for our morning outing to the park; it meant unmatched socks and scraped knees, the hiss of the kettle and the faded pinks and reds of the chequered table-cloth. It meant deadheading flowers in the front garden and watering pots of geraniums on the terrace of our tall, wisteria-clad house in west London. (The terrace doubled as a sandpit full of small diggers for Edward.)

Normal meant trying to rest after lunch while the children napped and making sure the prawns had defrosted for the fish pie in time for Sebastian's return. It meant calls to make, *Thomas the Tank Engine* to read, dry-cleaning to collect, friends to see, articles to read and pyjamas to sort. It meant snatching a look at the papers while breastfeeding George and then hunting for Edward's duck in the bubbly bath when all three of us got into the tub.

It meant swapping notes with Sebastian about our respective days and appreciating the blast he brought back from the outside world. That night he came home with my favourite apricot tart from the late-night Spanish patisserie nearby.

All this I did. But inside I felt no different. Physically I remained as helpless as if a spell had been cast on me by a wicked witch in a fairy tale. As I queued at the dry-cleaners I had tried to ignore the fact that the spacey lightness of being hadn't gone away. Now it felt as though my head had been scissored from my body and had a life of its own. There was a further tightening of the stomach and an alarming twitchiness in my arms and legs.

I had had short nights before; I knew that headachey feeling the next day. This was different, as if the symptoms had been forced into me with hostile intent. I felt as if I were a delicate glass bottle over-filled with a livid liquid that threatened to explode. I was bursting with an active sense of dread that disaster was about to strike. The car was about to crash, the boat to sink. Something terrible was going to happen and I couldn't do anything to stop it.

That evening, when Sebastian and I sat down to supper, I had to explain away hardly touching the food. After we'd eaten he went up to check on the children and I tidied up. The tablecloth was just as chequered and the radio was still tuned to Radio 4 and the door creaked just as it always had. But everything now seemed different and bewildering, as if I were at a fairground where all the shapes were distorted.

I sat down carefully and stayed very still, trying to remember what people did in emergencies. They drank hot sweet tea and flasks of soup. I was in such a rush to heat the tin of tomato soup I found at the back of the cupboard that I only half warmed it through and forgot to stir as I did so. I thought how odd it was that the soup could be streaked with hot and cold at the same time. I just managed to get to the downstairs bathroom in time but there was no disguising the smell of vomit afterwards.

I could not have imagined that by the end of the week I would have lost almost a stone and that I wouldn't even be pleased.

The next few days were blurred. I wish I could impose more chronological order on events but I know one thing was consistent: I had this terrifying sensation that I was continuously falling, hurtling downwards as if on a crashing plane. I had once been on a plane that landed under emergency conditions in Dubai. The feeling was similar: I was braced, rigid with fear, waiting for the crash. This time the landing didn't happen.

I no longer pretended I was fine to Sebastian, who hadn't believed me anyway. He now gave the children their bath, made supper and listened out for George at night. Any petty bickering about whose turn it was to load the dishwasher evaporated as we united against the common foe of whatever it was that was taking me over.

Meanwhile, our nanny Julie looked after the children in the day. Our two pressured careers with long hours based far from home had given us little option but to hire a nanny when I returned to work a few months after Edward was born. Being based in Wapping and working in a newsroom meant I often didn't return till seven and none of the nurseries I investigated were willing to cover such hours. Julie allowed me to return to the career I loved. She was a disciplined, trained professional who loved children and produced perfectly arranged plates of orderly food for them, little mounds of mashed potatoes and neatly aligned fish fingers. Even the peas seemed to line up in a tidy fashion for her. She had continued to work for us through this period of my second maternity leave. The house felt a little crowded with both of us at home, but we knew the arrangement was temporary.

Now, thanks to Julie, the household ran smoothly and the children were scrubbed and fed. I had nothing to worry about in the day, nor any person for whom I should wake at night.

I hardly noticed what was going on. Every ounce of my being was devoted to my own survival. I still felt as though I were falling. Naturally I kept trying to stop myself by holding onto something, ideally Sebastian. His arms were a livid red from my grip. My need to hold tightly on to him meant we mostly retreated from family life to our room, for fear of alarming others in the house. I cried much of the time, begging to be better and for what felt like madness to stop.

I longed to be pottering in the garden, with the sun on my face and my hands muddy from wet earth. I wished to be upstairs tucking the children into bed under their Bob the Builder duvets. Or in the kitchen making banana muffins with Edward. But my world had shrunk to one room. The strangeness of it was terrifying.

The only time I was quiet was when others came near. I hid under the covers if I heard Julie coming up the stairs. I felt I had to appear normal in front of her, be the competent mother who could get back to work with no problems; that was the deal that underpinned the household and our jobs. The pretence exhausted me further. I also hid if I heard the children, as I didn't want to frighten them, Edward in particular.

Sebastian stayed by my side as much as he was able while still caring for the children and going to work. He remained calm, seemingly taking in his stride my sudden strange behaviour, and helping in practical ways. While I didn't move from our room, he at least made sorties down to the kitchen to bring me trays of food. The apricot tart he tried to tempt me with lay untouched. Given that I now began to protest loudly if he left me alone, even if he went to the bathroom or nipped downstairs, he asked my mother to come and help. If neither Sebastian nor my mother were there, I held on tightly to the edge of the bed.

While the boys slept without a murmur, my insomnia continued as the week wore on. I might catch an hour or so in the night, but not enough to enable me to get up in the day. Bone-tired, I lay outwardly still, worn out by the effort of clinging on; inside, my body was furiously busy. I had a permanent headache, as though dozens of vicious, heat-maddened wasps were massed behind my eye sockets, stinging my soft, unprotected brain. My rancid stomach fiercely knotted and reknotted itself, spinning in a sharp-pointed pirouette. I no longer even seemed to be able to throw up. I kept repeating that I was going to crash.

The only faint relief came from lying underwater in a near-scalding bath emptied of plastic ducks and patterned flannels.

My head and stomach were soothed by the friendly warmth and only my mouth and nose were not submerged, like an otter. Sometimes I would almost fall asleep, only to be jolted back to consciousness by the slowly cooling water. I momentarily wondered if my symptoms had gone, only to realise they hadn't. I sat in the bath crying.

Very soon there was no difference between night and day. In the space of just a few days, my life had completely unravelled. A trapdoor had opened beneath me. I no longer struggled to get up. I stopped getting dressed. I couldn't think of a single thing I could do to get the crashing sensation to go away.

I worried I would never be well. I worried about Edward and George being left largely in Julie's care. I had long worried about tiptoeing out of the door every morning to go to work and only getting back at seven. Now I feared I might never be able to look after them at all, nor return to work. And I dared not confess any of this to Julie. Or to anyone. Saying it aloud might make it more true.

As the week progressed and it became clear that I was bedridden and always at home, Julie started taking the children out early to the park and staying out of the house as much as she could, naturally drawn to cheerier environments. Life was bleaker still with the house emptied of their jolly chatter. As a nanny used to being in sole charge, she didn't welcome having a mother and now a granny at home, too. I couldn't help feeling threatened. At least she couldn't replace my role of feeding George, which forced her back to base and a baby into my arms. This was my one moment when I rallied slightly and felt I was still a mother, my other faint relief from the crashing. But even this happiness was under threat. Given how little I was eating, it was hardly surprising that my milk was drying up. My appetite had not returned. My mouth was permanently dry.

And my worries continued to multiply, endlessly spinning round my head: that I would never recover, that I would never again care for the children or Sebastian, that I would never get back to work, that I couldn't fathom what was happening to me. What was this illness? Cancer? An impending heart attack? A brain tumour? Was something causing the sleeplessness, or was the sleeplessness causing everything else?

Answers came there none. The cloud of insects became ever blacker. My head was now bursting with the swarm within. A few black thoughts had been replaced with a lowering darkness of thousands of wasps devouring the insides of my skull, swarming relentlessly and stinging me with furious, hate-filled abandon. There was nothing I could do to stop the violence of their assault.

It seemed I would never sleep again, for all that I was permanently in bed.

Wednesday, mid-May 1997

From feeling normal to being bedridden had taken around three days and three nights. Each second of each minute of each hour of each day had been lived at such a pitch of intensity that to me it felt like an age.

On Wednesday my mother and Sebastian hatched a plan: maybe it would help if I went to my parents' house, just a few streets away. My mother scooped me into her arms in my dressing gown, drove me back and put me to rest in my rose-wallpapered childhood bedroom while she watched over me.

She brought up the supper I had most appreciated as a child when I was unwell: roast chicken and mashed potatoes. She sat down with me to eat on the edge of the bed, hoping her company and a properly laid tray with a linen napkin and a small bunch of flowers would defeat my nausea. But what had once been soothing in its familiarity was now as bewildering as my own beloved kitchen. I retched when I tasted the chicken; maggoty insects seemed to be crawling out of the rosebuds on the walls and the flowers on the tray. I caught a glimpse of red eyes as my mother walked towards the door with the barely touched food.

We returned to my house on Thursday morning. There was hushed whispering outside the bedroom door as my husband and my mother tried to decide what to do. My mother argued that they should turn to her doctor, who had known me as a child and might come to the house. Persuaded by the desperation in my mother's voice that this was an emergency, he agreed.

In his mid-sixties with pepper-and-salt hair and a face creviced from a life of caring for others, Dr Ross exuded certainty and competence. He had been our family doctor when we were growing up, though I had ceased to see him as an adult. However distressed we were as children entering his surgery, he would always wash his hands first with a lavender-scented soap, which suffused the room. Whatever was wrong, the slow deliberation of this ritual would mean we had quietened by the time he turned to us.

He kept up his imperturbable demeanour when he came upstairs and found me moaning in bed more than twenty years later. My mother's face was pale. Dr Ross had known her for forty years but he later confided that he had rarely seen her so stricken. He put his arm around her, reminding her that I had always been an anxious child. She steadied herself, thanking him for coming while expertly wheeling a curious Edward out of the door and telling him, 'No, darling, that's Dr Ross's briefcase.'

I was adamant that I didn't want to see any doctor. Doctors meant pills. Pills meant I might not be able to feed George. That was my only meaningful action, the delivery of the liquid gold I could still manufacture, just. So all the niceties that had governed my childhood relationship with Dr Ross dissolved. When he arrived, I asked him to leave. Even saying it was an effort, but as he approached the bed I surprised myself with the strength of my voice. I begged those who should have been my most loyal supporters: 'PLEASE tell him to leave. Take him away!'

My mother tried to calm me as I thrashed in an effort to escape him but I was encircled by the three of them, blocking the light from the windows and holding me still. Then I was shocked at the sudden ache of an injection in my arm. The jab of some mysterious sedative washed through me like a warm bath. I felt my eyelids close with the firmness of a door slamming shut. The much-longed-for sleep came quickly and easily. I was finally gone.

Chapter Two

My Grace Is Sufficient for Thee

MID-MAY TO MID-JUNE 1997

Friday, mid-May 1997

When I woke from a dreamless sleep, for a split second I felt elated. The black solvent of sleep had dissolved my worries and embraced me for a full ten hours. Now I had slept, I would be better. But a second later a hot jab of pain made me realise that I felt as ill as before.

I couldn't believe I could simultaneously be alive and feel such pain. Everything throbbed. It was a pain like no other, suffusing every bit of me. I had become pain, and pain had become me. If only it could just affect an arm or a leg. I would have swapped everything for a containable agony. If only there had been a gashed lip, some vomit or blood to demonstrate what I was feeling. No one realised how much I hurt. No one understood. There was nobody to whom I could explain this total disquiet.

I lay motionless. I felt I was without anyone or anything. I had seen Dr Ross and he didn't have the answer. There was no magic cure for this curse. Logically, there seemed little use in seeing another doctor. It was over.

Had I in truth been properly alone, I don't think I would have moved again. I don't know what would have happened.

Luckily those around me took matters into their own hands. The rapidity of my collapse, the speed with which I had lost weight, my inability to eat, my constant screaming, the physical agony, the sheer sense of not knowing what was going on – all these things alarmed them mightily. They knew something was seriously wrong; I was normally optimistic and uncomplaining. As a family we were out of our depth, not waving but drowning. It was too worrying to be left in the hands of a GP.

It was time to act swiftly. This time, we turned to a doctor who was a specialist in these mysterious matters.

Friday evening, mid-May 1997

We met Dr Fischer late that Friday evening at a hospital nearby. He had fitted us in as an emergency. The room was small and furnished with an orange sofa. Dr Fischer was bearded and focused. My husband did most of the talking initially. Naturally calm and with an air of authority, he had always been good at coping in times of crisis and was the sort of person to whom others turned for help

I didn't know what was happening, I began, when the doctor turned to me. 'Let's start with your date of birth,' he replied calmly. Born in September 1965, aged thirty-one. Yes, this was the first time I had felt like this. I thought he would be more impressed with my symptoms, but when he asked about the extent of the not eating and not sleeping he seemed unsurprised when I said I had all but stopped doing both. I told him about the pain and again he was unsurprised. 'Many of these physical symptoms are classic signs of a "depressive episode",' Dr Fischer said. It was the first time I had heard of such a thing.

'But I thought being depressed meant feeling sad and gloomy,' I said. 'I just hurt.'

Privately I thought Dr Ross must have referred us to the wrong specialist. Perhaps I should be seeing a cardiologist or neurologist. I wasn't feeling sad, just experiencing painful physical symptoms. The doctor must be wrong. I was maddened that I hadn't been able to explain the extent of the pain or to describe its nature in such a way that he could give me a proper diagnosis of this appalling illness. And I was disillusioned that this supposed specialist had no explanation, other than a diagnosis that was clearly a mistake.

As to treatment, Dr Fischer was respectful of my preoccupation with sleep and suggested that one response would be to start taking antidepressants, which could also help with insomnia. But I wasn't depressed, I reiterated, I just couldn't sleep. The notion that I should start taking antidepressants was crazy. Okay, then a sleeping pill might be the answer for now, he conceded. If we righted the sleep, my anxiety might subside. We need not start antidepressants straight away.

I still cried when I looked at the little blue zopiclone pills he had prescribed and Sebastian had collected from the hospital pharmacy. Surely I could sleep on my own? There was nothing wrong with me or my life to cause this degree of sleeplessness. Yes, I had some worries, but nothing that warranted symptoms as severe as those I was suffering. It was unfathomable that I had been diagnosed with depression and been given drugs.

After hours of argument with myself, I was finally persuaded by Sebastian that I should take the pill. Dr Fischer was highly experienced and we should respect his expertise, he said. It would be the first step to being better. So I took the first pill, my mouth saturated with its caustic taste. It was medieval in its power to bludgeon me to sleep. Later I would learn that a symptom of depression is feeling unable to make any decision at all, including whether or not to take a pill in order to feel better.

The next morning I managed to get up and proceed slowly through the day. Somehow the sleeping pill had worked when the injection hadn't. All my symptoms had shrunk to a horrid metallic taste in my mouth, but even the taste had gone by noon. I went downstairs, played diggers with Edward, who was gratifyingly pleased to see me, and I ate a proper lunch. Aha! I was right. There was nothing wrong with me – I just needed a good night's sleep, as my grandmother had always maintained. I could get back to being busy, and busy was good. I had snapped the trapdoor closed.

I was determined not to take another sleeping pill that night. If I did, I might fall into the addiction trap and then I really would be ill. No more pills. Nothing was wrong.

My mother agreed that I was better, delighted at the turnaround. 'You do seem quite all right,' she clucked when she popped in to see me. 'Never trust a man with a beard!'

My optimism had resurfaced. I felt reassuringly normal. And I managed to doze through much of the night, too, without a pill. Just as the bad fairies had temporarily spirited me away, now the good fairies were working on my behalf. It seemed like magic, as if someone had waved their wand. I even managed to hug my husband.

Monday, late May 1997

Despite my reservations, Sebastian took me back to visit Dr Fischer at the same hospital two days later. It was a precautionary measure, my family told me, just to make sure, though they all agreed I was back to normal.

I noticed more about Dr Fischer this time. He was neither distant nor overly intimate but had a manner that encouraged mutual respect. Though small, he felt substantial. He listened rather than talked and wrote on sheets of white paper with a silver fountain pen and smooth-flowing midnight-blue ink. I couldn't see what he wrote, other than the phrase 'high functioning'.

I explained politely that I didn't need him or his pills. I prided myself on my social skills and graciously told him how grateful I was for his help. I tried to charm him by saying how marvellous he had been in helping me out, while simultaneously glossing over what had happened to avoid any future dealings with him. For despite my positive talk, and however much I wanted to deny the whole experience, he had become associated with something terrifying. Later I would become more aware of this mind trickery: the ability of one part of me to mask something seriously wrong in an effort to keep up appearances and continue in what I believed to be a normal way.

So yes, I had managed to more or less get through the night, thanks. I really was okay, thanks so much. I had a very nice life, sorry to disappoint, no grand tragedy I could point to, very boring really. Yes, I was busy, and yes, it was true I worried about coping with everything and was often tired. But all our friends were tired! We were at that stage in life. I liked being busy. Job at a newspaper, husband working hard too, he had stood as a parliamentary candidate in the general election only a few weeks earlier, and yes, I had managed to be at the count despite just having had a baby. Okay, I had to admit I did at times feel overwhelmed. I had found it hard to support Sebastian's political life as well as look after a baby, yes. But I liked juggling everything. And things would be easier now the election was over. I just wanted to get back to normal.

When Dr Fischer gently raised the subject of how ill I had felt, I swiftly dismissed the severity of my symptoms.

We had a long and (it seemed to me) largely irrelevant chat about my life and my family. My loves were: planting bulbs, poetry (favourite poet George Herbert), watching thrillers, cooking with Edward, having friends to supper, altering clothes, matchmaking girlfriends and dancing to anything with a recognisable beat and tune. My dislikes? Nothing, really, apart from driving and lemon tart. Family consisted of an older sister (writer), younger brother (lawyer), loving childhood, professional parents. All in all something of a blessed life, not at all the sort that would suggest depression. Indeed, so lucky did I feel that it didn't seem right to tell him any more details of my charmed existence. He had got the wrong patient: all rather embarrassing, really, as clearly there were some very sick people out there for him to attend to.

As Sebastian and I got up to leave, Dr Fischer asked to see a photograph of me taken before I became unwell, which he had asked me to bring along. I showed him a recent picture, of me sitting on the doorstep hugging Edward and George, all of us bathed in spring sunshine.

I didn't realise the significance of the request. Dr Fischer later explained that it was a useful pointer to what I had been like before I became ill, and the state to which he wished me to return. Psychiatrists are in the unenviable position of not knowing their patients before depression strikes and robs them of their identities. I couldn't help noticing that he didn't return the photo.

We parted, as far as I was concerned, for ever. It had been lovely to meet him, I said. 'Best of luck,' he replied, shaking my hand deliberately, thereby setting up the professional distance he always kept from his patients. It was a handshake I would come to know well and a gesture I would come to depend on more than I could possibly imagine.

Then it was night-time. Right, I thought: steady now. I can handle this. For the first few hours I lay still and breathed calmly. Steady, I kept repeating to myself as if talking to a flighty horse. But then the worrying began: minor problems distorted in the small hours as in a fairground mirror till they became huge. If I couldn't sleep, what would become of me?

Mind swiftly led to body. All the agonising symptoms were back, taking charge once again of my stomach and head. I didn't know what was happening. My body gave physical expression to my fear. I went over the same ground, deepening the pathways as I trod over and over the same worries: the children, the job, the future, feeling so unwell. Now I was in a different part of the nightmare fairground, this time like a skater who carves ever deeper and deeper patterns in the ice. If I couldn't sleep . . .

I felt as though I had been inching back from oblivion on to solid land, collapsing in a happy heap on the clifftop and gripping the clumps of grass, only to be kicked back into free fall, as one by one my fingers lost their hold. My wounded hands were slipping; I was falling and once again there was nothing to stop me. The solidity had gone out of the world.

I was loath to wake the sleeping figure next to me but I

really was beginning to fear for my sanity. I eventually prodded Sebastian awake in the small hours.

I wept even more with an audience, as Sebastian held me in his arms and stroked my hair. I wept as I realised I was seriously ill. I wept as I realised I was indeed at the mercy of my mind, which was sickening my body, and I hadn't closed that trapdoor after all. I wept with the exhaustion of knowing that my spirit was slowly evaporating. I wept with the terror of the utter uncertainty of what was happening, and the longing to return to the life I loved. Maybe it was my fault. Maybe I hadn't appreciated my life enough, or the people in it. Maybe this was a punishment. But surely I had now been punished enough?

My night off had been an interlude, an illusion. The avalanche of the illness might have stalled but now it was relentlessly rolling forward again. Later I was to learn that the descent into depression often follows this jagged progression rather than a smooth curve, with tantalising moments of recovery punctuating the triumph of the illness.

Tuesday, late May 1997

The next day my husband phoned his office to say he would not be in until the afternoon. I persuaded him not to ring Dr Fischer. I still had the energy to argue, passionately, that this was a temporary blip. I was okay. This was still just about the sleep. I didn't want to start on any pills. Left to my own devices, I could right myself. I was a capable, sociable, multi-tasking person. My generation had been raised on a culture of self-empowerment, that with know how, medicine, and technology, problems could be solved. I would solve this problem. Why, I could write articles at high speed and edit feature pages on all matters to do with housing, homelessness and architecture and then come home and rustle up supper. I had gone back to work after Edward's birth without trouble. I would do it all again. Surely I would.

Yet I couldn't get up. My worries terrified me and were impossible to refute. They were no longer the more quotidian fears I had entertained in what now seemed a gentle early introduction to the madness. I didn't worry about getting to sleep or being a good mother or wife or even my own health. Now I imagined that George would die, Edward would die. Any attempt to distract me only confirmed my worst fears.

A friend had dropped off a video of *Dad's Army* in an effort to cheer me up. After the familiarity of the first bars of the theme music, my stomach retched at the sight of a uniform. Before my eyes, Captain Mainwaring turned from an avuncular part-time soldier, ineptly trying to mastermind the Home Guard, into a monster who might one day command my children to fight and crush their eggshell skulls. As their mother I would no longer be able to protect them. These thoughts seem unhinged in retrospect, but my logic then felt urgent and compelling. Even now, catching a glimpse of Captain Mainwaring is jarring, a reminder of how far I had lost touch with reality.

That afternoon Dr Fischer came to the house, joined the tips of his fingers in a steeple, and took charge. He would respect my obsession with sleep and I would take sleeping pills at night – for now. I would also begin on tranquillisers to keep the anxiety under control, but if that didn't work fairly swiftly, he would have to consider other approaches, including antidepressants. Tranquillisers can be highly addictive, he explained, so you can't use them for very long. My mother would look after me by day, while my husband would take over in the evenings. Dr Fischer himself would visit me at home, which was highly unusual for him. Normally he saw patients in hospital or at his surgery. But Sebastian had persuaded him I could be better looked after at home than in hospital and that it would be beneficial for me to remain in the same house as the children. Dr Fischer had agreed, on the condition that I wasn't left alone at any point.

I was too ill to care any more that taking the drugs meant that I would no longer be able to breastfeed George. I had pretty much stopped anyway. I took another sleeping pill, longing for oblivion. This was a better, muffled, calming blackness, not the terrifying blackness of my descent. As Dr Fischer left I clung to the belief that, with the help of the pills, I would be better the next day.

Wednesday, late May 1997

As soon as I woke, the pain woke, too. I was being stung, wracked, assaulted, every bit of me hurtling out of control, my mind haemorrhaging terror. Any sense of normal life had broken down.

I lay in bed, holding onto my mother's hand, squeezing it till my own was white-knuckled. If I let go, I would die, crushed by these blows, flashes, strikes, whirled into agony, lost to the pain and into oblivion. The bed was falling; I was falling. Every muscle was tense, every sense alert, fibre strained, cell taut as I lay clenched in the foetal position trying to hang on.

I had never been in such active, dynamic physical agony. It was worse than tearing in childbirth with a faulty epidural, worse than a tooth being wrenched through a fleshy gum without anaesthetic. No one understood. I wanted to explain quietly and rationally: 'I don't know how this has happened. I don't know where this has come from. I don't care. All I know is that I can't go on. Please. Stop it. Please.' But I couldn't get such a long sentence out. All I could manage was to howl again and again, 'I'm crashing.' I didn't have the physical resources needed not to howl. There was no one to rescue me.

Okay: new deal. If they couldn't save me, then I wished to die. Simple. I was happy to be buried in a hole, to be blind, dumb, deaf, to no longer feel or exist, to be put down like a wounded animal, anything to stop the fall into deeper terror.

I could no longer get out of bed to go to the bathroom but had to be picked up and carried in my foetal curl. Any change of position was out of the question; it was as if I were a victim at a crime scene, my position encircled in chalk. Once in the bathroom, I couldn't move back to bed. If I moved, I might fall further. So I lay on the floor, gripping the towel rail, refusing to let go. My mother tried to loosen my grip, finger by finger.

This was unfathomable. The only thing with which I could even begin to compare it was the time the plane I was on made its emergency landing in Dubai. As the oxygen masks came down, I felt the same racing head and clenched stomach and certainty of death. I said my prayers over and over. But despite all the emergency procedures we landed safely and everyone managed to disembark.

This time there was no getting off. I heaved with fear all day and all night, wincing with agony, metaphorically braced for the crash, hands covering my head as though I was about to be submerged beneath the wreckage. I had to stop screaming as my voice had almost gone.

Days merged into nights. Time had stopped. There was no getting up and no going to bed, no mealtimes, no dawn or dusk. All signposts of daily life had gone, there was just one terrifying merging of past, present and future, spinning out of control. I longed for a different future. But there was no escape.

The only respite over the next few days was to knock myself out with sedatives. My mother would consult Dr Fischer and give me his prescribed dose of tranquillisers, which made me dizzy and nauseous but momentarily lulled the demons. At night I would take both the tranquilliser and a sleeping pill. I devoured the pills, longing for oblivion, crunching them as if for nourishment.

A few days later, early June 1997

The strain of looking after me was taking its toll on my mother. One evening, feeling concerned for her and emboldened briefly by tranquillisers, I promised her I would be fine. She should go home. Off she went, reluctantly, turning at the gate to check if I was sure. I waved from the door. Yes, I reassured her. Sebastian would be back soon. I pottered back upstairs to the safety of our room.

But Sebastian was delayed. My anxiety levels rose. I slithered out of bed, down the stairs, and slumped on the doorstep, wailing in my nightdress. Just as a concerned neighbour was approaching the house, I saw Sebastian's familiar figure returning from work. He was horrified to find me there.

It hadn't occurred to me that I might worry our neighbours. Such was the intensity of my pain, I had no sense of others' feelings. My mind was racing as he carried me back inside, while waving at the neighbour to indicate that all was well. I had only one thought. There was no choice. I knew now I had to find a way to keep my husband at home.

Friday, early June 1997

The next morning I cracked it: I would ring his boss, a man I hardly knew. Relief suffused through me at the thought of having a plan.

I managed to dial his number, steadied by urgency, and left a message telling him how ill I was. I felt elated by my ability to take the kind decisive action I was used to. When I put the phone down all the symptoms returned. Luckily, so did Sebastian. That Friday evening he came back from the office, put his backpack down, changed out of his suit and assured me he would stay at home with me until I got better. I wished I had felt well to give him some sign that I was pleased.

Already mid-May had become mid-June. That's not to say the time went quickly. Those days were the longest of my life. The time according to the clock was one thing, the time I suffered, another. Seconds felt like minutes, minutes like hours, hours like days, days like weeks.

There was a rough household pattern. I was looked after mainly by my mother, who would arrive first thing in the morning. Even though Sebastian had promised me he would be at home, life at work meant that in fact he remained largely in the office. His work was demanding, his bosses equally exacting – disappearing was not an option. He managed to finesse his movements so that I at least believed he was more present. My mother contributed to making his subterfuge work, and also helped to look after the boys.

I hardly saw the children, who Sebastian later assured me had continued life as normal. I did not know or care whether they noticed my absence. I was a ghost in my own home. I didn't ask after Edward and George; I no longer even thought or worried about them. All my energies were focused on me. It wasn't egocentric in a vain way; it was a bitter fight to survive. My mantra was: 'I want to die. I can't stand the pain any longer. I've got to get off the plane.'

My only clear memories are of Dr Fischer's visits every two days. I would start waiting for his visit the minute he had left, even though I had no faith in him. His drugs didn't work; he didn't work: I would never get better. But there was, it seemed to me, nobody else. He tweaked my drug levels constantly, but more importantly he tried to reassure me that I would get better. This would end, he promised. Yes, because I will die, I thought. He gave me his business card and carefully wrote the words 'YOU WILL GET BETTER' on it in the blue ink I knew from his notes. The card was soon creased and yellowed with sweat; I could not put it down. I had to have something to hold on to: either the card or my mother's hand.

Sitting by my bedside, my mother had taken to reciting a phrase from the Bible that reminded me of my childhood: 'My grace is sufficient for thee; my strength is made perfect in weakness.'

It would have been impossible to learn anything new, but I could remember these words from my childhood without much effort. It was a different mantra, more positive than my previous chant that I wanted to die. 'My grace is sufficient for thee; my strength is made perfect in weakness,' my mother repeated. I clung to those few paradoxical words. Words were what I knew, what I had always relied on: loving poetry when I was growing up, writing essays at school and university and churning out copy at work. And aside from the sonorous beauty of the language, I was soothed by the idea that God's grace would be enough for me and that when I was weak, then I was strong.

Sometimes it didn't help. There were days when I was too weak even to complete the phrase and went back to longing for death, when I lost all faith in God or his words and bitterly resented what seemed like His false promises. Groans had replaced screams. I was no longer bartering with God that I would be better, kinder, more thoughtful if He would just let me be well. My bargaining hadn't worked. I wanted to die.

My thoughts of an easeful death were perfectly reasoned and logical. They weren't 'fears' as such. It was what I wanted. Death would be peaceful. Others would no longer suffer. I would no longer suffer. I didn't want to die because I hated my life, I just hated this present existence: I wanted the life I had before I was ill. But I had accepted that wasn't possible and acknowledged it was a shame I had never appreciated my life properly before, that I had sometimes moaned to Sebastian about how exhausted I felt or how stressful it was to combine home and work.

That was all in the past. Now I couldn't endure this agony any longer. It was no one's fault. I had to end it. My body had done good service and produced two sons. I'd had a good run as a wife and mother and journalist. Really, I was fine with what I had achieved. There was no 'if only'. My genetic continuity was assured. At some point, we all have to stop. Yes, there might have been more I could have hoped for, but that would always be true. I accepted life was short. I had done enough – a lot, even. Now I must be allowed to rest. It was too painful to be me. It was my turn. There was nothing frightening about suicide. It was a sweet and natural choice and would achieve the peacefulness I craved. It was the answer.

I longed for a stream of warm red blood from my wrists, which would quietly lead to blissful oblivion. The blood would be like a soothing river that would carry me away. No one could live in this agony, anyone else would think likewise. Hoping for death wasn't hysterical. It was utterly logical. Nobody could rescue me, so I had no option. And thanks to the pills next to my bed, it would be easy to put into practice. I could effortlessly go to sleep and never wake up. I figured that I had just enough energy to reach over and pop open the foil-covered blister packet.

I reasoned that my family would actually be relieved to see my suffering end. At least the boys would have each other; they would understand. My husband would be able to raise them. I wasn't even sad that I would never see them grow up. I would trade that for it to be over. I'd always liked a bargain and this was a good one. Or if it wasn't a deal, it was like a torture victim confessing because they can't take any more.

I opened the drawer of my bedside table. Perhaps Sebastian had sensed something. The tablets had gone.

Chapter Three

I've Got to Have Something to Hold on to

Those around me were clearly becoming more concerned. They talked quickly and quietly among themselves. None of them had seen anything like it before. My brother in particular looked very pale. They couldn't understand why something so extraordinary was happening to a perfectly ordinary family. Even my mother, who had raised three children and had a wide circle of friends, had not come across depression like this. She never normally cried but now she did. My sister was so shocked at the sight that she started crying, too.

My brother, sister and father found it unbearable that they were unable to ease my pain and that I was so pulled into myself that I barely noticed them. They questioned whether the doctors were doing enough, if they knew how sick I was. There were fears that I had gone crazy, that I would have to be nursed for ever more in an upstairs room, hidden from view.

Later I learnt that Sebastian was not sure I could recover. He imagined a future in which I would always be ill. It was the uncertainty that was so frightening, he recalls, the not knowing. Unimaginable though it seemed, I might even get worse. He felt he couldn't get through to me. Of course he couldn't. The person he knew wasn't there. Someone had stolen his wife. There was just a contorted figure, wholly detached from him. It was as if I didn't know him.

All he could do was try to keep steady, to protect me and to help me believe that we had a future. He was in charge of my pills now, a subject that we never discussed: I hadn't the energy to argue against his decisive action. It was safer for him to keep them and not to have anything lying around, he told me later. He would sit holding my hand, mouthing that it was going to be okay and I would get better. Sometimes he would talk about all the things we would do together when I recovered, the walks we would take and the suppers we would enjoy, the plays we would see. Sometimes we repeated together my mother's mantra: 'My grace is sufficient for thee: my strength is made perfect in weakness.' He kept going, despite the lack of any response from me. One evening I wondered if I had the energy to put my arms around him. I didn't.

He tried to separate the illness from the wife he loved: this was about a disease, not about me. But sometimes it was hard for him not to take it personally that our joint life had spun so out of control. The reasons for my illness were terrifyingly unclear. I had shown no signs of being unwell in the months before my collapse, when I had played the candidate's wife pushing a pram with a rosette and a toddler in tow.

He was the juggler now, working and looking after the children and me. They barely noticed my absence. He tells me there was no constant questioning from Edward, no 'Can I see Mummy?' or 'Why can't I see Mummy?', just ordinary chatter about their days, which, mercifully, were buttressed by familiar routines. Mostly I remained indifferent to Edward's musings and George's gurglings wafting up from the kitchen but occasionally I revived enough to focus and feel them tantalisingly just out of reach. I would weep at the impossibil-ity of hugging them or reading to them in my weakened state. Sometimes Sebastian would respond by bringing one of the children up to see me – two was too much. But he soon stopped when he realised I became worse when faced with a child with whom I could no longer interact. He carefully removed the pile of children's books I had always kept on my bedside table for such moments.

He was also managing the well-wishers, some calling with advice, some wanting to pay a visit. There weren't many, as few people apart from our immediate family knew what was going on. There was no deliberate attempt to keep my illness secret, or shame that I was unwell. It was simply that no one had the time or energy to try to explain what felt inexplicable. Besides, Sebastian didn't need other people to deal with, especially those who required gratitude for their sympathy. When the odd friend did come to see me, nervy calls to Sebastian typi-cally followed. He knew that what little energy he had left couldn't be dissipated reassuring others. And things were so uncertain, he might be so distracted that he offended a guest without knowing it. The risk wasn't worth taking. He tried his best to dissuade visitors.

I dimly recall a few such visits. One friend said I looked like her mother on her deathbed. I was as pale as the white duvet cover. She felt as if she was already grieving for a friend who had died. Another friend brought some potted lilies with a note saying 'By the time these bloom, so will you', even though Sebastian had tried to explain that I was miles beyond the flowers-might-make-a-difference stage.

A third visitor was different. She had experienced depres-sion herself, though mercifully was better now. As she left, she handed Sebastian a copy of the poem 'The Sickness unto Death' by Anne Sexton, who had also suffered depression. She was sensible enough not to mention that Sexton had committed suicide, and acknowledged that it wasn't obvious why she was giving him a poem among the bleakest ever written. But as a traveller who had returned from the horror of the land of depression, she was aware of the near impossibility of trying to communicate what was happening to others who hadn't. Sexton's poem, she said, had been useful to those looking after her. They had handed it out to anyone who wanted to know what she was experiencing. 'The poem describes how I felt at my very worst,' she told Sebastian, 'when I had utterly lost all faith in anyone or any God. Make some copies and then you need not talk to all the visitors. You can get back to looking after Rachel. Just don't show it to her!'

> *God went out of me*
> *as if the sea dried up like sandpaper,*
> *as if the sun became a latrine.*
> *God went out of my fingers.*
> *They became stone.*
> *My body became a side of mutton*
> *and despair roamed the slaughterhouse.*
>
> *Someone brought me oranges in my despair*
> *but I could not eat a one*
> *for God was in that orange.*
> *I could not touch what did not belong to me.*
> *The priest came,*
> *he said God was even in Hitler.*
> *I did not believe him*

for if God were in Hitler
then God would be in me.
I did not hear the bird sounds.
They had left.
I did not see the speechless clouds,
I saw only the little white dish of my faith
breaking in the crater.
I kept saying:
I've got to have something to hold on to.
People gave me Bibles, crucifixes,
a yellow daisy,
but I could not touch them,
I who was a house full of bowel movement,
I who was a defaced altar,
I who wanted to crawl toward God
could not move nor eat bread.

So I ate myself,
bite by bite,
and the tears washed me,
wave after cowardly wave,
swallowing canker after canker
and Jesus stood over me looking down
and He laughed to find me gone,
and put His mouth to mine
and gave me His air.

My kindred, my brother, I said
and gave the yellow daisy
to the crazy woman in the next bed.

With no sign of improvement Dr Fischer decided that I should go into hospital. This had always been an option but until now I had pleaded to stay at home, as I didn't want to be separated from the children. But after weeks of no progress and the mounting desperation of my family, I agreed. All I knew was that staying at home wasn't working and going to hospital might help.

Mid-June 1997

Dr Fischer set out the next steps. We had tried sleeping pills and tranquillisers while staying at home, he explained, the authority of his tone momentarily containing our collective fear. They were not working. After five weeks it was time for a different approach. Being in hospital would mean that I could be constantly supervised by experts. His tone didn't suggest he was consulting us. He was making the decisions now. I should go into hospital, and swiftly, Dr Fischer said. Time was against us. Sebastian and my mother agreed: they thought I was deteriorating fast – not that they told me so at the time.

Most people, faced with such a prospect, would be frightened. But for the first time in the weeks since I had been ill, I felt hopeful as we packed a bag. Going to hospital marked a change. Somehow the simple step of walking into a different building meant progress. It was true that I was very ill. Very ill people went to hospital, where they got better. I needed care dispensed by experts. This was the answer; it looked to me like a magical exit from the horror.

The hospital was a red-brick hybrid of Victorian main building and modern extensions in a quiet street off a busy road. I had often passed it but its appearance was so unremarkable that I had thought it was a block of flats. I brought some books with me, assuming that before long I would be able to concentrate on the printed page. I imagined bubble bath and magazines. The whole thing would be over as soon as I walked through those doors, I kept thinking. Staying at home had been a terrible mistake. All my symptoms would gather themselves up, pack themselves into a bag, and walk out of my life as quickly as they had arrived. I in turn would be allowed to go home and normal life would resume.

Walk through the doors we did. But my heart was pounding faster, not slower and I was squeezing Sebastian's hand even more tightly.

There was an ordinary reception area and long, anonymous passages with closed doors. I glimpsed day rooms and people I assumed were patients – it was hard to tell as they were dressed in normal clothes. A few purposeful nurses strode about. One patient did loom up and put his face very close to mine, saying he was sure he knew me. But other than that, there was no hint it was a hospital. It was very quiet, the only sound some soft typing, the usual buzz of office life as a printer offered up its page. There were no crazy figures, no muffled screams or haunted eyes – none on view, anyway.

I just about stopped myself from crying when Sebastian left. He handed me over to a nurse who spoke in breezy exclamations as if talking to someone whose first language wasn't English. She showed me to a fourteen-foot-square room, with primrose-coloured walls, a bed centred on the right-hand wall, a side table and orange curtains of a modern geometric pattern. For all that the nurse extolled its virtues, and those of an en suite bathroom, with an infuriating calm, I could find nothing remarkable about it. Clearly there was no such thing as a room deliberately designed for the treatment of this

illness, with special features that might help me, as I had opti-
mistically imagined. The room was no different to one you
might find in a plusher motel.

I minded the windows the most, grimed with dirt, their
1970s-style frames jammed closed for fear of suicide or escape
attempts and offering a view of industrial bins with not a sliver
of green. The air was leaden and I felt breathless. As I sat down
on the edge of the narrow bed, I was – and felt – completely
alone. The room could have been anywhere, at any time, in any
country. I wanted to be rooted somewhere particular, and that
somewhere was home. I wanted Edward's *The Very Hungry
Caterpillar* book, the one with a brown stain on the cover where
I had spilt the hot chocolate we were sharing. I wanted to fold
the boys' Thomas the Tank Engine pyjamas in a neat pile ready
to take up to their rooms. I wanted to watch Sebastian reading
his book in his favourite armchair from the door of the drawing
room where he couldn't see me. I wanted my own duvet, the
scent of our usual washing powder, the solace of my family. I
buried my head in my sleeve to suck up the smell of home.

Even the position of the bed was wrong. I needed to be
tucked into a corner, with the safety of the walls around the
bed frame, not in a bed in the centre of the room surrounded
by a scary nothingness. I wanted well-thumbed books and
cotton sheets, a miniature fireplace, and a rose-covered
bedspread, and a view of trees to remind me of the leftover
Eden that was home. But there was just the unmoveable bed
and the windows that wouldn't open. The only things I could
move were the lightweight blanket and the pillow. Wrapping
the blanket around me Native American-style, I retreated to a
corner.

Curled up in a ball, my guts seemed to be digesting pure

acid. I hugged the pillow tight, wishing it were Sebastian or one of the children, or even Edward's favourite cuddly panda, till even that became too much effort. I had become so tense I couldn't move, my exterior stillness contrasting with the violent movement inside me. Coming here had not made anything better. I would do anything to end the agony, to get off the crashing plane. I thought of cutting myself open. Then I could kill what now seemed like a crazed monster that was sucking the goodness out of my every cell right to the very tips of my fingernails, that was inhabiting me and attacking me and becoming me. Aha: I was in hospital. They must have an operating table. Cut me open. Cut me now.

Every sense was perverted. All I could feel was sick, all I could sense was sick, all I could speak was sick. I wanted to grab anyone, to shake them and scream, to rock their shoulders till their eyes were forced from their heads. No one understood. I wasn't the mad one. They were. Mad in their obtuseness, their blockheaded, wilful, wicked ignorance. There was a place called hell and I was in it. No one realised. There was no limit to my suffering. No one helped; they just did normal things like walk and talk. I didn't understand how they could. How dared they? Why didn't they rescue me?

The agony burned with more power than anything I had ever felt before, more than the force of being in love. My incomprehension, and my powerlessness, were complete. There was nothing else. It was as if I were screaming at top volume from a television screen, but the watching world had switched the TV to mute and couldn't hear me.

I'm not sure what I thought should have happened. Surely *something* was going to happen. I was left alone for what seemed like an age. It was a crushing anticlimax, having invested so much hope in an assembly of bricks and mortar, having mustered up the courage to come here at all.

Eventually, as it seemed to me, the nurse returned and took my blood pressure and pulse. Why had she left me for so long, I wailed. She said it had only been a few minutes. Now, the more I talked of planes and crashing and cutting myself open, the more other people, unsurprisingly, began to concentrate. A stream of doctors, nurses, psychiatrists, therapists came to call, with clipboards and questions and smiles and pills in white paper cups. Tapping their papers into place, they asked me a series of questions. I was asked to grade myself on a scale from a) mildly gloomy through to e) suicidal. ('Has she been in a plane crash?' one nurse asked another, assuming I was out of earshot.)

I realised with sickening certainty that these people couldn't rescue me. I was out of reach, theirs and that of anyone else. Their questions were absurd – how could a one-line answer elicit anything of the horror? That they were asking such questions showed they knew nothing of the unfathomably strange land I was presently inhabiting – they had no passports, nor could they speak the language. This pain was NOT normal, however reasonably they asked the question. This agony was NOT capable of description on ANY form, and yes, I WILL raise my voice even if yours remains steady. How could you possibly BEGIN to imagine otherwise? I only lowered my tone when I realised that I was in danger of being forcefully sedated.

Night fell. The only change the nurses could offer was switching off the light, followed by torch-lit checks to see that I hadn't tried to do anything stupid with the plastic knives. My pills had been taken away. I couldn't take any more as I had taken so many already.

My room did have a Bible, which was at least something to

cling to though the words were a blur. I remembered my mother's phrase, 'My grace is sufficient for thee . . .' and feverishly repeated the lines to myself. The next time a nurse came in, I dropped the Bible and held her hand just as I held my mother's at home. She soon understood I wasn't going to let go. Without Dr Fischer's card, with its words of reassurance, or anybody else's hand to cling to, the nurse was all I had. In the end, she slipped away by substituting the Bible. She didn't turn around when I howled at her to stay.

I didn't sleep at all, my anxiety so high that I was immune to all my usual drugs and more. Sobs tore my chest. Since the nurse had freed herself from my clasp, I clutched myself. I repeated over and over, 'I want to die . . . I want to go home . . .' The ache of separation from the person I had once been was unbearable. My life as a mother, wife and journalist my ability to touch and to be touched, to hear and to sing and to dance, had all been taken, quickly and efficiently, chopped up, sliced through and discarded in a neat pile in the corner of that room.

Naturally, the more I wept heavy tears, the more professionals kept heaving into view, the more anxious they made me, the more I wished to leave, and the more they wished me to stay. All I could focus on was the need to discharge myself the following day.

As daylight leaked in around the edges of the curtains and a slight rain began to fall, I realised that in order to get out, I would have to pretend to be better. My acting had never been slicker. It was the first stirring of positive will. There was no more talk of crashing planes. Despite the attempts of the hospital staff to keep me there and their insistence that they couldn't guarantee my safety once I was no longer in their care, my impassioned plea worked, and I was discharged. It helped that Dr Fischer supported my bid to return home; he had come to visit me briefly in the morning and seen the swift deterioration that followed my admission. I was blessed with the option of at least lying panic-stricken in my own bed. I had somewhere else to go. My husband took me home, carrying me to the car, as commuters streamed down the pavement in the direction of the Tube.

I believed at the time that all the hospital had given me was the confirmation that there was no answer. As I later grasped, there was one small consolation: the fact that Sebastian could tell family and friends that I had been admitted, albeit briefly, helped people to realise that I really was sick. Previously some of them had said things like, 'It's all very odd. She's not the sort to be depressed. I've always thought she was so cheerful. Are you sure it isn't something else?' It was almost as if they thought we had invented the illness. They seemed to think that if they came to cheer me up I would quickly recover.

I couldn't blame them; I had thought the same a few weeks earlier. Previously I had had only the vaguest notion that depression could have physical symptoms, certainly not the agonising ones I was experiencing. Nor had I imagined that anyone as privileged and happy as me could become unwell. Depression was entwined in my mind with old age, unemployment and vulnerability.

In terms of treatment, Dr Fischer once again fashioned a sense of order out of the chaos that followed the hospital visit, almost as if my disastrous night was to have been expected. As I was going to stay at home now, he said, we would need to be able to contact him at all times. He gave me, Sebastian and my mother his home number. We could call him even in the middle of the night.

I now realise this was exceptional. I have never heard of another psychiatrist offering his patients this kind of access. But at the time I took it for granted. Of course I couldn't survive at night on my own. Of course I needed someone to call. It was essential. The agony was so acute I might die and the only person who could save me was Dr Fischer.

So call I did. Dr Fischer could instantly gauge my symptoms from the fact I'd rung: no conversation was required. He would tell me which drug to take and how much. 'Call me back if you need to,' he would always say. He was nice enough to imply that he often worked at night anyway.

Dr Fischer proposed that we stop using only tranquillisers and sleeping pills. We had given them a sufficient run. Now it was time to move on. The anxiety had gripped me despite the tranquillisers, and we had already discussed their addictiveness. Even I no longer insisted that it was just about the sleep and that I couldn't possibly be 'depressed' – it was clear that something serious was going on. Whether I liked it or not, the time had come to start on antidepressants.

My family would be even more important during this next stage, Dr Fischer told them privately. He believed that the antidepressants he had selected were the right drugs for me, though they were not the most conventional choice. One reason why doctors are cautious about prescribing this particular variety of antidepressants, known as tricyclics, is that even a small overdose can be fatal.

Late June 1997

The new pills were called dosulepin and were white. Initially, I didn't want to take them. I had admitted that I was properly unwell but I feared I might become a different person thanks to their mind-altering properties. Even feeling this sick, I wanted to be in control. They were my only option though. There was no middle ground: I could take them or leave them, and my desperation to get better won out. I had no choice but to surrender to Dr Fischer and my family.

One advantage was that my drug had no aftertaste and worked as a sleeping pill as well as an antidepressant, so I need not take the zopiclone as well. The downside was that it wouldn't start working immediately, though the side effects would. Dr Fischer swiftly listed them as if they were a shopping list: weight gain, dry mouth, drowsiness, constipation, blurred vision. In an earlier incarnation, I might have minded. Now all I could hear was that I would soon feel better.

But I hadn't listened carefully enough. What I didn't realise was that the side effects meant I would feel much worse in the short-term. This is one of the most terrifying aspects of the treatment of depression and the reason so many patients give up on drugs before they have actually started to work, a process that can take several weeks.

From the moment I started taking the pills, they made my body balloon. They affected me in multiple ways. I didn't just feel drowsy; I literally couldn't move. My tongue was furred, a desert behind my teeth, my lips cracked. Doused in chemicals, my speech was slurred and as a result, I simply resorted to sign language, chiefly putting my thumb up, down or in between to convey 'yes', 'no', and 'don't know'. I could hardly even open my eyelids. They felt like stone. It was as though I was dressed in lead. Even my blood seemed to be clotting. The crashing sensation had abated, but now I was like an insect trapped in amber.

Despite all this, I now believed in the pills with the fervour of a convert. Previously I had been drawn to all things alternative; I had even written a column about complementary medicine. Now my entire life had led to this one moment, and shrunk to this one action: swallowing something small and white. The new pills had to start working, I would scream. They had to start working. NOW.

I still hurt all over, all the time. 'But where does it hurt?' my mother would keep asking, perplexed. I couldn't explain. Everywhere. Even my fingernails hurt.

Sebastian or my mother acted as nurse and would dole out the right dosage as I wasn't capable of administering the pills myself. I no longer felt tempted to take an overdose, though that was less a sign of progress than of being completely numbed by the new drugs. But I might easily have consumed the wrong dose by mistake as I simply wasn't well enough to focus. I might have died by accident had I been left alone.

Meanwhile, the household continued around me. Julie ensured that the children ate their fish fingers and played in the park and listened to the weekly story at the local library. My husband took photographs, perhaps subconsciously believing that it would help me to fill in the memory gaps at a future, happier time. He later told me that this represented the first stirring in him that I might get better: the time would come when we could enjoy the pictures together.

He was wise enough not to share anything of the children's lives with me, and he warned others not to either. My maternal feelings had dried up like my breast milk. I shunned anyone who tried to recount some cheery anecdote about a funny thing one of them had done in an attempt to distract me. I couldn't bear the agony of being reminded of them:

Sebastian became adept at hiding any signs of their existence. Many people around me found my lack of interest baffling and almost unbearable.

Mostly my children's lives appeared to me as if from behind a thick pane of glass but there were moments when they edged into my consciousness: a sudden stray appearance by Edward, a dropped teddy bear on the landing. Then my sense of responsibility for these little beings appalled me, but I still couldn't act on it. I was incapable.

Sebastian was finding looking after me and the children exhausting. He was harried at all hours of the night and day and continuing to work a highly involving job. So he and my mother decided that, to take some of the pressure off him, George would go to stay with Sebastian's family, who were keen to help but were hampered by not living in London. I wasn't party to the discussions.

I remember weeping at my bedroom window one morning as a small figure in a buggy was pushed down the street and into a waiting car. I might not have been able to look after them, but I realised then that I needed to know my children were asleep under the same roof as me and breathing the same air. I knew it to be true in the very marrow of my bones. The decision to remove George was understandable and well meant, but some elemental connection between us had been broken. Something whole had been ruptured. I felt a continuous ache of missing. I would think of him last thing at night and first thing on waking. My only compensation was relief that despite being utterly incapable of being a parent, I could still feel as any mother would about her child.

Chapter Four

All Things Are Passing

LATE JUNE TO LATE JULY 1997

Late June 1997

The next six weeks passed in a blur of heavy sedation. Days slipped by in which nothing happened, whole weeks left no mark at all. The terror wasn't gone, it was just hidden deep inside me. These chunks of unmarked time were interrupted only by the taking of my beloved pills, gobbled down with relish as a way of suppressing the return of the crashing horror. Sometimes my mother would have to run to find the pills in time. Then once again I would return to being semi-comatose in a darkened room. New visitors were shocked at the state of me. I didn't react when one left the room, sobbing.

There was nothing worth remembering, nothing that interested me from my earlier life. I no longer cared about being a mother or having a job. The idea of being able to work seemed laughable. Any notion of competence had gone out of me. I assumed Sebastian had explained to my employers that I was so unwell that I would never return to an office. I wasn't able to discuss the matter with him. All I could concentrate on was trying to defeat the beast of the pain.

Nothing made the contrast plainer than when I got a get-well-soon call from the newspaper I worked for. I had always admired the journalist who rang me yet I felt neither nervous nor excited that such a figure had been kind enough to call. I struggled even to answer the phone. When you expect death, no one can seem frightening. We are all equals before our maker in our final days.

A second colleague, George, sent me weekly missives with news from work. All his keen journalistic skills were displayed in witty accounts of office politics: sharp descriptions of news-room romances and scoops from the front line, material that I would once have devoured eagerly. Sebastian would try to read me the letters, but I wasn't interested. It seemed like news from another planet.

I had become disconnected from real life. I had never been more conscious that we are born and die alone. I was existing in a state of solitude and selfishness of such acute-ness I could barely comprehend it. There was not one scrap of feeling left for anyone else. My heart seemed as unfeeling as stone. My only concern was to lessen the terror; the only role of others was to be there at all times so I didn't face the terror alone.

Sometimes prayers helped. There were moments when I was soothed by the act of repeating certain phrases. I am still unsure whether it was the healing power of great words that helped me, or faith itself. They say there were no atheists in the trenches and I too believed I was facing death.

When I was a child, church had often been a boring thing I was dragged to on a Sunday by my parents but I had always loved the poetry of the Bible, almost in contrast to how disap-pointing I found the actual services. The greatest excitements were the thrill of the white confection I wore for my First Communion service, aged eight, and then a grey serge dress with a white poplin collar that I wore when I was confirmed at fourteen. The language of the King James Bible had rarely disappointed me in the past, and it began to reach me now.

To begin with I could only manage to repeat my mother's line: 'my strength is made perfect in weakness'. Now I returned to prayers from my childhood, the first being 'Matthew, Mark, Luke and John', which I had recited on the night I fell ill. The prayer was particularly suited to being bed-bound, especially its second line, 'Bless the bed that I lie on.' I graduated to 'Hail Mary', though I still sometimes muddled the words. At times it felt as if someone had thrown the well-ordered deck of my mind into the air, and now all the cards were strewn in chaos on the floor.

Initially, my mother would read the prayers aloud. Luckily, her head was richly stocked with beautiful examples to which she introduced me. I also had plenty of my own favourites from long ago. Then I started to be able to recite the prayers myself, again and again, the words strong enough to bear the repetition. They temporarily laid my anxiety to rest by fixing me in the present. It was as if the words had become embodied, almost physical in their power, something to hold on to and rub, like prayer beads for the mind. At other times it seemed as if I was swallowing them whole, almost as if they were nourishment for my wounded being.

St Theresa's writings were another particular favourite. The prayer found in her breviary when she died felt to me as though it had been written for exactly this moment, especially the line 'All things are passing', which I would repeat like a mantra, over and over, leaving no gap to allow the horror to intrude. This too would pass; her compelling wisdom and companionship from the past turned the prison of my mind

briefly into a peaceful place, and reclothed me in a more rightful mind.

> *Let nothing disturb thee*
> *Nothing affright thee*
> *All things are passing*
> *God never changeth*
> *Patient endurance*
> *Attaineth to all things*
> *Who God possesseth*
> *In nothing is wanting*
> *Alone God sufficeth.*

Later, I read about the attempts to investigate how prayer may
help people feel better. Some recent studies have tried to
explore the relationship between prayer and positive thinking.* The evidence is complex and its implications debatable,
but findings suggest that people who pray show more of the
sort of brain activity thought to be associated with positive
characteristics such as gratitude and charitableness. (Though,
of course, a great many brutal acts through history have been
committed by those who claimed to pray.) At the time I didn't
feel grateful or positive in any way; all I knew was that the
prayers were something I could cling to.

---

* Andrew Newberg and Mark Robert Waldamn, *How God Changes Your
Brain* (Ballantine Books, 2009).

End of June 1997

Very slowly, my anxiety continued to subside, but only in pockets. There were moments when I felt present in the room once again. It was as if I had cleared a space around me, a crucial distance between me and the horror. My old self and personality returned to say hello momentarily, as if my reflection was waving back at me in the mirror. Some mornings I wished I could peel off that smiley face and pocket it for good. At other times, I could not recognise my reflection. It was the same with photographs: sometimes I would chance on a picture of myself and find that person familiar; at other times it looked like a stranger.

I found I occasionally had the ability to notice detail: my heart skipped as I caught sight of the lilies I had been given when I first became ill, their green buds now in bloom. Nature was reaching out and grabbing me by the collar, my mood perfectly summed up by Gerard Manley Hopkins's poem 'Pied Beauty', with its celebration of even the smallest miracles of creation. The language performed for me, rekindling my enthusiasm for words and refreshing my own stale vocabulary.

> *Glory be to God for dappled things –*
> *For skies of couple-colour as a brinded cow;*
> *For rose-moles all in stipple upon trout that swim;*
> *Fresh-firecoal chestnut-falls; finches' wings;*
> *Landscape plotted and pieced – fold, fallow, and plough;*
> *And all trades, their gear and tackle and trim.*
>
> *All things counter, original, spare, strange;*
> *Whatever is fickle, freckled (who knows how?)*

With swift, slow; sweet, sour; adazzle, dim;
He fathers-forth whose beauty is past change:
Praise him.

Nestled in the fold of the lily leaves was a ladybird that adventured its way onto my hand. It paused, its wings slowly opening, before – thinking better – it folded them. Then very tentatively it took flight. Seconds later it landed on my hand again. It seemed as if it were willing me to get better and fly again. The familiar had become unfamiliar. My faded world was taking on colour.

There were times when the pain diminished to the point where the normal rhythms of the day reasserted themselves. I can remember managing to help Edward complete his favourite jumbo-sized farm puzzle. The uninterrupted crashing feeling was briefly arrested as I slotted a black-and-white cow into a bright green field with a satisfying click. Edward took full advantage of the unlimited number of times I was happy to tip all the pieces out and start again.

The recovery was bumpy. It was as if I were climbing out of my tunnel up onto a mountain with multiple false peaks. I would get to the top, only to slip back down the other side, having glimpsed another peak ahead; but each time, I slipped a little less. On his next visit, Dr Fischer drew a picture for me of a jagged line, as if outlining the Himalayas, but on an upward curve on the graph. This was how I would get better, he said, just as this was how I had become ill. I pinned the picture by my bed.

He also sat down and explained a little about the drugs I was taking, as he had found that it helped his patients to understand something of what he was prescribing and why.

There are roughly three different types of antidepressants, he said. The first generation of 1950s antidepressants, known as MAOIS (MonoAmine Oxidase Inhibitors), are rarely prescribed now, because they can interact with food and some other medicines and cause problems.

But doctors still occasionally use drugs from the second wave of antidepressants, known as tricyclics or TCAS, which included the drug I was taking, dosulepin.* Such drugs were discovered accidentally: they were found to improve mood when being tested as a treatment for Parkinson's disease. One advantage is that they are cheap and generally not addictive. But some psychiatrists have now rejected them as they have strong sedating side effects, as I had discovered.

Then there is the newer generation of pills, which have become well known under brand names such as Prozac and Seroxat.** These more recent drugs were developed in the 1980s and are supposed to have fewer side effects. They tend to elevate the mood of those struck down by lassitude and negativity. For all the advantages of this new generation of drugs, with my variety of what Dr Fischer called heightened anxiety and frantic nervousness, he felt the tricyclics were a better choice. I needed calming down rather than cheering up.

* The names of antidepressants are confusing. Each drug effectively has two names: its generic or chemical name (in this case dosulepin) and its brand name, or names, if sold by more than one drug company (dosulepin is sold as Prothiaden, among other names). This is just like the difference between a vacuum cleaner (its generic name) and a Hoover or Electrolux (the brand names chosen by different companies). The easy way to remember the difference is that the generic name is lower case, and the trade name has a capital letter.
** The generic names for these drugs are fluoxetine (Prozac) and paroxetine (Seroxat).

He told me that he was continually adjusting the drug levels to try to control the anxiety without knocking me out, a process doctors always need to manage carefully when treating a depressive illness. He was slowly increasing the level of antidepressant. As soon as I had absorbed a certain level, he would increase it again. He thought of it like straightening a picture frame, he said: now up, now down, now just level.

It was much less clear how exactly the drugs work, and Dr Fischer was not given to glib explanation along the lines of 'increasing levels of serotonin'. Even now, with far more sophisticated brain-scanning techniques and after years of research, the precise way antidepressants affect brain chemistry is opaque and poorly understood, even in the corridors of neuroscience. There was only one certainty: Dr Fischer believed in their efficacy and I believed in him.*

That day I enjoyed a little pocket of lucidity and felt a glimmer of understanding of this difficult subject. The clarity evaporated the next day. Then it returned, in what became a pattern: shafts of optimism and clarity piercing through the gloom, but only sometimes.

The mornings were the worst. Typically, I would wake up, momentarily euphoric that perhaps I would feel different today. Perhaps it had all been a dream. Then, just as quickly, I would despair as I realised I felt the same, and it was real. There was no guarantee that I would ever be well, ever be released from that crashing plane. Worry would pile on worry, fear on fear, panic on panic in what was by now a familiar

---

* Later, I would become more aware of the debate about whether, in fact, antidepressants work at all. Some argue they are no better than placebos for the majority of patients. I was not well enough for such discussions and Dr Fischer wisely didn't initiate them.

pattern. It was still far too frightening to make even the simplest decision, beginning with whether or not to get up. Subsequent decisions required monumental courage: to brush my teeth, get dressed, say hello, even go to the bathroom. I never knew at what point I would be defeated and need to return to bed and more sedating drugs.

Later in the day the antidepressants seemed to take hold. By adding some tranquillisers through the day to up their impact, I could slow these moments of spiralling angst without knocking myself out. The interludes during which I struck the right balance between sedation and panic were few, however. The picture frame wasn't yet level.

First week of July 1997

One day, my concentration seemed suddenly to return. At breakfast I managed to finish reading a newspaper article – a report of Britain's handover of Hong Kong to China – and then I found I could remember what I'd read, ten minutes later. I also consumed a plate of scrambled eggs: previously, particularly at this early stage in the day, I could only swallow something liquid.

Inspired by these achievements and an azure sky, I felt a surge of optimism and said to my mother that I wanted to post a letter at the post box round the corner. Was I sure, she ventured? It would be my first proper foray outside since I was discharged from hospital. I was determined. She agreed to accompany me. My heart leapt as I shut the front door: I felt I was walking back to normality and freedom.

We set off. Each step was a huge effort. My legs felt like swollen tree trunks as I tried to manoeuvre myself down the street. It was like swimming through mud. We had to pause every two or three houses, to the surprise of our neighbours against whose gates we rested. They didn't recognise me. Then we simply stopped. I could neither will myself forward nor back; I was frozen in fear. My mother could do nothing to unfreeze me. We finally managed to return to my room when the panic subsided. I was so disheartened by the experience that I did not venture outside again for another week.

The walk to the post box reminded me that I had become fat. My thighs touched and my clothes didn't fit. The indicator on the scales had whizzed up as quickly as it had previously gone down. I was now more than two stone heavier and weighed almost eleven stone. (Weight-gain is so common on antidepressants that some psychiatrists have scales in their offices.) I felt the weight was a price worth paying, given that the drugs seemed to be beginning to work. But the downside was that my new girth fed the well of my anxiety. While that well seemed bottomless, no amount of liquid could relieve the terrible dryness in my mouth. I sipped water constantly. It was something to do.

During the day, I mostly did and felt nothing apart from the fear. All other feelings had withered, in contrast to my physical bulk. My clothes were enormous but I was shrunken inside. The only exception was bedtime, when I took my anti-depressants and felt a momentary elation that another day was over. I was completely sedated for the first few hours of the night. Even that sleep was odd: dreamless for a start, and as if I had been captured by the drugs which had led me to a different place not of my own making.

My family tried to make me at least go through the motions of normality. There was now typically a moment at around eleven in the morning when the day was poised on the brink of success or failure. My mother would seize the moment to try and dress me. Getting up was the start of a virtuous circle, which would give me the confidence to make the next move, which in turn gave me more confidence. Other days the circle would turn vicious. I would feel a huge sense of failure, return to bed and feel more depressed, making it even less likely that I would be able to get up again.

Throughout this time Dr Fischer stayed calm, continuing to impose order with his prescriptions in their carefully measured doses and his own carefully measured tones. He had sanctioned my release from hospital confident in his own care and that of my family. It was beginning to look as if he had been right.

Mid-July 1997

The picture frame was beginning to straighten.

The first clue was that I continued to be able to pay attention for more than a couple of minutes to matters other than my own panic. I could often read the front page of a newspaper now, and as a journalist it seemed natural to measure my recovery through how much of the day's paper I could digest. At times returning to my old reading habits proved unsettling: I was alarmed by news of a nanny accused of murder in America. Sebastian acted as a censor when the newspapers arrived in the morning, reading to me instead the letters that George from *The Times* continued to send me. Now I listened keenly to each one.

The second clue that my analytical faculties were returning was that I managed to make my first decision – which nightdress to wear. Previously my mother had decided, just as the children had their pyjamas laid out for them every night. A small step, yes, but it felt significant.

As I got better Dr Fischer continued to explain more about my symptoms. He would reveal a little more about depressive illnesses on each visit, only sharing what he expertly judged I could absorb and might be helpful. Previously I had been too ill to take much on board. While it seemed like the longest journey of my life, in fact I had now been unwell for only eight weeks.

I liked our chats. He explained things clearly, without condescension, and fully acknowledging uncertainty. The more I learnt that my experience was fairly typical, the more normal I felt, and the more humbled that I wasn't the only person ever to have felt this way and that I hadn't known such illness existed.

On his next visit, he explained that depression is an umbrella term covering many different types of emotional or mood disorders. The term itself is misleading, as it has become commonplace to say 'I feel depressed' as a proxy for feeling briefly gloomy. 'It may be easier to use the phrase "depressive illness" as a way to distinguish depression from ordinary sadness,' he said.

The separate illnesses that make up 'depression' include bipolar depression, seasonal affective disorder, major depressive disorders and postnatal depression. While each ailment has different characteristics, they all share the main symptoms of depression, notably insomnia, lack of appetite and lack of enjoyment in life. Moreover, symptoms can overlap, and a patient can suffer from several different types of depression at once, which is why diagnosis is often complex and time-consuming. Doctors need to give patients a diagnosis, but there can be a certain arbitrariness to the operating categories for severe mental illness.

The obvious culprit in my case was postnatal depression. I told him I found this odd. I thought I had been coping well for several months, and the illness had come seemingly out of nowhere. I hadn't suffered from depression after my first child was born. I had always thought that postnatal depression was very different from other kinds of depression. I had no idea it could descend so dramatically.

But Dr Fischer explained that my symptoms were no different from those who suffer depression at different times in their lives, whether young or old, male or female. My illness had been treated in the same way as that of anyone else suffering from a depressive episode. The symptoms are the same, even if the triggers are different. That was another way to understand what had happened.

Presumably my hormones were at fault, I suggested. Postnatal depression does have some special characteristics, chiefly a mother's concern about her baby, he said. That had certainly been true of me. But postnatal depression is not 'caused' by changes to hormonal levels he said, to my surprise; the research is inconclusive. Levels of oestrogen and progesterone (and other hormones connected to conception and birth) do drop suddenly after a baby is born but it's not clear exactly how this affects your mood and emotions and there was no indication that it had been a factor in my case. No significant differences in hormone levels have been found between women who do and those who do not get depression. Having said that, hormones might play a part, just as they might be implicated in the depression suffered by adolescents or those experiencing the menopause. In any case, I couldn't just blame my hormones. It took several days to absorb this news, which seemed to overturn conventional wisdom.

Third week of July 1997

My curiosity, so long dormant, was now furiously alive. Why had I become ill? I felt entitled to an explanation for my suffering. Up to this point the physical pain had been sufficiently all consuming as to crowd out any attempts to analyse the reasons for the illness. Now I counted the days till Dr Fischer's next visit as if I were an inspector about to interview a key witness who would provide the vital clue to the case. As I quizzed him my reporter's training came to the fore. Life was rational and so was I. Once again I believed problems could be solved. If I could get to the bottom of the illness, the mystery would be solved and hey presto! I would be better and never fall through this mysterious trapdoor again.

But as I was increasingly to learn from talking to Dr Fischer, depressive illnesses do not lend themselves to one-word answers to the who, what, when, why and where questions I was asking. To paraphrase him, depression wasn't like cancer: you couldn't identify the rogue cells that caused it. There are currently no urine tests, blood tests or other biological tests to determine who is mentally ill. There was no single answer as to why I had been unwell, he said, though clearly the stress of having a second child and my worries about combining motherhood with my work provided the context in which the depression had taken hold.

Any major life change makes you vulnerable to depression, be it childbirth, separation, redundancy or bereavement, he explained. That struck a chord; I had always hated change ever since I was a small child, especially if the change involved loss. It might not be obvious, but having a child could mean a subconscious loss of independence and a previous way of life, however joyful the addition.

I was physically vulnerable, too. I had been very tired and I had in retrospect been pushing myself beyond my limits, though this wasn't obvious at the time. The trigger had been one particular sleepless night. But it could have been anything that tipped me into such a state of heightened anxiety that I felt unable to deliver all that I imagined was required of me.

A part of me relished this piecing together of the clues after weeks of bafflement. I had previously prided myself on getting things done – that was how a former English teacher once summed me up. Now, Dr Fischer gave me licence to reflect on what had indeed been massive challenges: the arrival of two children in quick succession, both of us having careers, a busy social life. He gently prompted me to consider that I might be more compassionate to myself and feel less guilty about what had happened. Others too might have succumbed to illness had they faced similar pressures. Perhaps I could be gentler in future in terms of what I asked of myself. After all, I now had startling evidence of my own physical vulnerability. He paused to pass me a box of tissues.

A second part of me didn't want to dwell on the cause of the breakdown. My pattern in the past when faced with setbacks was to move on swiftly, to return to the chase and the life I knew. I was eager to get back to being a mother, wife and journalist, and it didn't help to analyse the whys and wherefores of what at times I tried to dismiss as nothing more than a temporary blip.

Such a description hardly did justice to the last few months,

Dr Fischer lightly corrected me. We talked about the language surrounding depression. We had already agreed that the word itself doesn't sound particularly severe, nor did it suggest how frantic I had felt. At least the description fitted my emotional need to downplay what had happened, just as I had tried to diminish the severity of my symptoms when I first met Dr Fischer. Part of me still didn't want to admit to being ill or that beneath the smooth surface I could be so seriously adrift.

Another part of me thought that 'nervous breakdown' at least seemed to approach the horror of what had happened and would convey the severity of the episode to outsiders, even if doctors don't like the phrase. Its meaning is so unclear: there are no medical guidelines to define what a 'nervous breakdown' means.

Call it what you will but during a 'depressive episode' or breakdown, those parts of one's brain that are non-essential, including memory, shut down in the battle to survive. Often those recovering from a breakdown are amazed to discover that, when ill, they had no sense of time. They assume they have been unwell for far longer than they actually were. That was certainly the case with me.

Nor had I realised the intensely physical nature of depression. As I told Dr Fischer, I had thought it was a case of lying around in a vaguely disconsolate mood and had absolutely no idea it could make you feel physically ill. Yes, he agreed, it was a common misconception. But mind and body are indissolubly linked. No human activity can be said to be wholly physical or wholly mental; all human activity, in whatever sphere, is psycho-physical. So the depression causes bodily symptoms – what doctors call somatic symptoms.

Like any other organ in your body, your brain can go wrong;

but unlike other organs, the brain is of extraordinary complexity and we have relatively little understanding of how it operates. Dr Fischer explained that, very roughly, as someone suffering from acute anxiety and panic, my adrenaline levels were so high that they were stopping me sleeping and eating and this contributed to the physical pain. My body meant well: it went into the fight or flight response the body resorts to in order to cope with life-threatening challenges. All my priorities switched from long-term to short-term survival. My systems were on a permanent emergency response; fuel reserves were mobilised and dispatched to my brain and muscles. Extra oxygen to burn the fuel was required so my heart had been pounding non-stop for months as my blood pressure and breathing increased. My appetite disappeared as my body shut down energy-consuming digestive processes and slowed down the production of saliva (another explanation, apart from the side effects of the drugs, for my dry mouth). My pupils dilated to let in more light, my reaction time speeded up, all in readiness for attack. Even my early nausea had a reason behind it: in a life-threatening situation I would need to vomit or defecate to make my body lighter and less appetising for any animals seeking me as their prey.

All these physical responses would normally be short-lived, the result of temporarily high anxiety. They were the same symptoms I had exhibited when I feared our plane might crash on that ill-fated journey to Dubai. But in my state of heightened arousal they were maintained, exhaustingly.

Doctors now agree that the physical pain of a major depressive episode can be even worse than severe physical illness. One doctor was quoted as saying in a classic book on depression that if he had to choose between suffering from renal

64

colic, a heart attack and an episode of severe depression, he 'would prefer to avoid the pain of depression':

> *It is a surprisingly physical sensation, with a surprising resemblance to coronary pain, because it too is total. But it cannot be relieved quickly. It even threatens life. It is oneself and not part of one's machinery, a form of total paralysis of desire, hope, capacity to decide what to do, to think or to feel except pain and misery.**

I have never experienced coronary pain but every other word of this rings true.

---

* Dr John Horder, a former president of the Royal College of General Practitioners, quoted in Lewis Wolpert, *Malignant Sadness: The Anatomy of Depression* (Free Press, 1999).

Chapter Five

Love Bids Me Welcome

END OF JULY 1997

Late July 1997

The magnolias in our street had long since shed their pink waxy flowers and were sporting green leaves instead. A new little Portuguese café had opened around the corner selling gooey custard tarts with scorched caramel tops served by a handsome dark-eyed patron. George had remained firmly at home after his brief stay with Sebastian's family and was now able to sit straight-backed. He laughed if you squidged his tummy.

I was beginning to reclaim some of my roles. When I managed to be a mother to the boys, sharing their evening bath for example, it felt like being back on an island of delight-fully solid ground. When I stopped, I was soon in danger of crashing again. So it was good to do things, to do anything. I was slowly reintegrating myself into family life.

Sometimes I could pray or simply concentrate. I discovered a fresh relish for music and art, slowly allowing myself to feel emotions that had until recently been obliterated in the narrow battle to survive.

I found music the most accessible. A friend who had nursed her dying mother agreed, telling me that as her mother's faculties faded, her last bodily connection was with music, the notes communing directly with what was left of her.

There was a moment when I felt a new dimension of consciousness as I listened to Sebastian's favourite piece, Handel's *Messiah*, shivering with the pleasure of the music. Art of all kinds introduced me to a different world: an opportunity to live as many unlived lives as I wanted, an escape from the hell in which I had been living, but deeply real, too. The music I was listening to was not separate from my life: it was part of my life.

Inexplicably, the heat-filled anguish and fear I had become so accustomed to sometimes gave way to a cool, calm higher power. At these moments I became certain of God's presence and utterly grateful for it. I felt freed from any anxiety or expectations as to who or what I was, a sense of my own ego dissolving and the embrace of something bigger. St Paul talked of 'the peace of God which passeth all understanding': this too was a sense of glimpsing the invisible and the divine beyond any conscious rationalisation. I stared up at the clouds and remembered the words of e.e. cummings. On occasion the black sky was turning blue.

> *i thank You God for most this amazing*
> *day:for the leaping greenly spirits of trees*
> *and a blue true dream of sky;and for everything*
> *which is natural which is infinite which is yes*
>
> *(i who have died am alive again today,*
> *and this is the sun's birthday;this is the birth*
> *day of life and of love and wings:and of the gay*
> *great happening illimitably earth)*

how should tasting touching hearing seeing
breathing any–lifted from the no
of all nothing–human merely being
doubt unimaginable You?

(now the ears of my ears awake and
now the eyes of my eyes are opened)

Yet days later any faith evaporated again. My belief in God seemed to wax and wane in a dizzying fashion. I was intermittently acquiescent and rebellious, an uncertainty which left me confused, ill at ease and troubled. But like many of those who battle with their faith, I felt that belief beset by uncertainty was better than no belief at all.

Sensing rebellion returning, and perhaps feeling that a second motherly figure might help, one late summer afternoon my mother suggested we try to walk to our local church. After the drama of our previous outing to the post box, both of us were nervous of venturing out. But this expedition proved a happy one, perhaps partly because our family had a long association with the church. It felt as if we were returning to a safe haven. It was where I had been baptised a Catholic and bored as a teenager, where Sebastian and I got married in 1993 and where we christened both the boys. George had smiled in my arms despite the cold water, though now it seemed as if joyfully standing around the font was a scene from a different life.

I had never much noticed the interior of the fine Victorian building before, or the way the light shafted through the stained-glass windows and illuminated the motes in the air. Once I left home my visits had become intermittent, defeated by the supposedly superior claims of work and family. I gave the matter of religion little thought. Sometimes I was baffled by how much it could mean to others and sometimes I was a little jealous of their certainty. If we did manage to get to a service my focus tended to be more on enjoying the poetry of the language than dwelling too much on my faith. My feelings about it had been muddled for a long time. Sometimes I believed in a Christian God in heaven and his church on earth, sometimes not. My only certainty was that my faith was highly personal.

Yet at the height of the illness there had been moments when any doubt vanished and my faith had seemed real and concrete, expressed through my beloved prayers, while God's existence seemed personified in those taking care of me. As the intensity of the illness ebbed, so did that certainty. I felt nostalgic for that conviction and thought perhaps a trip to the church would help revive it.

Once inside, my mother led me to look at the statue of the Virgin Mary cradling the infant Jesus, which I had never noticed before. To the left of the main aisle, the statue was of blue and white china, life-sized without being imposing, with delicately sculpted roses encircling the base. We sat and looked up at the Madonna. There was sweetness to her face, mingled with sadness.

I felt a flush of faith return. Sitting in the quiet comfort of Mary's accommodating gaze, I felt she had a message for me. She accepted me and my vulnerabilities and I should accept myself – all that I was and all that I failed to be, in all my child-ish fraility: for her there was no conclusive division between adult and child. She had a second message too: that I wasn't alone, that I could come and find her. She might not be able to hold me, but there seemed to be a warmth in the very air that surrounded her.

From then on I visited the church whenever I felt well enough to travel the two streets that separated us and sat quietly looking at that face, hoping that infusion of peace would descend. Sometimes it did.

But even if I didn't always feel God's presence, I still relished these little trips. I might not always experience religious conviction, but sitting on that pew, looking at that statue, allowed a different part of me to find a home, the part that needed quiet and peace and contemplation, the part that just needed to be, to be accepted for what I was and not for what I might achieve, to be accepted for just being. So much of my life was about doing. Satisfying, yes, but the doing, I began to realise, would never end. The relief of having accomplished things would only ever be short-term.

Poetry was proving a second deep spring of satisfaction on which I increasingly began to draw. Again I felt blessed that, now I was unwell, I had some reserves from an earlier life. Like most children, I had loved rhythm and rhyme. My mother would read poetry to me when I couldn't get to sleep and it always soothed me. But I also loved poetry as an adolescent, to the point that I learnt 'The Lady of Shalott' off by heart, fully aware it wasn't fashionable to wander around with a volume of Tennyson in my pocket.

Knowing my enthusiasm, when I first suffered a broken heart my mother slipped me a copy of Louis MacNeice's 'Apple Blossom', with its opening verse:

> *The first blossom was the best blossom*
> *For the child who never had seen an orchard;*

For the youth whom whiskey had led astray
The morning after was the first day.

While my lost love seemed like the 'best blossom', in time I too would see an orchard and love and live again. It was another poem I learnt by heart, burying its treasure deep within, a store of images that I could draw upon later, against adversity.

Throughout my twenties and early thirties, whenever a friend needed comfort, be they facing illness or divorce or heartbreak of some other kind, I would send them a poem that had helped me. Some joked that I ran a sort of poetry pharmacy, prescribing words instead of pills. The texts were better than self-help books, confided one, as they were better written and more nuanced in every way.

Now, in sickness, I was the one in need of poetic consolation, and my mother was once again a rich source. I was a child again, lying in bed as she read to me, my mother as protector. It was a role she had never abandoned, but it had become buried as I got older; it reasserted itself now as she read aloud in a strong, true voice.

It turned out that all these years she had been keeping a commonplace book of snippets of poetry, prayer and anecdotes that had particularly struck her, entitled 'Consolations'. I devoured the collection as if it were ice-cool water offered to a parched traveller. I resolved that I in turn would begin my own collection as soon as I was better, noting with astonishment that I was starting to believe in being better.

Some mothers and daughters are bound by a shared love of baking; others bond over their enthusiasm for a particular television show: my mother and I had always been united by a love of poetry. When I was a child she had furnished me with several gorgeous illustrated anthologies. My favourite was *The Golden Treasury of Poetry* selected and with a commentary by Louis Untermeyer. Inside its front cover I wrote 'This book belongs to Rachel S. Kelly January 8th 1976'. For the avoidance of doubt I added a book plate on which I inscribed 'Rachel Sophia Kelly' in turquoise italics.

A second favourite anthology she introduced me to was *The Golden Journey: Poems for Young People*. We learnt Edgar Allan Poe's 'The Raven' together from its pages. And as a teenager I particularly cherished the edition of *The Rime of the Ancient Mariner* she gave me one birthday, with its swirling studies of the sea by Gustave Doré in a rainbow of blacks. A leather-bound *Oxford Book of English Verse* was a present as I left for university.

Her knowledge of poetry far exceeded mine. As a schoolgirl, she had learnt reams of verse by heart as was more common at the time. ('There was nothing else to do,' she told me.) It astonished me how much she could still remember: great chunks of Shakespeare, Keats, Wordsworth, Byron, all the classics. She knew how one poet had influenced the next and once wrote a potted history of poetry on two vast sheets of paper for us three children.

I would like to say that I in turn introduced her to new poets and voices. But the traffic was largely one way. The poems I dispensed to my friends had largely come from her. Sometimes I would chance on a poet's voice that especially resonated with me – Emily Dickinson was a particular enthusiasm at one stage – and I would share my passion with my mother in a glorious moment when it felt as though I might be able to pay her back for all she had given me. But mostly, as if by magic, it was she who would send a copy of the poem that most perfectly answered my needs. This was how we shared our passion: not by talking about poetry, but by exchanging copies of poems. The point was that the poem expressed what needed to be expressed so much better than we could ourselves. We lacked the words.

Poetry was the perfect medium for me when I was ill. For a start, I wasn't well enough to listen to, let alone read, anything longer than a few verses. Even that could exhaust me. I didn't have the attention span to read an entire novel. So poetry's brevity was a blessing. So too was the way it dissolved the feeling of solitude: I wasn't alone, others had suffered and made something of their suffering. They had re-ordered the seemingly random cruelty of the illness into some kind of sense.

Then there was the way poetry absorbed and revitalised me. Its condensed nature and sophisticated vocabulary required a concentration that shocked me into the moment in an almost physical way, thereby freeing me from worries past and future. The rhythm and rhyme made the words speak with the necessary weight to command my attention. Images had to be unpacked and savoured, meaning discovered, the specificity of each word and phrase enjoyed.* I might not have been literally incarcerated, like so many others who have turned to poetry, from Primo Levi reciting Dante in a concentration camp to

---

* Research by Professor Philip Davis from the School of English at the University of Liverpool used scanners to monitor brain activity, researchers monitored how thirty volunteers responded to literature by Wordsworth, Shakespeare and T.S. Eliot, among others. They compared the results with readers' responses to simpler, modern translations. Electrical activity jumped when they read Shakespeare, because they had to decipher so many unusual words and images.

Nelson Mandela turning to W.E. Henley, but poetry helped free me from the imprisonment of my anxious mind.

Later, I read more about the healing power of words. Primitive societies made use of cures involving the spoken and then the written word: invocations and runes. The ancient Egyptians wrote remedies on papyrus, which was then soaked in water and the liquid drunk by the patient. In Greek and Roman myth, Apollo was the god of both poetry and medicine. The Greek playwright Aeschylus wrote 'Words are the physicians of the mind diseased.' and the philosopher Longinus believed in langauge's power to transform reality. In 1751 Benjamin Franklin founded the first American hospital, the Pennsylvania Hospital, where reading and creative writing were among the treatments prescribed for mental illness. In modern times recognition of the power of words to heal began with the psychologists Freud, Adler, Jung and others and led to the founding in 1969 of the Association of Poetry Therapy.*

I had read history at university, not English literature, so I had a rather eclectic view of what I should or shouldn't like, or what was supposedly good or bad poetry. I hadn't studied poetry, so I wasn't frightened of it or flummoxed if I didn't grasp something intellectually: my enjoyment was almost a physical one of the sound of the words. Actually, I didn't really think about poetry at all, just whether an individual poet spoke to me and I could empathise with what they were saying. If the language was too highly wrought or the allusions too incomprehensible, I would simply move onto the next poet that did reach me.

My mother and I naturally began with short poems. One

---

* Now the National Association for Poetry Therapy.

favourite was this little poem entitled 'New Every Morning' by Susan Coolidge, who wrote the children's book *What Katy Did*. It particularly helped at the painful start of the day.

> *Every day is a fresh beginning,*
> *Listen my soul to the glad refrain.*
> *And, spite of old sorrows*
> *And older sinning,*
> *Troubles forecasted*
> *And possible pain,*
> *Take heart with the day and begin again.*

Another favourite was this song by Oscar Hammerstein's 'You'll Never Walk Alone', which my mother would repeat as she held my hand.

> *When you walk through a storm*
> *Keep your head up high*
> *And don't be afraid of the dark*
> *At the end of the storm*
> *Is a golden sky*
> *And the sweet, silver song of the lark*
>
> *Walk on through the wind*
> *Walk on through the rain*
> *Though your dreams be tossed and blown*
> *Walk on, walk on with hope in your heart*
> *And you'll never walk alone*
> *You'll never walk alone*

Later, as my concentration improved, I turned once more to the seventeenth-century poets, particularly George Herbert. Though he is best known as a religious poet, and his verses lend themselves to a Christian interpretation, that was not the only way I experienced his poetry. For me, it was about how he had gone through desolation but made something extraordinary of it. As he was dying, Herbert asked that his poems be given to a trusted friend to decide if they were of use for any poor 'dejected souls' and if they should be 'made public'. Luckily the friend published what had hitherto been private prayers. From his poetry I would imagine Herbert himself suffered from a depressive illness, undiagnosed at the time. When I read the first verse of 'Love (111)', I felt a bolt of electricity pierce through me. All the hairs on my arm stood on end.

> *Love bade me welcome: yet my soul drew back,*
> *Guilty of dust and sin.*
> *But quick-eyed Love, observing me grow slack*
> *From my first entrance in,*
> *Drew nearer to me, sweetly questioning,*
> *If I lacked anything.*

Yes: my soul had been drawing back. Yes: I needed love to bid me welcome. The idea that my soul was 'guilty of dust and sin' seemed the most perfect description of the depressive illness. The poem pinpointed a sense of guilt that I should be depressed even though I was blessed with a loving home, husband and children, something I had not previously fully acknowledged. Herbert's words were bursting through the clouds of my mind, giving clarity where there had been chaos. It seemed we had been to the same place and spoke the same language, albeit that his visit was centuries ago. At last I had found a companion on my journey.

As the poem unfolded, it was as if we were having a conversation across the ages. I was the unkind, the ungrateful, the shamed; but Herbert had created a second voice in my head, a more compassionate, gentle yet firm voice – 'Love' – that spoke of forgiveness. In the end it is Love that matters. I was welcome at the table. I could sit and eat.

> *Love bade me welcome: yet my soul drew back,*
> *Guilty of dust and sin.*
> *But quick-eyed Love, observing me grow slack*
> *From my first entrance in,*
> *Drew nearer to me, sweetly questioning,*
> *If I lacked any thing.*
>
> *'A guest,' I answer'd, 'worthy to be here:'*
> *Love said, 'You shall be he.'*
> *'I, the unkind, ungrateful? Ah my dear,*
> *I cannot look on thee.'*
> *Love took my hand, and smiling did reply,*
> *'Who made the eyes but I?'*
>
> *'Truth Lord, but I have marr'd them: let my shame*
> *Go where it doth deserve.'*
> *'And know you not,' says Love, 'who bore the blame?'*
> *'My dear, then I will serve.'*
> *'You must sit down,' says Love, 'and taste my meat:'*
> *So I did sit and eat.*

It was an active process, brilliant as a way of engaging me beyond my own drama, in one experienced by someone else. The poem's value was that it seemed to me universal. I too had a debate in my head between the forces of darkness and 'sweet-eyed love' – all that that was good and true and positive in my life, all the forces of love, were willing me to be better, fighting the 'dust and sin'.

I would also repeat endlessly certain phrases and images from 'The Flower', another Herbert poem. One of my favourites was 'Grief melting away/Like snow in May': I wrote it out on a Post-it note and stuck it on the bathroom mirror, as I had done with key facts when revising for my history finals a decade previously at Oxford. It felt equally urgent. Two other favourite lines were 'Who would have thought my shrivelled heart/Could have recovered greenness?' The experience was similar to the way I had repeated prayers or lines from the Bible (many of them highly poetic, of course).

In those moments of the day when I held hands with Herbert, the depression couldn't find me. It felt as though the poet was embracing me from across the centuries, wrapping me in a cocoon of stillness and calm. Here was a new and welcome voice in my head, preaching the virtues of acceptance and hope rather than struggle and despair.

> *How fresh, oh Lord, how sweet and clean*
> *Are thy returns! even as the flowers in spring;*
> *To which, besides their own demean,*
> *The late-past frosts tributes of pleasure bring.*
> *Grief melts away*
> *Like snow in May,*
> *As if there were no such cold thing.*

Love Bids Me Welcome

Who would have thought my shrivelled heart
Could have recovered greenness? It was gone
Quite underground; as flowers depart
To see their mother-root, when they have blown;
Where they together
All the hard weather,
Dead to the world, keep house unknown.

These are thy wonders, Lord of power,
Killing and quickening, bringing down to hell
And up to heaven in an hour;
Making a chiming of a passing-bell.
We say amiss
This or that is:
Thy word is all, if we could spell.

Oh that I once past changing were,
Fast in thy Paradise, where no flower can wither!
Many a spring I shoot up fair,
Offering at heaven, growing and groaning thither:
Nor doth my flower
Want a spring-shower,
My sins and I joining together.

But while I grow in a straight line,
Still upwards bent, as if heaven were mine own,
Thy anger comes, and I decline:
What frost to that? what pole is not the zone,
Where all things burn,
When thou dost turn,
And the least frown of thine is shown?

And now in age I bud again,
After so many deaths I live and write;
I once more smell the dew and rain,
And relish versing. Oh, my only light,
It cannot be
That I am he
On whom thy tempests fell all night.

These are thy wonders, Lord of love,
To make us see we are but flowers that glide:
Which when we once can find and prove,
Thou hast a garden for us where to bide.
Who would be more,
Swelling through store,
Forfeit their Paradise by their pride.

There were certain lines that spoke so powerfully to me it seemed as though they had been injected into my body. Like Herbert, after so many deaths I too would live once more. I too was part of nature, a 'flower that glides', and there was a garden for me 'where to bide'. Hope seemed to sluice through me, rinsing away all the terror and tension.

The poem had a second message, one which flew off the page like a spark: that of the need for acceptance. 'Who would be more,/Swelling through store,/Forfeit their Paradise by their pride.' I couldn't wait to tell Dr Fischer. It seemed like a revelation: that accepting being ill rather than raging against it had calmed me.

It felt as if I had discovered the world wasn't flat, or as though I was, in Keats's famous phrase, 'stout Cortez, when with eagle eyes/He star'd at the Pacific'.* I told everyone I chanced to talk to of this amazing discovery. It seemed odd to me that it wasn't written on billboards or adorning the front of the newspapers. Later, the notion of acceptance would loom even larger in my life, not just of illness but of feelings such as anger that I had previously found difficult to acknowledge.

When I did tell Dr Fischer, he replied that this is a well-known pattern of recovery. After all the rage and fear provoked by illness, if we can accept and no longer be fearful of what has happened, our path to recovery is eased. This is not to say acceptance proved easy. Yes, there were moments when I seemed effortlessly to be able to hand over to a belief in a higher power whose compassionate love was all encompassing. Those times were lovely. But they came and went. At other times I lost all faith and had to resort to trying to believe in the power of time or Dr Fischer and his drugs or my own efforts to be better. This too will pass, as the mantra goes.

Science is also on the side of acceptance. Fighting the panic stimulates what is known as the 'sympathetic' nervous system – the fight or flight response – which is in reality far from sympathetic. The sympathetic nervous system releases stress hormones and gears up for battle by getting blood to the muscles. Acceptance and slow breathing can help prompt our alternative nervous system into action, thereby slowing down our metabolism, heart rate, blood pressure and brain chemistry. The rhythm of the breath produces a feeling of detachment, allowing us to observe ourselves from a calm place in the present: it is impossible to breathe in the past or the future.

I found another piece of writing that also suggested

* John Keats, 'On First Looking into Chapman's Homer'.

acceptance. It argued for seeing unhappiness and pain as part of God's purpose. Cardinal Newman's understanding of his own purpose, contained in his *Meditations and Devotions*, struck home:

> *If I am in sickness, my sickness may serve Him; in perplexity, my perplexity may serve Him; if I am in sorrow, my sorrow may serve Him . . . He does nothing in vain; He may prolong my life, He may shorten it; He knows what He is about. He may take away my friends, He may throw me among strangers, He may make me feel desolate, make my spirits sink, hide the future from me – still He knows what He is about.*

I did not know what my purpose might be or in what way I could serve. But it was comforting to surrender to Newman's view that God at least knew what He was about. I smiled to myself the night I fell asleep after reading Newman's words: my last few months had not been in vain.

Chapter Six

Folding Up My Map of Desolation

EARLY AUGUST TO MID-AUGUST 1997

Early August 1997

My next encounter with Dr Fischer was different. I was well enough to visit him at his Harley Street consulting rooms for the first time; my first two encounters with him had been at the hospital and the others at home. Stepping out of my sickbay gave a palpable boost to my confidence, though I was amazed at the noisiness of London traffic and the unaccountable aggression of its drivers, who seemed unaware how lucky they were to be well enough to drive.

The building was large and Georgian with an impressive black front door flanked by a shiny brass plaque embossed with the names of the magicians within and the mysterious letters after their surnames. I waited with my faithful mother in the grand reception room at the front, quiet but for the ticking of the carriage clock and bordered by chintz sofas inhabited by a gentleman in a suit and a lady in a burqa.

'It's funny,' ventured my mother, her eyes fixed firmly on the magazine through which she was idly flicking. 'It's turned out that Dr Fischer is the one. He's wonderful, really. I had my joke picture of a psychiatrist with a beard. In fact, he's very profound—'

She broke off mid-sentence, startled by Dr Fischer's silent

entrance. I accompanied him to his office at the back, which housed a large mahogany desk in the centre of the room and had a bay window giving onto an inner courtyard. There was a huge wing-backed armchair that enveloped me and therefore felt safe. An old-fashioned electric fire marred the grandeur of the ornate fireplace, above which was a painting of a multi-coloured market scene full of brightly coloured vegetables and their sellers in equally vivid dress. Dr Fischer later told me the painting proved useful as a conversation starter with some of his more reticent patients.

It felt as if he had been to my house, and now I was coming to his.

He gave me a questionnaire to fill in. The form was an attempt to assess the severity of my symptoms in a more orderly and scientific way than the information elicited by our chats. The questions were designed to monitor my response to different treatments and are a classic tool in diagnosing and treating depression. Given how difficult this is, a cynic might say the forms give a patina of medical certainty to what is a very imprecise art.

The form Dr Fischer used is one of the most common, known as the Beck Depression Inventory. It lists statements about the patient's physical symptoms, such as sleeping and eating patterns. It also lists statements about emotional health, such as feelings about the future or whether you are experiencing suicidal thoughts.

Week by week, I was asked to pick the statement in each group that best described my feelings over the past seven days. So, I could choose from statements ranging from 'I do not feel sad' to 'I feel sad' to 'I am sad all the time' to 'I am so sad or unhappy that I cannot snap out of it'. There are twenty-one questions and each statement is given a numerical score. The higher the total score, the worse the depressive disorder. I came top of the class.

The good news was that I was filling in the forms at all. I had initially been too ill to do so. In a typical pattern of recovery, once you get a bit better, it becomes easier to check the boxes and try and work out what you are feeling. Still, it struck me as being a rather imperfect scorecard, as often my responses were more complicated than the form allowed me to explain.

By having me consistently fill in the forms over time, Dr Fischer gradually built up a clearer and more scientific sense of how I was coping. Even so, it is still difficult to describe accurately a patient's symptoms. Since I first became ill the process has become more sophisticated, using technology to plot mood on a daily basis, often with a series of electronic scorecards.* There are plenty of examples from other areas of life to demonstrate that the simple act of monitoring something can lead to positive change: people who wear a pedometer walk, on average, a mile a day more than those who don't; problem drinkers who are asked to keep a diary of

---

* I've found moodscope.com to be a particularly effective online method for measuring mood. Each morning, you assess your emotional state by visiting the website and responding to twenty double-sided playing cards, each of which registers an emotion like 'alert' or 'nervous'. The cards can be flipped back to front or spun head to toe to choose one of four degrees to which you might be feeling that emotion, from 'Very slightly, or not at all' to 'Extremely'. You are then given a moodscope score: a percentage between 0 and 100, indicating how happy you are. moodscope stores your scores every day and plots them on a graph so you can track your ups and downs as time goes by. The website also sends you a supportive email every morning, especially helpful as those with depression are often at their worst in the mornings.

their alcohol consumption tend to reduce their drinking over a period of time.

The tablets had calmed me down to the extent that I could now try other approaches to getting better. Dr Fischer suggested relaxation tapes. Talk of tapes now sounds very antiquated in a world of CDs and audio downloads, but changes in technology aside, at the time, relaxation techniques were seen as a newish approach. We didn't discuss my having ongoing counselling at this point, which might sound odd now that it is prescribed far more routinely. But my experience suggests it was less usual then.

As with prayer, guided relaxation techniques relax the body one muscle group at a time, which in turn relaxes the mind. It is impossible for your mind to be tense if your body is relaxed, a truth that devotees of yoga have known for centuries. Your metabolism, heart rate and blood pressure all slow down. Equally, if your mind tenses, then so does your body.

'Just allow your body to relax,' the soothing baritone would begin. 'Just allow yourself to enjoy that lovely warm feeling as you just allow' – there were plenty of 'just allows' – 'yourself to relax. Find a quiet place and make yourself comfortable, neither too cool nor too hot . . .' Then the relaxation 'coach', as he described himself, would work his way through all the different muscle groups in the body. He would repeat phrases over and over to the point where I went into a semi-hypnotic trance.

This was attacking the problem the other way round, as it were. Mend the mess in your head by attending to the mess in your body. And the joy is that the mental peace that physical relaxation imparts is automatic. You can't stop it happening, however hard you try.

Such approaches are now a standard part of psychiatric treatment. Many of the best 'guided relaxations' can be found as apps: my favourite is relaxiapps.com,* featuring the soothing voice of Ross Puddle. Psychiatric hospitals offer a variety of approaches to treating depression, addressing a patient's physical and spiritual health rather than simply treating them with drugs. Patients at the hospital I attended can now benefit from different types of counselling, courses in mindfulness, sleep management, yoga, massage, and even salsa dancing for the endorphin release, as well as the more conventional drug treatments, all within a structured timetable to suit each patient.

Had I stayed in hospital, one part of my treatment would have been learning how to relax with the help of the tapes. Unlike therapy, guided relaxation is free, once you've made the initial, small outlay. It is also relatively easy to master. All you need to do is choose which of the various voices you prefer.

Over a period of about three weeks I began to follow the instructions of a soothing voice emanating from the tape recorder on my bed. Lengthen the breath. Slow the heart rate. Enjoy the afterglow as the muscles relax. I was amazed to discover muscle tension I hadn't even realised was there as I explored my body through breathing. My mother was once again my main companion as my accelerating recovery had meant that Sebastian had been able to spend more time at work. She would listen to the tapes alongside me (she almost

---

* www.relaxiapps.com has made two meditation and relaxation apps available for download from iTunes: 'Complete Relaxation – Full' for 69p and 'Complete Relaxation – Lite', a shorter version of the full app, which is free. Both apps guide the listener through relaxing each muscle in turn, followed by positive affirmations.

invariably nodded off to sleep). Later I was struck by the thought that actually, I didn't need to feel alone: I could imagine my breathing as being like a companion, and my breath would never leave me till the day I died.

Soon I didn't need to listen to the tape at all. The soothing voice was in my head, and I could conjure it up at a moment's notice. I would relax all the muscle groups in turn, from my feet to my head, till my whole being loosened. Unlike my mother I didn't fall asleep; instead I stilled my racing mind for the blissful half an hour it took to work through every muscle group. If I did tense up during the process I would just observe what was happening without judging it or identifying with the anxiety. I was not my anxiety. Perhaps I could control my mind after all.

Worries take a physical toll. If we can relax our minds, our physical exhaustion can be reduced. And the technique can work wherever you are. More and more research is being conducted on the practical physical changes to the brain that result from breathing techniques.

I got better and better at switching off. The joy of such techniques is that you are in control. No doctor has to be on standby advising how many tranquillisers you need to consume. You can decide when and where and for how long you need to zone out.

It was time for our annual street party. Every year the council blocked either end of our road, residents hauled their kitchen tables out of their front doors, gladdened them with tablecloths and flowers and invited their friends to come and celebrate. There was a band and bunting, dancing uniting young and old, and good cheer for all.

My first assumption was that of course we wouldn't be able to be involved this year. We would hunker down, close the curtains and keep very still. It was not for us to invite friends over and join the thirty other makeshift outdoor dining rooms. As the sun went down, though, I could hear the band start up. I crept to my window and couldn't resist peeping out from behind the curtains. The first dancers were beginning to jive, the singers to sing.

> *Let's twist again, like we did last summer,*
> *Let's twist again, like we did last year . . .*

I was reminded that I had once been someone else, could be someone else again. Whatever the horrors had been, there were now these violent flashes of joy. In Siegfried Sassoon's words, the singing would never be done.

> *Everyone suddenly burst out singing;*
> *And I was filled with such delight*
> *As prisoned birds must find in freedom,*
> *Winging wildly across the white*
> *Orchards and dark-green fields; on – on – and out of sight.*
>
> *Everyone's voice was suddenly lifted;*
> *And beauty came like the setting sun:*
> *My heart was shaken with tears; and horror*
> *Drifted away . . . O, but Everyone*
> *Was a bird; and the song was wordless; the singing will*
> *never be done.*

I got up and tentatively slipped my hand in Sebastian's, struck that it wasn't fair how blue his eyes were. Initially he protested, worrying that I wasn't well enough to go out and join the celebration and to engage in conversation with our neighbours. Seeing my keenness to dance, he relented and took me by the hand. We sneaked together to the darkened end of the street where no one could see us. We began to rock gently from side to side, enveloped in the balmy night, the music pouring from the stars and me singing along. This stranger knew me so well. He held my waist just where it was meant to be held. Then we started giggling and couldn't stop.

My emotional numbness dissolved. I felt about fifteen. The illness had brought a special gift: a new kind of intimacy born of long absence and renewed appreciation.

I would have danced all night, but as the couples and grannies and children began to peel off in the late evening, thinning the cover of the crowd, we retreated indoors. Suddenly the acid-orange glow of the street lights seemed overly bright and intrusive and the night was no longer safe. It was indeed too complicated to explain to our neighbours what was going on and why I was suddenly dancing. All I knew was that as we turned the key in the lock, we also turned a corner. We walked upstairs hand in hand, a married couple once again, and Sebastian a nurse no longer.

Early August 1997

I began to grasp the real meaning of phrases I hadn't previously understood. So it was with the term 'occupational therapy'. Lying in a darkened room in a heap would be enough to depress anyone. In the words of the famous proverb: we all need someone to love, something to hope for and something to *do*.

But one enormous challenge for those recovering from depression is to find that something to do. I needed to find a task I could manage, challenging without being too mentally strenuous. I kept remembering the story from a book I had enjoyed, on the craft of fiction, *Bird by Bird*. The author, Anne Lamott, remembers her then ten-year-old brother trying to write a report on birds that he'd had three months to complete and that is now due the next day. The child is close to tears at the kitchen table, surrounded by paper and pens and unopened books on ornithology, immobilised by the hugeness of the task ahead. Lamott's father sits down beside his son, puts his arm around him and says, 'Bird by bird, buddy. Just take it bird by bird.' I too needed to take life the proverbial one step at a time.*

I couldn't pray and recite poetry all day, and there were only so many times I could go and sit in church. I considered myself so unwell that I still didn't imagine I would ever work again and had not been in touch with my employers: I left any liasing with the office to Sebastian. My job was being ably done by another journalist in the newsroom, appointed when I first went on my six months' maternity leave, which was still under way. Now I needed something more practical. Far easier to 'do' yourself out of the gloom than to 'think' yourself out of it.

So in those moments when I was able to get up or concentrate, my family ingeniously invented little tasks to distract me

* Anne Lamott, *Bird by Bird: Some Instructions on Writing and Life* (Anchor, 1994).

while letting me believe the jobs were real. It was better to be told to do something than to be given an option. Choice is paralysing for those with depression. It could not be a case of waiting till I felt like doing something. Had I waited, that lovely dynamic energy might never have come. I needed to act first, without demanding that my thoughts and feelings change too. There was no place for a life based on contingency or waiting till the conditions were right. They never would be. In the twelve-step tradition, there is a saying that it is easier to act your way into sober thinking than think your way into sober acting.

One friend of mine acts, when all else fails, by peeling vegetables. Another likes sharpening pencils. I too became motivated by undertaking as many small, manageable tasks as I could, sloughing off the anxiety in a magical release as my mind was set free. Domestic chores became the soul of life, washing-up a form of salvation. Several mornings were whiled away matching the children's abandoned story tapes with their cassette boxes. I stuck on freshly printed labels and lined them up in rows. Another morning was spent sorting the jars in the kitchen, matching savoury and sweet like a child rearranging the pantry in her doll's house.

But the problem with that kind of acting is the awful moment when it's all done. The question is what to do next. Stopping and starting made me anxious and decisions were beyond me. Far better to be absorbed in something long-term.

As it turned out, the garden provided the answer: we were lucky enough to have a handkerchief-sized space at the back of our house and one at the front, too. I preferred the front garden as it had mopped up the strength of the late-summer sun and had burst into colour and vibrant leaf. There was a straight path to our dark-green front door, flanked on one side by a narrow bed that I planted with a scarlet climbing rose and thick, packed spikes of pale-yellow hollyhocks. To the other side of the path was a paved area, bordered on two sides by more flower beds stuffed with sweet peas. At its centre was a large terracotta pot overflowing with trailing geraniums around a white mop-headed hydrangea.

The garden was an endless source of sustenance and release. It revived me. Reconnecting with nature was a way of reconnecting with myself, as of course we are, though we forget so easily, a part of nature and the animal kingdom. It was a way back to the person I used to be.

One fellow resident in our back garden was a cheery robin. He (or was it a she?) would perch on the bay tree. There was something so generous-spirited about the way he puffed out his chest and sang his heart out as if he were performing in a concert hall. This little bird required nothing in return. He made me think of Emily Dickinson's poem 'Hope':

> 'Hope' is the thing with feathers –
> That perches in the soul –
> And sings the tune without the words –
> And never stops – at all –
>
> And sweetest – in the Gale – is heard –
> And sore must be the storm –
> That could abash the little Bird
> That kept so many warm –

I've heard it in the chillest land –
And on the strangest Sea –
Yet – never – in Extremity,
It asked a crumb – of me.

I loved watching my robin, symbol of abundant hope. It seemed as though the storm described in the poem was the gale I had lived through, but now I had a sense that all along hope had indeed perched in my soul. Now I was hearing its triumphant song.

My gardening job was never done, which meant I never got to the anxiety-inducing point when I didn't know what to do next. There are always more plants to grow, weeds to extract, wilting blooms to dead-head, soil to enrich. The pleasure is like that of any creative activity, be it painting or writing. Something wasn't there before, and now it is, and I have made it, and it is beautiful. Luckily, that August seemed particularly long and hot. If all else failed, I could always unfurl the hose. Our garden must have been the best-watered in the city.

It turned out that science, once again, was on my side, not to mention history. Court physicians in ancient Egypt prescribed garden walks for the mentally unwell. The benefits of sunlight on mood are well known. We are similar to animals that hibernate. We tend to feel gloomy and lethargic in winter and happier and livelier as spring arrives. Mental health charities encourage gardening schemes, knowing their value full well: gardening decreases anxiety, takes us out of ourselves and – literally – into the light. Studies have found that patients with rooms overlooking trees recover faster than those who face buildings.* The

---

* Professor Roger Ulrich, a leading expert on the benefits of green space, studied a group of American patients recovering from gall-bladder surgery.

scent of flowers bypasses our conscious mind, smell being our most direct sense. It can instantly change our emotions and trigger memories, as well as lower heart rates and reduce stress. It really does make sense to slow down and smell the roses.*

The methodical digging and weeding and sweeping soothed me and returned me to happy days I had forgotten from my childhood, pressing sunflower seeds into terra-cotta pots stacked either side of the mossy pathway at the bottom of my parents' garden. My nails were rimmed with black and my lower back ached, while my cup of tea was specked with earth and my hair full of the dust from sweeping between the paving stones. But I hadn't felt so calm in months.

Edward came to help, sploshing water from the hose onto the grey dust, turning it a glorious glossy black and consuming the pair of us in mud and laughter in the process. Time passed as swiftly as it had once passed slowly. It seemed as though both Edward and the garden were flourishing in my care, thoughts I had to suppress as they made me giddy with happiness. Flowers were appearing on the earth and an apricot bloom in Edward's cheeks. The words from the Song of Solomon came unbidden, delivering an emotional charge straight to my heart:

Half had rooms with views of trees, half not. Those with a natural view needed less pain relief, were more cooperative and went home two or three days sooner than the other group. See www.healthdesign.org.

* Dr Charles Spence of the Department of Experimental Psychology at Oxford University, quoted in the *Daily Mail*, 5 April 2009.

For, lo, the winter is past, the rain is over and gone.

The flowers appear on the earth; the time of the singing
of birds is come,
and the voice of the turtle is heard in our land.

The fig tree putteth forth her green figs, and the vines
with the tender grape give a good
smell. Arise, my love, my fair one and come away.

The calm seeped out of the very plants and enveloped me. The exercise released endorphins, those rightly trumpeted chemical messengers in the brain that inhibit activity in the amygdala, its fear and anxiety centre. As the weeks passed, I was receptive to the cycle of the seasons, summer's abundance naturally dovetailing with my own recovery. I planted for next summer, too, a statement about the future as much as the present. Gardening activated this sense of hope and renewal, not just the notion that I would get better but the belief that my bulbs would come up next spring and my strawberry plants would bear fruit in their own time. There is no rushing gardening, just as I couldn't rush getting better.

The depression may have been unfathomable but so too were the workings of God witnessed in nature. I found it miraculous that all of life was packed into a single seed, that everything needed to grow into leaf and flower was contained in something so small. Not everything was knowable. I was but a small part of Mother Nature's master plan. New life was and always would be bigger than me. The vastness of my ignorance, the brilliance of that seed, rescued me from my monstrous ego: it shrank in size by comparison. There was nothing I could do to make the seed more brilliant. Its marvellousness and creativity was all its own.

Or, as Muriel Stuart puts it in her poem 'The Seed-Shop':

Here in a quiet and dusty room they lie,
Faded as crumbled stone or shifting sand,
Forlorn as ashes, shrivelled, scentless, dry –
Meadows and gardens running through my hand.

Dead that shall quicken at the call of Spring,
Sleepers to stir beneath June's magic kiss,
Though birds pass over, unremembering,
And no bee seeks here roses that were his.

In this brown husk a dale of hawthorn dreams;
A cedar in this narrow cell is thrust
That will drink deeply of a century's streams;
These lilies shall make summer on my dust.

Here in their safe and simple house of death,
Sealed in their shells, a million roses leap;
Here I can blow a garden with my breath,
And in my hand a forest lies asleep.

No one, it seemed to me, had better described the magic sealed into the tiniest seed. It was magic that I relished that summer.

Even what might once have seemed dull or unsightly in the garden now made sense. Rotting bulbs or diseased leaves had their place, too. The perfection was in the balance, the right-ness of things together. The garden's beauty existed next to its ugliness, just as my anguish had given way to this joy.

Gardening even helped with my insomnia. Occasionally the antidepressants were slow to work. When I couldn't sleep, I would walk around the sunlit garden in my head, visualising the roses in bud and the sweet peas clambering up their bamboo canes, the daisies I had planted and the trachysper-mum and wisteria that were beginning to romp over the brick walls. I particularly liked it when the rain was heavy and I could imagine it softening the dry soil and succouring the plants. Somehow it seemed that the rain was also healing me. Before I could mentally examine the pots lined up outside the kitchen door, I was often fast asleep.

Indoors, I found open-plan, anonymous, minimalist spaces bleak. I needed the cosy and the snug; a primal response to having somewhere to hide, and pockets of seclusion. Luckily our house was full of warm, small rooms. I only had to watch the children playing houses to find they also instinctively reflected those basic needs.*

Not only was I now able to garden; I was able to read about

---

* The Academy of Neuroscience for Architecture (ANFA) is an American organisation that studies the effect of architecture on our brains: how our external environment affects our internal one, and how we might design hospitals, homes and schools to be more in tune with our emotional needs. Researchers have found that people find it stressful in a kitchen, for example, where activity happens facing a wall. (Our backs are vulnerable to attack – hence the popularity of kitchen islands.) Heavy curtains, small intimate corners and fires were unsur-prisingly found to be comforting. Window seats with long views were also found to be soothing, as we feel relaxed when we know exactly where we are in our environment.

it, too. Illustrated gardening books were a gentle way to return to the printed page. I was naturally drawn to books about small London gardens, especially those with striking 'before' and 'after' pictures of run-down plots that had been transformed into inviting outdoor rooms; the transformations seemed to mirror my own recovery. John Brookes's *The New Small Garden Book* with its enticing subtitle 'A Completely Fresh Approach to Transforming any Small Space Outside' became particularly well-thumbed.* On the days when I wasn't well enough to garden, I imagined how I might follow Brookes's design strictures in our own plot and was soothed by pictures of what the book described as a 'leafy-ceilinged room' in which 'dappled sunlight falls gently through the vine-entwined pergola to make this a perfect spot for leisurely meals outside.'

The Concise British Flora in Colour had long been a favourite, a gift I had received as a child and enjoyed ever since (once again the frontispiece is dominated by my bookplate stickers).** The book is the outcome of sixty years of study, research and draughtmanship by the Reverend W. Keble Martin. Born in 1877, he combined his work in parishes in the north of England and as a chaplain to the forces in France in 1918 with his life as a botanist. At once a reference book and a work of art, the book contains thousands of species precisely described in the text, alongside exquisite botanical drawings. Each page of illustrations is crammed so full of flowers it is like a miniature garden, a triumphant hymn to nature's glorious abundance. On the

---

* John Brookes, *The New Small Garden Book: A Completely Fresh Approach to Transforming any Small Space Outside*, (Dorling Kindersley, 1991).
* W. Keble Martin, *The Concise British Flora in Colour*, (Ebury Press: Joseph, 1974).

facing page were sharp descriptions of each plant's characteristics: 'stems arching; leaflets narrow, tapering to base . . .' I didn't know what all the words meant but there was something akin to poetry about the long incantatory lists: 'Burnet Rose', 'Trailing Rose', 'Long-styled Rose', 'Dog Rose', 'Short Pedicelled Rose', Downy Rose', 'Northern Downy Rose', 'Soft-leaved Rose'. It soothed me in the same way as did listening to the shipping forecast on the radio.

Mid-August 1997

Originally I had only been able to read poetry, then I began to enjoy my picture books. Now I felt able to tackle something longer.

The first proper book I read as I recovered was *I Capture the Castle* by Dodie Smith. The novel was recommended to me by a friend whose sister had committed suicide. She said it was the first book she had managed to read, a year later.

Its sweet tale of young love is related by the narrator Cassandra and tells of her sister Rose, stepmother Topaz and two handsome American brothers: the characters' lives are so compelling, and the sense of their castle home is so effectively evoked, that the book transported me to different places; it was the perfect antidote to my self-absorption.

Slowly I began to pick up other books, mainly ones I had read before: I didn't wish to risk being thrown by the description of violent acts or anything that might induce anxiety. I was drawn to authors who created magical and humorous self-contained worlds, such as P.G. Wodehouse or Nancy Mitford, where nothing more worrying than a stray aunt was likely to appear. Returning to novels felt like being back at the wheel of a much-loved but rusty car that had been oiled so that once again the motor could start. It felt good.

Being able to read is not just a sign of returning concentration and that you are getting better. It can actually help your recovery: reading triggers that part of the brain that governs empathy and liberates you from your own personality by connecting you to others. While I was absorbed in the dramas of Cassandra, Rose and Topaz, I was rescued from thinking only about myself. The more connected I felt to others, the more stable I felt in turn.

This was particularly true when I started reading to the children again. This had always been a pleasure, but there was no denying that at times I had skipped chunks of text in an effort to finish and dash on to the next task on my to-do list. Edward was never fooled. 'You've missed a page,' he would complain, identifying which precise one, despite the fact that he could not read. Now I no longer skipped even an adjective.

My gentle occupational therapy was beginning to work. But for those moments when free fall beckoned again, I discovered more about the power of breathing thanks to Jenny, a yoga teacher friend who would sometimes come over for a cup of tea. I was already breathing differently thanks to my relaxation exercises, but Jenny told me that breathing could help to reduce my anxiety even when I did not have half an hour to spare.

She explained that, although for children nothing is simpler than breathing, as we become adults we can lose the power to breathe properly, especially when gripped by anxiety. Typically, I would hyperventilate. My breathing would become shallow and short in an adrenaline-fuelled flight or fight response.

I found it useful to understand what actually happens when you hyperventilate. Jenny explained that when you breathe normally, oxygen is transferred from the lungs to the haemoglobin in the red blood cells and carried to the tissues. The body cells use the oxygen, producing carbon dioxide as a by-product, which is then carried back to the lungs and breathed out. But when you over-breathe (or hyperventilate), you take in and breathe out too much air in short, sharp breaths. In particular, you breathe out too much carbon dioxide, leaving the body depleted. It is low carbon-dioxide levels that make you feel spacey. Too little carbon dioxide shrinks the veins and means less blood for the brain and the rest of the body.

Luckily, we can learn to breathe differently. The answer lies in breathing with the muscle at the bottom of your lungs, the diaphragm. This means you use the whole of your lungs to breathe, rather than just the upper half, as is the case when you hyperventilate.

That was enough science, she said. Far better to just do it. I felt rather self-conscious as the two of us sat there breathing, our efforts interspersed with giggles, especially as I was worried that our nanny, Julie, would interrupt us and think that I was displaying odd hippy-like behaviour. I gradually learnt to prolong my out breath, which stopped me forcing in too much oxygen in the first place, thereby upsetting those all-important carbon-dioxide levels. It felt deliciously calming. 'And you don't have to lie down,' Jenny enthused. 'You can do this anywhere, whenever you feel frightened. Even simpler is to simply block one nostril, which will force you to breathe more slowly. Pretend you've got a cold if someone asks why you've got your hand over your nose.'

By the time our tea cooled I had learnt the following method, which is so simple that to describe it as a technique makes it sound overcomplicated. Breathe in and count as you do so. Count to around five or six. Then breathe out, again counting as you do so. You must breathe out for more than five or six counts. This is the only rule: your out breath must be longer than your in breath. Experts in the method can breathe out to the count of eleven. Despite having practised the technique for nearly ten years now, I can never count for very long when breathing out, perhaps because I am small. It doesn't matter, just as long as you breathe out for longer than you breathe in.

The reason for making the out breath last longer is that exhaling stimulates the parasympathetic nervous system, the body's relaxation response. Inhaling, on the other hand, stimulates the sympathetic nervous system, which arouses us. The reason for counting is that it helps distract you.

My shallow breathing was so ingrained that it was surprisingly hard to change. I seemed to be able to manage when Jenny was there, but once she had gone I didn't feel relaxed on my own and panicked that I would forget what I had learnt. It took me several days after her visit to find a rate of inhaling and exhaling that was comfortable. Initially, I could inhale to a count of three and exhale to a count of six, and then I gradually built up. I practised in odd places. It was something else to do, breath by breath. If only I had known about such a powerful tool earlier, I said to my friend as she waved goodbye.

'Stand up, breathe, and fold your map of desolation,' she laughed, blowing a kiss as she walked down the front garden path. I recognised the phrase from W.H. Auden's love poem, 'Underneath an Abject Willow'.

Underneath an abject willow,
Lover, sulk no more:
Act from thought should quickly follow.
What is thinking for?
Your unique and moping station
Proves you cold;
Stand up and fold
Your map of desolation.

Bells that toll across the meadows
From the sombre spire
Toll for these unloving shadows
Love does not require.
All that lives may love; why longer
Bow to loss
With arms across?
Strike and you shall conquer.

Geese in flocks above you flying.
Their direction know,
Icy brooks beneath you flowing,
To their ocean go.
Dark and dull is your distraction:
Walk then, come,
No longer numb
Into your satisfaction.

Chapter Seven

The Pearl of Great Price

MID-AUGUST TO LATE AUGUST 1997

Mid-August 1997

The summer eased into fullness. The moments of calm I was experiencing coincided with the resumption of more normal relations with my family. My sister was away in Russia, but often my brother would bundle me up and take me across to his flat where he was studying for his solicitor's exams. I would lie on his sofa while he sat at his desk, working, before he stopped to make minestrone and help me eat.

While I had been seriously ill, the usual irritations of family life had been suspended, rather like politicians uniting in wartime. As I recovered, they returned, albeit in a subtly different way. My nearest family members now often found themselves dealing with someone more akin to a whiny child than a functioning adult. Life was conducted very much on my own selfish and sometimes angry terms. There was nothing necessarily ennobling about getting better.

I could be at my most juvenile with my mother. To my horror, I all too easily reverted to being the grumpy adolescent she used to describe as being like a dying duck. Some days I might refuse to get dressed if I disliked the socks she had chosen for me. Or I might turn against the lily plant I had been given, thereby depriving my ladybird of its home. Or maybe I would randomly reject the boiled egg with toast arranged in a star around the cup that she had carefully carried upstairs, just as she had done when I was a child.

'I'm not hungry,' I would say, after a brief, strategic pause, even if I was secretly ravenous and knew I would have to choose my moment to sneak downstairs and eat later when no one could see me. I had gradually returned to eating solid food after months of soups and smoothies. George was making the same transition at the same time. Or, I might hurt my mother's feelings by saying that I wanted Julie to look after me instead, as if Julie was an adequate substitute for my mother.

Partly I was angry at still being dependent on others, so I was prone to lashing out. I longed to be fulfilling my role with my children in the kitchen downstairs, but my uneven recovery meant that I was still being forced to read from a different script upstairs. It was all too easy to snap at the innocent court gathered around me.

In my defence, sometimes I was nervous of being too well, too quickly. Displaying an appetite or other signs of getting better might lead to being thrust back into life's hurly-burly too soon for comfort. I feared resuming responsibility for my to-do list and being required to remember everything from the washing powder that needed replacing to the children's stories that needed to be read. But sometimes I was just being plain difficult. My moods swung alarmingly and suddenly. A few seconds could separate a good day from a bad one, my confidence either growing steadily or snapping like a dry branch.

My mother rightly suspected that sometimes I was feeling better than I let on. I could tell by the way she smoothed the sheets a touch too firmly. Naturally she longed for the moment when I was officially 'better'. Not only could she then resume her own life; she could also rejoice at my recovery. At this stage, I was too mean to share such joy. Perhaps a bit of me had become accustomed to being the victim and the centre of attention, what some call the secondary gain of being ill. Much as I was loath to admit such a thing to myself or others, there is some advantage to being unwell: recovery could seem dull in comparison.

But forcing me to get up or telling me to get a grip would never have been my mother's way. She couldn't abide telling others what to do because she hated being bossed about herself. The closest she got was to suggest, once, that a new pink dress might cheer me up. There was never a moment when she turned soothing noises into 'You might actually feel better if you damn well got dressed and got up!'

'I felt helpless,' she told me later. 'There was no point mouthing platitudes. All I knew was that you couldn't be alone. Someone had to be with you at all times. That was my role.' If she couldn't be there, then Sebastian took over, or my brother. My sister was desperate that she was away and couldn't help.

Outwardly, my mother was steady. Her calmness was bred in the bone. One secret to it was her love of books. Brought up in Hampshire in a solid late-Edwardian house near Basingstoke, her family's life revolved around riding outside and reading within. Every spare inch of the bathrooms and landings were lined with books. Only convention stopped her and her two brothers and two sisters reading at the table. At least meals were an opportunity to discuss the books.

Books had sustained my mother through various previous crises. She gave birth to me in the middle of the 1960s to the sound of my father reading *The Wind in the Willows*; Erle Stanley Gardner's detective stories were her alternative to tranquillisers. My father would say 'She's curled up with an Erle Stanley Gardner' when I enquired where she was. Indeed, as a child, for many years I thought an 'Erle Stanley Gardner' was some kind of medicine.

Books were her solace, too, when my father was struck down by a stroke and left partly disabled in his early fifties. I was twenty and in my last year of university at the time. With an awesome effort of will, he gathered himself up and made a remarkable recovery, but it took the best part of the subsequent decade. After nearly six months in hospital he learnt how to walk again thanks to intensive physiotherapy and his own immense determination. The memory of his courage during those years helped inspire me now as I too struggled to recover. He hadn't complained. Nor would I.

Despite his efforts in the aftermath of his stoke, my father was left with limited movement in his left leg and none at all in his left arm. Inevitably it was my mother who therefore played more of a practical role in looking after me, while, unbeknown to me, my father lamented to her that he felt useless. She lugged trays up and down stairs, changed the sheets, remade my bed and nipped out to the shops for groceries, as well as helping more generally in the house and with the children. Looking after someone with depression is no different to looking after anyone who is unwell: much of the time it involves boring, repetitive and physically demanding tasks with very little thanks.

Meanwhile, my father would visit every few days. Typically, he would sit quietly by my bed and squeeze my hand. He seemed to know how little energy I had, perhaps remembering his own exhaustion after his stroke. If I seemed more responsive, he might share something of his day or a snippet he had read – he loved historical biographies and we had both studied history at university. Our conversations didn't dwell on my illness but were much as they had always been. His main concern was that I should be getting the best possible medical care. While my depression had taken him by surprise, he had long experience of dealing with doctors, as indeed did my mother after years of nursing a sick husband.

My mother's second secret weapon was her three best friends, whom she had known since childhood and whose lives and families interwove with ours. For as long as I could remember, every week she lunched with each of the three in turn. We grew up with their children. We swung together on the same swings when we were little and went to the same parties as we grew into teenagers.

In troubled times, these families were accustomed to supporting each other. It was a bit like a flock of geese flying in a V formation: if one bird faltered the others would sense it and would slow down to support it. Throughout my illness my mother had felt the rhythm of those beating wings. Her friends would take her out for little treats in her moments off from my bedside.

Her third weapon was how much she valued her work: I inherited from her a similar belief. She was a scholar and a writer whose interest was the eighteenth century, the first century in which she felt people were socially more or less the same as us, and she had devoted twenty years of study to the subject. Whatever the immediate horrors of a sick husband or child, she could retreat into another world in her work on the biographies of the playwright Richard Brinsley Sheridan, the poet Thomas Chatterton or the actress Sarah Siddons. She always said that there was only one thing she really cared about apart from her family, and that was trying to write as well as she could.

Late August 1997

While my mother's response to dealing with a difficult patient was to indulge my moods, my husband's approach was to try to humour me out of them. The two of them worked in tandem, united in their joint efforts and bolstering each other in dark times.

In one such moment, when all hope had fled, my mother recalls saying to Sebastian, 'You must remember, Rachel couldn't have done all she has done if it hadn't been for you.' He replied that he in turn couldn't have done what he'd done without my help.

In Sebastian's expert hands, laughter was a salve. While on the whole poetry didn't soothe him in the way that it did me, he did enjoy the taut writing of Dorothy Parker's 'Résumé'.

> *Razors pain you;*
> *Rivers are damp;*
> *Acids stain you;*
> *And drugs cause cramp.*
> *Guns aren't lawful;*
> *Nooses give;*
> *Gas smells awful;*
> *You might as well live.*

Sebastian helped me live. He defused the sickbay tension by asking me to put my worries in order. Large concerns vied with small. My still-fuddled brain couldn't distinguish between them. Each time I got to the end of one anxiety – I would never work again, the children were suffering – he would say, 'Next worry.' But gradually the worries got more and more trivial.

By the time we got to worry number eight or nine, which might be something as random as getting a spot, I would be giggling. 'If we've got to "getting a spot", then you're fine,' he would reassure me. He had managed to dissolve each worry in turn as if it were an aspirin disappearing in a glass of water.

He combined jokes with trying to tempt me beyond the confines of the house. We began to go on little expeditions to counter the boredom of having been confined for months to our bedroom. There were obstacles we hadn't foreseen, such as the time when he first tried to take me to our local swimming pool. We hadn't calculated on separate male and female changing rooms, and I still couldn't be on my own. So we abandoned that plan.

A few weeks later we tried again, this time with a girlfriend in tow who could accompany me to the changing rooms. Kate had been a friend since childhood and felt more like a relation. But even with her continuous support and encouragement as well as Sebastian's, I hadn't foreseen how challenging the trip would be or how easily my flimsy self-belief could evaporate like the steam coming off the hot showers. It was an indicator of quite how much the illness had knocked my confidence that I wasn't sure if I could remember how to swim. And if part of confidence is decisiveness, it had taken me weeks to say yes to Sebastian's idea.

It was Saturday and busy when we arrived, after all the palaver of Sebastian reassuring me we hadn't forgotten anything and finally managing to leave the house. For months all my senses had been muffled, so the first shock was noticing the smell of box-fresh trainers mingled with chlorine and sweat that suffused the changing room. Catching a glimpse of myself naked in the changing-room mirror was the second. I didn't recognise the round figure who stared back. I was equally amazed at my lack of physical prowess in the water. I felt threatened by the noise and seeming aggression of the other swimmers after the quietness of my room. In addition, I was so overweight that the effort to get through the water was monumental. And I was weak, having stayed in bed for the best part of four months. The water felt too choppy, the chlorine too caustic and my bathing-suit too exposing. The other swimmers seemed to be attacking the water and I feared I would be next. I wanted to return to the changing room to gather a protective towel around my shoulders and snuggle inside. In future I would be wary of positioning myself to fail by setting my expectations too high.

This unpromising start meant that it was several weeks before we ventured to the pool again. This time my anxiety levels had reduced to the point that I felt confident enough to go without Kate. I was not yet preoccupied with losing the weight I had gained as a side effect of the antidepressants: I was more drawn to the well-known mood-enhancing and stabilising effects of exercise. Swimming suited us both well: it had always been Sebastian's exercise of choice and he needed an endorphin boost as much as I did. Meanwhile, measuring the number of lengths I managed to complete was a good way of mapping my progress, giving me a sense of achievement. The pattern mirrored that of my recovery more generally. It was a case of two lengths forward, one back.

Not long afterwards, when I was confined to bed yet again after a relapse, I recognised Sebastian's familiar bouncy tread on the stairs. He burst in, clasping a big plastic bag containing a large parcel and smiling broadly. I have always loved the giving and receiving of presents, never more so than in this period when I reverted at times to childish ways. I couldn't pretend to be sicker or crosser than I was as I tore off the wrapping paper. It was a multi-coloured kite, red and yellow and blue and green.

Later that blustery day our little band set off to fly it in the park. Sebastian unreeled the twine, yanking the contraption into life and releasing it to freedom high in the air until it was as small as a postage stamp. We laughed, our heads tilted to the clouds, and George in my arms. Sebastian ran, almost falling over backwards and his muscles straining as the kite swooped and flew, its feathery tail snapping in the wind, only to collapse in a tree. It became officially Day One of Being Better.

Being my cheerleader round the clock inevitably took its toll on Sebastian. He had shouldered much of the burden of keeping our family afloat.

My style of friendship had always been highly confessional. I liked to build intimacy by sharing and respecting confidences. By contrast, Sebastian was less gushing about personal matters. As I recovered, though, he began to be more open about the illness now at last we all knew what was going on. Even though at times it was difficult for him to include someone in a narrative that had been running for so long and seemed hard to believe, he chatted straightforwardly with friends about what had been happening. After months of silence, being open helped him feel more normal about the situation. It also allowed him to explain our absence from our usual social life for the last few months. In particular, he wanted to discuss the striking physicality of the illness, which he believed was not widely appreciated in our circle. 'I felt our friends should know. It was hard for them to understand how seriously ill you had been without knowing the sheer pain of your symptoms, the screaming agony. That always seemed to surprise people.'

When he felt under strain, he tended to fuss about food. As the child of a French mother, one of his particular delights was fresh bread. While I had been very ill, he had been responsible for buying it but as I continued to recover, it became a pleasing challenge for me to try to incorporate a daily trip to the baker. After all, I was at home all day. I set myself the challenge of buying a loaf of bread. And as I became better still, it was time to return to one of my favourite pastimes while I had been on maternity leave: taking the children out for a buttery croissant at one of the local cafés, typically full of other lucky mothers doing the same. I loved witnessing Edward's delight as he deconstructed a *pain au chocolat*, carefully isolating the chocolate strip to eat last by delicately picking off the flakes of pastry.

Sometimes I managed to buy the bread, sometimes I didn't. The days when I did, a baguette on the chopping board became a symbol of our life continuing to knit back together. On his return from work Sebastian would tear off its rounded nose and crunch into it, ravenous from the day.

One evening there was no fresh bread. I hadn't got out that day. 'I forgot to get the bread,' was all Sebastian said as he came upstairs. It was always a sign that he was stressed when he blamed himself for failing to complete a task which had never been his responsibility.

A balance shifted that evening. I had a fresh thought, one I hadn't had for months: I had my part to play in steering our small family ship once again. I had, I remembered, a living, breathing husband who was affected by what I did. It was as if I had only been able to hear one monotonous chord for months, living life at such an extreme pitch of selfishness. Now the whole piano keyboard of emotions was opening up again.

Buying the bread became a symbol of being able to think of others. Some days I feared going to the baker would tip me back into illness. But beneath my unease was a sense of returning joy. It was undeniable that once again I was starting to hear that full range of notes. I had felt needed by my husband and I wanted to please him.

I was even more pleased when I discovered one day that I could feel bored, an emotion I hadn't experienced for months while living through the high drama of the illness.

It happened when I went to the hairdresser for the first time. The trip was self-evidently a good sign that I once again cared about my appearance. It was also a good sign that my image in the mirror now seemed to be stabilising. Most days it was definitely me looking back to say hello, rather than a stranger.

It made me smile into the glass. My internal world might have been sliced to shreds, yet outwardly I was unscathed. I had to stop myself waving at my reflection. The only noticeable difference was that I had somewhat chubby cheeks, resembling my childhood self.

I resumed my lifelong quest for the perfect hairstyle. As my hairdresser wrapped a robe around me and we began to chat, I found my hand being drawn inexorably upwards towards my mouth. I instinctively hid the sound of my yawn. It was small, certainly. But it was a yawn nonetheless.

Even better, when I left the hairdresser I glimpsed myself in a shop window. No, the hair wasn't quite right. Some familiar restless itch had returned. Hooray! Life was getting back to normal. Normal was very good.

Alongside the mundane, there were extraordinary moments when the everyday became exquisite. I was surprised at the force of my attraction to Sebastian as it returned after months when all sensuality had vanished. Extreme times had summoned forth extreme emotions, good as well as bad.

One evening, after Sebastian and I had had supper, I went to shake out the tablecloth on the little balcony outside the kitchen. My heart lurched at the glimpse of the moon, flawless and new, sitting so comfortably in the warmth of the night sky. The dark, which for so long had triggered thoughts of sleepless nights, now seemed welcoming. I jumped up to sing and twirl in a trance of joy, throwing myself into the air as if I had been sitting on top of an oil well which had suddenly spurted into life.

As I danced, I was suffused with a sense of Sebastian's devotion and self-sacrifice and uncomplaining acceptance of all that had befallen us. This really had been a case of 'in sickness and in health', of his love having to bear all. He had created the scaffolding on which I had clambered to the light, been my taken-for-granted respite and buffer against violent uncertainty, partner in trouble and always at my side as we beat down the tremors together. I had a fierce sense of gratitude. I was no longer beyond love. My prayers had been heard. I determined that I would never, ever take him or the life we shared for granted. Knowing I couldn't find the words, I borrowed those of Elizabeth Barrett Browning: it felt as if I was reading and dimly understanding the poem for the first time.

> *How do I love thee? Let me count the ways.*
> *I love thee to the depth and breadth and height*
> *My soul can reach, when feeling out of sight*
> *For the ends of Being and ideal Grace.*
> *I love thee to the level of everyday's*
> *Most quiet need, by sun and candle-light.*
> *I love thee freely, as men strive for Right;*
> *I love thee purely, as they turn from Praise.*
> *I love thee with the passion put to use*
> *In my old griefs, and with my childhood's faith.*
> *I love thee with a love I seemed to lose*
> *With my lost saints – I love thee with the breath,*
> *Smiles, tears, of all my life! – and, if God choose,*
> *I shall but love thee better after death.*

While my evenings could be exuberant, in the mornings the physical pain would return. The medical term for this is diurnal variation in mood. It affects everyone to some extent (though in varying ways), but those with depression have more extreme variations in their mood during the course of the day.

I had only been able to bear to see the oldest of friends and the nearest of adult relatives. As the days wore on, I gradually began to set about restoring other relationships, chiefly and most importantly the children I had neglected for so long.

One Saturday morning I woke up to their presence as

summer began to fade and the leaves yellowed on the trees that lined our street. Sebastian had left Edward playing on the floor with his Duplo. George was lying quietly by my side. My usual early-morning fears dissolved as I noticed him properly. I had regained the ability to pay attention.

For months, my concentration span had been almost non-existent. My brain had been moving so fast that I had been unable to focus properly on anything, as if every thought or concept was like water slipping through my fingers. Now it was as though I could cup my hands, hold onto a little of the liquid and briefly observe it.

It was his hair that caught my eye. It was almost a physical pleasure to observe it properly. When he was born, it had been thick and black. Now wisps of gold were nudging from the still-soft crown of his head. Light was pushing out dark, right in front of me. Momentarily, he was neither brown-haired nor blond but an extraordinary combination of the two. I was caught out by my tears.

I studied the rest of him. Delicate fingernails sheathed the pink tips of his fingers. He was straining out of the Babygro he had failed to fill only weeks before, the outline of his perfect toes visible. Sparrow-like cries and little purrs and hums gurgled out of him, all begging for a response from me. Just at the moment when I could once again hear, he had reached the point where he could communicate.

I could hold him properly, too. George's rounded little legs seemed like miniature unleavened loaves where his soft flesh folded into itself. He instinctively wrapped them around my side as I balanced him on my hip. He could hold his head up now and my breast was once again useful, this time as something to nestle against. The warmth of his skin made me shiver. For a moment I had to put him down. The exhilaration was such I felt I might faint.

I recovered enough to scoop him back up into my arms, weeping softly into his hair as I remembered his departure to stay with Sebastian's family a few months earlier. I resolved then, that however ill I might be, I would never again be separated from either child. 'It's never going to happen again,' I promised him, looking into his fiercely blue eyes. His returning gaze seemed to say that even he could have told me it had been a mistake to send him away.

My husband was momentarily taken aback to see me up and about as he emerged from the bathroom towelling his hair. He smiled and picked up Edward, who hadn't stirred from the floor. 'I want to go to the park,' Edward said. Of course he did.

Over the next few weeks, the children's natural insistence on living in the present and their instinctive joy at discovering the world helped dissolve my fears of past and future. A friend to whom I had once sent a poem returned the favour: she introduced me to R.S. Thomas's poem 'The Bright Field' with its lines 'Life is not hurrying/onto a receding future, nor hankering after an imagined past.' Instead, Thomas asks us to embrace the present. Life is here. Life is now.

> *I have seen the sun break through*
> *to illuminate a small field*
> *for a while, and gone my way*
> *and forgotten it. But that was the pearl*
> *of great price, the one field that had*
> *treasure in it. I realize now*
> *that I must give all that I have*

> *to possess it. Life is not hurrying*
> *on to a receding future, nor hankering after*
> *an imagined past. It is the turning*
> *aside like Moses to the miracle*
> *of the lit bush, to a brightness*
> *that seemed as transitory as your youth*
> *once, but is the eternity that awaits.*

I became more steadfast in my enjoyment of the children and their hidden treasures, fixing on them like Thomas's bright field and re-establishing myself in their immediate lives. Their unconditional love pulled me from my bed in the mornings to a world that tingled with possibilities. Perhaps being over-whelmed as a mother may have triggered the depression, yet spending time with the children and acknowledging their needs was reviving a sense of hope. I was needed, and I was needed now.

In the 1970s, residents in a home for the elderly were divided into groups for an experiment. Half were given pot plants to look after; half were told that their plants would be tended by nurses. Those who had to look after the plants had better outcomes in terms of health and longevity than those who didn't. My children were like those pot plants.*

Another challenge I set myself was my weekly attempt to take Edward to story-time a few streets away at the library with its wood-panelled interior, deep, soothing shelves and its old-fashioned loo without any heating. I was accompanied by a sympathetic Italian friend and we walked arm in arm,

---

* Karran Thorpe and Lynn Basford, *Caring for the Older Adult* (Nelson Thornes, 2004).

resembling the pairings familiar in southern Europe at *paseo* time. Though we were the same age, I walked like a little old lady.

As time passed, I was able to walk a few more steps before losing my nerve and returning home, whereupon my friend would continue the journey with Edward. He didn't like it when I abandoned him, but would nonetheless slip his hand in hers and continue. He was too young to articulate anything about my illness. It was just what was happening in our house. But once he looked back just as I too turned round and his little face was crumpled and red.

I gave a small, self-conscious skip the day I managed to get to the front door of the library, much to the consternation of the librarian. I'm not sure what was different about that particular morning. I was conscious that my thirty-second birthday was approaching on the nineteenth of the following month; it was a sunny day with a wide reach of sky, the glancing light on reddening leaves somehow gave me the confidence to will myself on the few extra yards.

I became more and more able to look after the children. One evening I realised I was feeling sufficiently better, even this late in the day, to have a bath with them, as I had on the night I fell ill. I was once again emptied of fear, safe in the warm water, the mirror opaque with condensation. Afterwards I read them another of Edward's favourite bedtime stories, *The Elephant and the Bad Baby*.

Nothing, I thought, could interrupt these happy moments of senseless and sudden joy. But as I walked back downstairs the phone rang. It was an editor from *The Times*, kindly wanting to know how I was getting on. He was just saying hello: there was no mention of when I might be coming back. In the drama of the recovery, I had continued to avoid any thoughts of work. This phone call was enough to totally unnerve me. I only managed to get to sleep that night by taking some extra tranquillisers: any decisions about the future were still beyond me.

Meanwhile, I had plucked up the courage to start seeing some friends who were also at home with their children. I looked forward to the day when I could escape with them for a shared expedition. Such mother-and-children trips would have been part of my usual pattern as a working mother, given that I didn't want to waste a minute of the precious time I had with Edward and George, but I wanted to keep up with my girlfriends, too. At this point I still felt too fragile to contemplate such a trip with the children: while my confidence as a mother was returning at home, I didn't yet trust myself in public. It was enough of a challenge to leave the house on my own.

So I settled for a trip with a friend while Julie held the fort at home with the boys. The canvas of life presents big pleasures, such as music, art and literature. But that summer it was largely around small treats that I continued to try to build my life. Going out for a simple cup of coffee assumed huge importance as a luminous symbol of my much-longed-for recovery.

I fantasised about the airiness of the frothy top of the milk and the bitterness of the espresso beneath, about the way it would transport me to warmer, more forgiving places and remembered holidays. Long abstinence would make the pleasure all the sweeter. It felt like my passport to happier times ahead.

But I was still chilled with fear of the outside world and

random encounters that might derail me. On my rare outings I usually wore a hat that I could pull down over my eyes in case I bumped into anybody I knew. Before my illness I had been highly sociable but now I could only cope with those I had scheduled to meet.

It was my friend Rebecca who suggested the next logical step: we could drive to a café in a different neighbourhood where she used to live, in another part of the city. Then I wouldn't bump into anyone. She was an expert companion for someone recovering from depression: another friend of hers had suffered from the illness, and in addition she seemed to know instinctively how to behave with those who were unwell, whatever the reason. Specifically, she decided exactly what we were doing, thereby relieving me of the still difficult decision-making process. She arrived, got me dressed and marched me out of the door.

My elation at getting to the café that afternoon was dashed by the fact that there was no corner table available. Sitting at a table in the airy middle of the room frightened me. My anxiety flared up. There was no safety without a wall to cradle me. As we sat down, my carefully constructed defences began to crumble. All the bounce that had propelled me into the patisserie escaped like air from a balloon.

I began to gather my things as if to leave. Rebecca tugged my sleeve and motioned for me to sit down again. Sit I did, but I couldn't stop fidgeting. I felt as if I were an eight-year-old at school who didn't know the answers to the teacher's questions. I found it impossible to sit still or to focus on Rebecca. It felt as if everyone was looking at me, waiting for the right answers, judging me and finding me inadequate. If only the waiter would arrive and take our order. For me to relax and feel safe, the café 'show' should begin – I needed the curtain to rise and the actors to say their words. The uncertainty was agony. Each second dragged ever more slowly as no one came. A few more seconds and I would have to leave.

Oh for a quiet, safe place in which to make my camp or to dig a burrow in the comforting cool of the sandy earth. It was just too noisy. There were too many people. Far from enjoying the vivid display of happy familiarity on show, I found it disturbing that others seemed to be experiencing such a different world. It only served to complete the sense of being alone although surrounded by others.

As I clamped my hands to my ears, I realised that an elderly waiter was watching. Judging by his hushed exchanges with another younger waiter, he seemed sympathetic to my erratic behaviour. Maybe he too had been close to someone with depression and recognised how difficult I was finding it to re-engage with the world. With the kindness of a stranger, he approached us and quietly helped move our things to a different table in a corner that had become free. He calmly took our order from Rebecca.

There was still the agonising wait for our drinks to arrive, for the stage to be full, for me to finally have some props on hand with which to do something. Rebecca sensed my concern, putting her arm around me. 'It's going to be fine,' she reassured me. 'The drinks are coming. I understand.'

I finally began to relax as the same kindly waiter arrived, only to tense again as he placed a cup of tea in front of me. But I had asked for a coffee, I began, close to tears. He turned, nonchalantly it seemed to me, to give the tea to someone else, a new look on his face that I translated as 'She's officially not my problem anymore.' Don't be so certain, flashed my eyes back at him, angry as well as panicked. I can scream and it won't be my fault. You brought tea. You didn't care about me enough to get my order right. This was a profound rejection. Everyone was watching and everyone could see. My humiliation was complete. I began to shake as time speeded up again. It was getting physical.

Rebecca swooped like a defending eagle protecting her young, wrapping two arms around me. It was too late. I was breaking open now. I began to cry, appalled by the noise I was making but unable to stop. The more Rebecca tried to soothe me, the sorrier I felt for myself and the louder the wailing.

Hearing my cries, the waiter doubled back to see what was wrong.

'She' – sob, sob – 'didn't want' – more sobs – 'tea,' Rebecca explained swiftly in a down-to-earth voice as if it were perfectly normal to have a customer behave in such a way. Her change of tack from dispensing sympathy to dealing with the waiter proved my salvation. Her assumption of normality allowed me a drama-free window in which to begin to recover, almost as quickly as I had unravelled.

No wonder not many friends wanted to go out with me. No wonder that, for me, the prospect of meeting up with them could induce a night's insomnia. Some friends understood. They were of my tribe, able to tread that line between tempting me out and protecting me when needed.

We prepared our operations into enemy territory in advance. A recce was required to reserve a discreet table. Check. Quiet places were better than noisy ones, small spaces better than large. Check. We needed to be armed with supplies of tranquillisers. Check.

I needed my friends to be aware of how much courage was

required to engage with the noisy, scary world of other people. Those who accompanied me had to submit to the inevitable trial and error involved and dig deep to find stores of patience and unselfishness. They knew that we might have to turn around at the door and abort our attempted mission altogether.

My need for control meant that we had to agree an end time as well as a start time for all such meetings. This was a godsend. It defused any embarrassment about leaving early. I relaxed in the sure knowledge that however difficult the expedition might prove, it would not be for long. Initially, some of them lasted as little as twenty minutes.

I always had a plan for a fast exit if I needed to retreat even earlier. I would deliberately start to stutter or mumble, or unnervingly just stop talking altogether. I found it too challenging to explain I felt unwell; it was for others to work it out by my behaviour and to ensure I returned home.

Going far from the house was out of the question as I never liked to be far from my pills, even if I did carry spares. I was still taking the dosulepin and could top it up with anti-anxiety medication if needed. Even my first, disastrous café trip with Rebecca was only a ten-minute drive away, much as it seemed an epic journey to me at the time. That adventure proved a one-off, and I didn't venture out of the neighbourhood again for some time.

As I still didn't dare drive and I didn't want to risk relying on others, my expeditions tended to be within walking distance from home. This became a rule. I increasingly found that having routines helped me. It was far easier just to remember the rule than to make a decision: to eat the same thing for breakfast every morning (porridge and bananas) to go to church on Sundays. On Saturday nights we watched a soothing film. The normal, the everyday and the repetitious might seem boring to others but were of great comfort to me, even if our lives had come to resemble those of the elderly.

Other rules were to avoid being overstimulated close to bedtime for fear of insomnia, so no watching thrillers into the night or engaging in challenging chats that might upset me after eight o'clock. Sebastian had learnt to be highly disciplined at winding down in the evenings and parking, as he put it, the worries into tomorrow. I adopted some of his already established patterns.

My rules included limiting the commitments I took on in any one day; never making a plan much before eleven in the morning, both in case I had slept badly and also because the need to get up early might provoke a bad night in itself; setting myself small-scale goals (such as going out to buy Sebastian's fresh bread); keeping a window after lunch to recuperate if it had all been too much.

At this stage the rules made sense and I delighted in the sense of control they imbued me with. Later, as I recovered more fully, I recognised that their rigidity was part of being unwell. They sprang from a fear of, rather than joy in, life. One definition of good mental health is the flexibility to react and adjust to life's flows and ebbs and to delight in the uncertainty of that unfolding.

However, for the time being, rules allowed me to operate and for that I was grateful. Though I still worried whether I would ever fully recover, I was functioning, as Sebastian reminded me. He made a list of all the ways in which I was better. (He was a great one for lists: he helped me by getting me to list my worries.) I was getting out of the house every few days, looking after the children, seeing the odd friend, going swimming. In addition, I was eating normally, sleeping at night (mostly), only crying occasionally and no longer screaming. The number of good days now easily outweighed the number of bad. It was true: I had come a long way.

Chapter Eight

That's the Way for Edward, Georgie and Me

My life became strictly local. Even though I lived in a big city, I experienced it as if it were a village and relied more on neighbours than my friends, who tended to be young, well and at work.

I now had time to get to know everyone who worked in our street. I became attuned to the soothing noises of the comings and goings of the milkman, the dustbin men and the family in the corner shop. I had never met any of these people before, when I was rushing between home and work. This was my new office life and I was enjoying it, and the cheery exchanges that greeted me.

I became very friendly with Felicity, who lived a few doors down. She was an artist in her early forties but she seemed younger. She favoured striped matelot tops and three-quarter-length trousers, her scarlet toenails encased in studded high-heeled clogs. Her two children, Victoria and Paul, were older than ours: Victoria had babysat for us in the past and was turning fourteen, while nine-year-old Paul liked riding his bike up and down the street.

Had she been able, Felicity would have lived somewhere warm and indeed she did decamp to Greece whenever she could. As it was, she had to make do with catching whatever meagre rays an English sun could provide. She would be out with her mug and newspaper at the first sign of sun, sitting on the wooden bench in her front garden, reading while she stroked her cat, before retreating to her studio to work on her canvases of fuchsia flowers and lime-green foliage against cerulean skies and bright sunsets.

Our exchanges had previously been friendly but brief, flavoured by concealed urgency as I was always trying to get to work, metering out my time like a precious drug. She lived life to a timetable of different priorities.

Once, before I fell ill, I asked her whether she was working towards another show that autumn. No, she replied. Her show was temporarily on hold. There were elderly parents to care for, a friend who was getting divorced, Victoria was starting a new school. But Victoria and Paul were both at school all day. So didn't that leave Felicity free? Such thinking was to misunderstand her. Her creativity lay in adding to the canvas of other people's lives by being properly available, as much as contributing to her own exuberant pictures. People were her priority. For a while she treated me as if I were part of the family she cherished.

The process happened gradually. At first we would just chat briefly on the rare occasions when I ventured out and she was sitting in her front garden. As my sorties outside the house increased in number, so did our conversations. It seemed perfectly natural when she began to pop round, often to drop off the book we had talked about or to supply me with more of the chocolate biscuits that she had tempted me with previously. She would normally ring the bell at about eleven, knowing that I was unlikely to be up before then. Sometimes

I was, sometimes not. She would settle down in an armchair in the dining end of the kitchen, even if I remained upstairs. Sometimes, merely knowing that she was there would tempt me down. Then she would simply live her life alongside mine, as though we were characters from an earlier century. Eventually she became such a part of our household that my mother gave her a spare key so she could let herself in.

She would make her own cup of tea, as well as one for me. Correctly, she discerned that I might feel as if I had to entertain her, so she more often than not brought a piece of sewing or a sketch she was working on. She might chat. Once she told me the fable of the butterfly that inadvertently fell into a bowl of milk: in order to survive it flaps its wings furiously, thereby turning the milk into butter on which it can safely stand. Or she might be quiet. She didn't require me to do anything. She just was.

Sometimes she brought a little present. One day it was a small pendant on a silver chain to ward off the evil eye. Another day she would bring round some homemade soup. Victoria and Paul would come too, and play with Edward and George. Instinctively she knew when to come and when to leave.

Felicity's easefulness warmed the atmosphere in our kitchen or our little front room. When she was there I felt able to come downstairs. Upstairs was still more the domain of my mother and husband, charged with looking after me at those times when I felt very sick. Those days were becoming less frequent, but they did happen. When I was feeling better, they would often leave me in Felicity's care, allowing themselves a break.

Felicity made our downstairs rooms a good halfway house on my return to the world outside, bringing news of neighbours and even, occasionally, the neighbours them-selves. I could trust her to keep both me and others in check.

She also protected me from what I felt was occasional hostility from a sharp-eyed Julie. Felicity's sheer pleasantness defused the tension by relieving the claustrophobia of a house-hold that was increasingly composed of just me, the children and Julie. As the number of good days increased, my mother set about reclaiming her own life and Sebastian had returned to working intensely hard.

When I was alone with Julie and the children I often had a sense I wasn't welcome in my own kitchen. Our previous rela-tionship had relied on me leaving: to go to work, to take the children out, to see friends. She was the nanny, and her role was to take care of the children when I was absent, her long hours on duty matching mine at the office. Now we were spending our days together, one of us keen to reassert her role as mother, the other struggling with a new dynamic. The previous delicate balance of household power had been achieved by the simple fact that I wasn't there. Now I was, and Julie was finding it hard.

I felt her actions become brusquer and brusquer. Her slap of the dishcloth on the kitchen counter or the shove of the closing dishwasher could slice through me, though to others she appeared as calm and composed as ever. Sometimes, when I was feeling well enough to emerge from my room, I would be met by wafts of delicious fried chicken emanating from the kitchen. I would creep back, unable to find the courage to descend. I was, after all, officially a sick person. I should stay in my box. Once, I waited till the chatter and scraping of plates had died away, then snuck downstairs and fished the still warm leftovers out of the bin.

Taking part in communal meals was not part of my job description. My role was either to get better and get back to work, or to stay upstairs, eating off a tray. There was no room for convalescence, certainly not by Julie's side. As she told me one morning, she had not applied for a job that involved looking after a grown-up.

One afternoon the atmosphere became particularly tense, perhaps because of the heat or because we had been tripping over each other in our kitchen as I attempted to cook with Edward. The battle for space culminated in me knocking over her cup of tea

Julie's pristine indifference and professional silence evaporated. As she put down a bowl of rice pudding on the table, she turned to me. 'I don't believe in depression,' she said, before turning her back on me and walking the few yards to the dishwasher. 'Some people have nothing to be depressed about,' she continued, managing with her voice to convey inverted commas around the word 'depressed'. 'It's all just made up.'

At this point she turned to face me with a look that dared me to disagree, continuing her speech, which had clearly been prepared.

'It's obvious – if you lie in bed all day then you'll be depressed. I don't understand why people don't get it. I mean, if I lay in bed all day' – she looked at me with particular intensity – 'I'd feel depressed too. Only I can't be depressed because some of us have got a job to do. And by the way, can I ask when you are going back to work?'

It struck me then how difficult it is to be suffering from something that others may or may not believe in. It is not as though people routinely don't 'believe' that someone has got cancer or diabetes. There is proof: a scan or blood count, an operation that may have to happen, a timetable and a prognosis.

Depression offers no such measureable proofs. Even its victims may wonder if they really do have an illness. Many sufferers believe it may make them feel worse to acknowledge something is wrong and they are, scarily, 'mentally ill'. Despite huge strides in awareness, some stigma still surrounds mental health in the way that it once surrounded cancer.

Julie's 'some people' made my heart thud and my stomach lurch; I found myself wondering if she was right. Her comments inflamed my own uncertainties, especially as there was no denying that I was now feeling better. Yes, I had been very ill, but it was true that now, if I were honest, my own behaviour could affect my mood. Some days I did just lie in bed when I could have roused myself if I had really tried.

It was a false division to say it was either all about the illness or all about my own behaviour. The truth was a more complicated, nuanced dance between the two. I knew that if I tried to exercise, eat well, see supportive friends, positively practise breathing, recite my prayers and poems, I could allay many of my symptoms. The reverse was equally true. The sense that I was in some way responsible for getting better or worse was daunting. Probably this is the case with all illnesses to some extent, but it felt especially so with depression.

This was frightening. At the time I shied away from examining my own role in what had been happening. It was far easier to blame outward circumstances than to look inwards, far easier to shirk my own responsibility for recovery and to look to pills, doctors and other experts to sort out this alien force that seemed to have come out of nowhere and could safely be blamed on chemical imbalance, as if I might have eaten a very bad oyster.

So it was easier to move on and agree with Julie. I was all back to normal now, I told her, though I avoided talking about my work plans which I hadn't properly considered. I didn't really believe in depression either, I continued. (I felt ambivalent saying this, even if I did allow myself the 'really'.) Perhaps I said it because I knew I didn't have the strength to argue with her. Perhaps it reflected the complexity of the reality. Anyway, I wanted to please her, at least partly as I still needed her help with the children, to whom she was devoted.

We never resolved the upset nor referred to it again; we just continued to tiptoe around one another. Her outburst had frightened me and I didn't want to risk any further confrontation that might derail my baby steps to recovery. Arguing would imply an emotional intimacy that we had never enjoyed when I was well. Not arguing meant a return to normal, and normal was what I craved.

Sebastian agreed. If I wished to discuss what depression involved, I could talk to him, or to my mother or Dr Fischer. I should respect the fact that Julie was a professional fulfilling a job, which was critical to our way of life, and doing so well despite much uncertainty and confusion. He reminded me of the pressure she had been under and how hard she had worked while the household had been in crisis. He would have been unable to continue working if he hadn't felt able to rely on Julie. This wasn't just about me, he said, with apologies if that sounded bracing; but it was true.

As I continued to recover I felt almost as if I were inhabiting two personalities: I was one person with those who thought depression was nonsense and another with those who realised that I had been very ill. Felicity was in this second category and all the more special to me as I didn't have to pretend anything at all when I was with her. I felt sufficiently safe to be truly myself. This made her company relaxing, though I don't think I realised why at the time. I just knew I felt calm, my heart didn't race and I found myself talking to her freely.

I didn't have to keep up any kind of appearance with other friends who had also suffered from depression. One said she felt like a tree whose bark had been scraped off: at once vulnerable and more open and, most importantly, more honest. For me, being more honest meant being able to express difference. My usual pattern was to prioritise being friends to the point that I would always agree, even if I didn't. Or I would remain silent instead of speaking the truth as I saw it (the therapeutic term for this is 'speaking your truth', I would later learn).

This ability to be more authentic around certain people was a blessing. I had been beaten into a new and better shape, it seemed. I could admit to finding life difficult and let my upper lip soften. I could say if I was angry or happy, and all parts of me were acceptable. I didn't have to pretend I felt better or worse than I really did.

These new relationships contrasted with some older ones. At this stage, all I observed was that I felt tired when keeping up appearances, having to rest afterwards, but was energised in the company of those with whom I felt I could be myself. I did not yet seek to analyse why. Later I would begin to realise that although it might seem easier at the time, pretending requires huge amounts of emotional energy and is exhausting. At this point, though, I was unaware of the cost of pretence and willingly and ignorantly inflicted it on myself, especially in the company of unbelievers.

The passing weeks saw me deepen my bonds with the tribe who understood what a depressive illness was, some of whom I had known for years without realising that they had struggled in this way. There was always the moment of admitting to membership, almost as if we were part of a secret society with a funny handshake: 'What, you too? I never would have thought it' – all in whispers mixed with the occasional slap on the back about joining the club.

Then there was the slight danger of one-downmanship, as we swapped notes on how long exactly we had been in hospital, how many drugs we had taken and who could claim to be the greatest victim of this illness. Some were competitive about their superior knowledge of the depression game, missing no chance to condescend to newcomers like me who were fresh to swapping tales of beating the blues and 'benzos', as we called the benzodiazepine we took to reduce our anxiety. But it never went on too long before we pulled ourselves up short. This thing was too terrifying to be a platform for showing off. We returned to goodwill. 'Don't worry about forgetting your drugs,' one friend said as we settled down for a cup of tea. 'I've got a cupboardful upstairs.'

Recovery reminded me of the time when I had lived abroad, when I was much younger. Here was the freedom to reinvent myself, to reframe my life through the prism of a depressive illness and start afresh. So I used the fact of having been ill as an opportunity to speak more truthfully about my feelings, and thereby heal grudges and resolve issues that had festered in my mind for too long. Being ill gave me a one-off carte blanche to behave differently, at least with certain people – not that I managed with Julie.

I could now acknowledge anger where before, I had

smoothed it over. Previously any conflict felt frightening as I had been brought up in a household where we didn't have rows. Having come through the terrifying months of illness, angry feelings no longer felt so daunting. Pah! They were nothing in comparison to what I had survived. Avoidance had always been my default way of operating but now it felt safer to express difference or explain why I had backed off certain relationships. In addition, my delight in recovery meant that I was brimful of forgiveness and a desire to patch up any old quarrels.

Such shifts were an immense drama for me. The changes surprised some of my friends, who weren't quite sure what the fuss was about. For me, it was all deadly serious. The fear of death still stalked me on occasion, and I was keen to get my house in order, just in case.

End of August 1997

The peaks and troughs became less noticeable as the days began to cool. I was reading the newspapers with interest, spotting ideas for articles and noting bylines. George was beginning to crawl, albeit backwards; Edward was becoming chattier by the day. He liked our bed, not his, he told me one morning, as his was 'too noisy'. Another evening, as I tucked them both in, Edward told me he wanted to marry me.

I seemed to be taking the right dose of antidepressants to keep me stable but not incapacitate me with side effects. I would do so for around a year or possibly longer, depending on my progress. Then, after a prolonged period of stability, very, very gradually over several months, Dr Fischer would reduce the antidepressants till eventually I would be able to manage without any medication.

The process continued to be bumpy. It was as if a crust had temporarily hardened over bits of me and had to be cut or sloughed away. As I began to re-engage with different areas of my life and my relationships with different people, I broke free in fits and starts, poking my head out like an animal after hibernation.

Up until now I had only been well enough to see my immediate family. Now we even felt well enough to go and stay with some friends outside London, although I insisted that my girlfriend came to pick us up in her car. I required a soothing maternal figure at the wheel. 'Oh, don't worry,' joked her husband. 'If I drive you anywhere I will wear a peaked cap and you won't notice me.'

Emboldened by the success of this visit, the next step was to believe myself able to travel not just out of London, but across the sea. We had planned before I became unwell to go on holiday to France that summer, renting a house with another family who had two children of their own. Dr Fischer sanctioned the trip. I would be fine to go, he said. He reassured me that the flight would be okay.

The days before our departure passed badly. I packed and repacked my suitcase, convinced I had forgotten my drugs. Sebastian took a spare set. After leaving the house, we had to go back as I was certain I had left the oven on and the hose running. I clutched a small lavender-scented pillow in the car to the airport and was sick despite its supposed calming powers.

On the plane I clung to Sebastian throughout the journey, much to the amusement of Edward, who loved the bumps. Nor would I let go of a small bag in which I had put another spare set of drugs: my worst fear was to wake up in a strange country without medication or any hope of acquiring it.

At first feeling fragile in France wasn't any different to feeling wobbly in England. But gradually the house's setting, surrounded by meadows and woods that meandered out of sight, was restorative in a way that London could never be. The house was long and low, one storey high, with doors leading from the bedrooms directly onto a wild garden with clumps of cornflowers, valerian and campanulas. Edward and I particularly liked trying to spot fish in a nearby stream, and he was fascinated by the clouds of iridescent dragonflies. It was quiet but for the droning of the insects. George meanwhile preferred staying closer to home, rolling around on the lawn and pointing at butterflies. I read James Hogg's poem 'A Boy's Song' aloud for the boys, swapping the name Billy for Edward and Georgie. 'Again, again,' Edward would say when I got to the last line of each verse.

> *Where the pools are bright and deep,*
> *Where the grey trout lies asleep,*
> *Up the river and over the lea,*
> *That's the way for Billy and me.*
>
> *Where the blackbird sings the latest,*
> *Where the hawthorn blooms the sweetest,*
> *Where the nestlings chirp and flee,*
> *That's the way for Billy and me.*
>
> *Where the mowers mow the cleanest,*
> *Where the hay lies thick and greenest,*
> *There to track the homeward bee,*
> *That's the way for Billy and me.*

That's the Way for Edward, Georgie and Me

Where the hazel bank is steepest,
Where the shadow falls the deepest,
Where the clustering nuts fall free,
That's the way for Billy and me.

Why the boys should drive away
Little sweet maidens from the play,
Or love to banter and fight so well,
That's the thing I never could tell.

But this I know, I love to play
Through the meadow, among the hay;
Up the water and over the lea,
That's the way for Billy and me.

I was best when busy. Lying on a sun lounger or taking long siestas allowed for too much reflection on the dramas of the last few months. It was better not to dwell on all the story-times I had missed or how frightening my life had been; far better simply to make up for lost time: I rolled around on the grass with the children, balancing Edward precariously on the end of my legs as he turned into a rocket being launched into space, or tickled Georgie until I had to stop as both of us were in danger of choking on our laughter. There were *boulangeries* and *boucheries* to enjoy, as well as walks through the woods and butterflies to chase. This was a joyful return to the plain happiness of domesticity, whether with children or cooking or shopping.

Returning one afternoon with an empty basket after the local *boulangerie* was closed, I remarked that the shop was shut to an elderly man leaning over his front gate, near our house. 'Yes, isn't it amazing that shops aren't open seven days a week and that people do things their own way here?' he said. He smiled, and it took me several moments to understand his point: life was lived to a different pace here, and rightly so.

My worst moments were when, by mistake, I bowed to well-intentioned suggestions that I should go and rest. As soon as I lay still, my thoughts began to whirr into regrets about the past and worries about the future, in the classic pattern of someone with depression. Had Edward drowned in the pool? Had I lost my pills? It was my supposed siestas that were in danger of tipping me back into turmoil.

On the whole, the less I talked about having been unwell with the family we were holidaying with, the better. I wanted to spare both them and myself from retelling the story.

We returned home on 31 August to the news that Princess Diana had died in a car crash in Paris. She had been part of the furniture of my life for as long as I could remember. I had watched from the Mall when she married Prince Charles; I had followed every turn of her life as she became a wife, mother and then a divorcee. Her death was a startling reminder of life's pitiless uncertainty, just as I was beginning to feel I was on steady ground. The news unsettled me to the point that my usual dose of sleeping pills didn't work properly that night. On Dr Fischer's advice, I increased my dosage.

September 1997

Diana's death only added to the sensation that August had been the longest month. It felt as if so much had happened in the last few weeks, partly in contrast to the previous months when I had been less aware of the outside world and time had limped by.

Come September, I had managed to further right myself and was able to go out for a birthday supper to a Thai restaurant as I turned thirty-two. Yes, I had been ill, I told my neighbours and new friends over the pad thai; now the drugs had made me better. It was a happy, sparky evening. The beer circulated and the dishes sizzled and shone. The conversation took wing, open-ended and free, and I felt full of joyous gratitude. I wanted to thank them for all their love and support, I said in an impromptu, teary speech. Really, the best thing about being ill had been realising who my true friends were. 'I love you,' I ended in a whoosh of emotion.

I didn't discuss having been ill in any detail. I didn't find it therapeutic to talk about it, just frightening. I didn't want to be reminded of what had happened. I was also bored with that conversation. Yes, yes, I had felt frightful . . . yes, physically frightful; no really, you actually feel ill . . . yes, it actually hurts . . . yes, I am fine now, yes, yes, the children are fine . . . There was just too much to explain that was too difficult to comprehend for most listeners. Apart from anything else, it would take too long. I was relishing my pockets of feeling better and didn't want to squander them on talking about being ill.

Moreover, Julie's scepticism had left its mark. Part of me continued to wonder sometimes whether I had made it all up, especially as I re-engaged more and more with my previous existence. The episode felt so unconnected with the facts of my life. I enjoyed strong friendships, a happy marriage, a fine education, two glorious sons and had been brought up by loving parents in conditions of tranquillity. It was not for me to feel depressed. I felt ashamed that I was so hopeless. (At these times I conveniently ignored a second, more emotional voice that spoke of the relentless pressure of our two jobs, my habitual exhaustion, how much I demanded of myself.)

The more I dismissed and belittled what had happened, the safer I felt. In retrospect, didn't lots of people fail to get to sleep? Hadn't most of my worries been petty? I hadn't worried on the whole about world poverty but trivial details. After all, other women in the worst of circumstances didn't complain, I told myself, and nor would I indulge the illness again – goodness gracious, not someone like me with so many blessings.

'Never complain.' This was another saying beloved of my family, probably born of my mother's wartime childhood when making a fuss felt inappropriate; move on, put on a brave face and pull yourself together. Nothing was served by what felt like an indulgent raking over the past, and anyway, as my family kept reminding me, most of the time I had been ill had been spent in a fog anyway, so it was not exactly readily available for analysis.

Just as I did not dwell on why I had been ill, neither did I think too much about what had made me better. I was unsure whether it was the tapes, my poetry and prayer or the breathing that helped the most. I would later come to understand that I couldn't have got through those months without all of them. But in general, at the time, I put much of my recovery down to the miracle drugs. It didn't occur to me that I should think more deeply about how I might guard against a recurrence or why I had been ill in the first place. I was now in a tearing rush to get better, and though still struggling, I would soon be completely well again.

Night and day had returned. I was getting up, staying up and going to bed in sequence. The pack of cards was back in order, albeit with a few different cards from the bottom of the deck now nearer the top. The days followed the same pattern, but in a less dramatic way. I would still be at my worst in the morning, but as the day wore on, I relaxed in the knowledge that my mood would improve as night fell. If you had only met me after about eight o'clock in the evening, you wouldn't have believed there was anything wrong with me. If anything, I was even more cheerful than usual. I was so thrilled to be better and not to feel ill. One friend who came to supper said I was like a prisoner who had just been released from solitary confinement.

Such had been the drama of the past few months that nearly all thoughts of work had receded. That identity had been swapped for someone struggling with an illness. Being ill had become my job. I was recovering my other roles of mother and wife. But going back to work seemed to require such an improved state of health that it was only now that I began to feel the pressure return.

Chapter Nine

Kindness in Another's Trouble, Courage in One's Own

SEPTEMBER 1997 TO MAY 1999

End of September 1997

It was Dr Fischer who gave me the confidence to reclaim my career. By now I was well enough to go and see him unaccompanied. In his efforts to reassemble my life, he combined talking to me with chatting to my family separately to get second opinions on how I was doing. His psychiatric skill allowed him to ascertain my mood levels as much by our general chats as through specific discussion of the illness. I still filled in the forms, though, and my scores were steadily improving.

So preoccupied had I become with the illness, I was astonished when Dr Fischer mentioned my return to work as if it had never been in question. My job was being handled smoothly in my absence and in due course I was expected back. But mention of work made my whole body shake: I was sucked back into that first night and my fears of trying to combine both roles and failing.

Throughout my treatment Dr Fischer had been continuing to try to piece together my previous self and life as a well and working person, what doctors sometimes call a patient's pre-morbid personality. This in turn helps doctors build up what is termed a patient's 'bio-psycho-social model' or profile. Treating other illnesses may not require such a detailed account of someone's life, but depression does.

This process had begun all those weeks ago when he had asked me for a photograph. He had been closely involved in my life since then. Now he wished to build more of a picture of life before we had met in such dramatic circumstances. Only now did I have the capacity to focus on my past as well as my present.

In job interviews, candidates are sometimes asked how they think a friend would describe them. It's an approach some doctors find helpful when they try to piece together what their patients were like before they became depressed.

Sitting in the wing-backed armchair that had become my home from home, I told Dr Fischer of my upbringing in a Victorian house in west London. My father ran a small steel manufacturing business but longed to spend more time writing about his Russian history (his father had been a diplomat in the Soviet Union after the war) and my mother would tap away at a typewriter in her bedroom. My mother remembers me as an outgoing little girl, though I look pensive and anxious in some childhood photos. I didn't share with Dr Fischer a nagging memory that I always longed for more hugs as a child, however much affection I was given by my loving parents. Surrounding our immediate family was a much larger extended one of cousins and aunts and uncles: I had twenty-two first cousins alone, and one uncle had eight children.

I paused. I felt self-conscious talking about myself: that wasn't our family's way. But after an encouraging nod from Dr Fischer, I continued. I went to St Paul's Girls' School between 1976 and 1983 – 'enthusiastic' was the most common comment on my school reports – and read modern history at Magdalen College, Oxford between 1984 and 1987. I met Sebastian when we were both seventeen and I was staying with my cousins in Ireland. He too read history at Oxford. We had the same group of friends at university, began dating shortly after our finals and married when we were twenty-seven at the same church that had been so important to me when I was ill.

My first job after university was a disastrous stint as a secretary at *Vogue*. After nine months and no longed-for appearance on the magazine's masthead, I left to become a reporter on an advertising trade magazine called *Campaign*: much more fun, a world awash with fiddled expenses and drunken creatives. Eighteen months later I moved to *The Times* as a diary reporter. When I became ill, I was the paper's property correspondent, and also wrote features on other topics.

Specialising in property might sound dry, but I had learnt that the more glamorous a job seemed, the drearier it often was. The housing market was hot news in the early 1990s. There was the potential for front-page bylines as housing became an important political issue, homes were repossessed and homelessness soared; there were architects, planners, civil servants, estate agents, designers, developers, house-builders and conservationists to meet. I would return to the office full of what I hoped were good stories with which to try and tempt my editors in the newsroom.

Then there was the exhilaration of trying to write the stories at high speed. I was entranced by the thrill of picking up the phone and saying '*The Times*', while struck by how much I had to learn about constructing a news story or feature article. One of my first attempts at an article had to be rewritten from beginning to end by someone else. But there were highs: I queued at midnight for an early edition of the paper the first time I wrote a front-page story. I loved telling people where I worked, slipping it in to conversation at the earliest opportunity.

I kept working after Edward was born. I managed by convincing myself I didn't have a choice: working was what all my friends did and what I had been raised to do. But I was agonisingly torn. The day I went back to the office, I was sick in the front garden as I left the house: it had been a mistake to wave goodbye to a child being held by his nanny at the window. At times it could feel as if there were a perpetual moving staircase to climb and no possible resolution to the conflicting calls of home and work. My life was busy, busy, busy and the to-do list could seem never-ending. Sometimes I even struggled to dry myself after a shower: my clothes seemed perpetually damp in the rush to avoid being late in the mornings.

I longed for more time with Edward. I would cry at odd moments, especially if I read about a small child or spotted one on my way to work. Every day when I handed my boy over to Julie, my stomach lurched. The worst moments were in my lunch breaks. I was neither busy in the office nor with Edward but marooned far from home observing other young mothers. Somehow they always seemed to be laughing with their children in the café in the local supermarket, where I would sit alone picking at my lunch.

But equally I was competitive and wanted to be part of a world of highly educated, well-connected achievers where the pressure to succeed was unspoken but real. The women in my circle all wore the same sharp suits and discussed the same recipes from the River Café cookbook. Few of us had the time to actually make the Chocolate Nemesis. Everyone we knew seemed to have a book that was about to be published, or an internet start-up to launch, or a think-tank they were starting. Everything was always just about to happen, and often did. Our contemporaries had embarked on careers in politics, journalism, finance, law and academia, and would in time become well known in their fields. I was even featured in a glossy magazine in a round-up of 'Bright Young Achievers': not surprisingly, as I was friendly with the journalist compiling the list.

Outwardly, I was managing: the job, the children, the husband, the friends, as I told Dr Fischer. But I couldn't deny to him how I was anxious, suffered mood swings and insomnia, and worried about how I was performing as a wife, mother and journalist. Our existence might have seemed idyllic to some but we had little time to ourselves, worked very hard and were constantly stretched.

It was then that my life was stolen from me and Dr Fischer had entered the scene of the crime so dramatically. He didn't need me to recount the events of the last few months.

Throughout our chat, he had been making notes with his fat silver fountain pen. He stopped writing and explained he was less interested in the facts of my life than the way I was unknowingly reporting them. It mattered less what I had supposedly done than how I had experienced it: how my voice strengthened and my posture became more confident describing some subjects, how I seemed more subdued when mentioning others. Despite the demands of my job, for example, Dr Fischer said it was perfectly obvious from hearing me that I also found it exhilarating. At the mention of the word job I began to shake.

From his long experience, Dr Fischer continued, he felt that the structure and steadiness imposed by the routine of work could help with the mood swings and anxiety and tendency to introspection. Journalism in particular, with its requirement to discover facts about others, might be especially helpful. On balance, despite my fears, he thought work would be good for me.

My body continued to shake, and so did my voice. Returning to work so soon, while managing two children, might be too much, I pleaded. After all, I had become ill even without the pressure of the office. The familiar spiral of worry re-emerged.

While acknowledging my fears, Dr Fischer said much of my terror was about the prospect of change and having to make a decision, rather than the job itself. Even a simple deviation could trigger panic at the moment. He was taking decisions for me. A long run-up to going back would be a disaster, he said. The way I would get back to work was just to go, Dr Fischer told me. It was Thursday. I should ring my editor and be back at my desk on Monday. The less it was a matter of choice, the better it would be. Being a journalist was what I did and what I did well, he reassured me, as I gasped at the suddenness of it all.

So I went back to work on doctor's orders, just five days after I phoned my editor to say I wanted to return. He was supportive, though I later realised that the speed of my return was difficult for him as well as for the person covering for me who didn't expect me back so soon. I was too absorbed in my own drama at the time to consider fully my impact on others.

My first Tube ride was briefly disorientating. Everyone moved with such determination and focus, yet they seemed unaware of those crammed next to them on the escalators and

in the carriages. But after a few stops it felt reassuringly familiar, and I too had my eyes forward and mind elsewhere. On
arrival at Wapping, the security guard at the front gate was
just as tubby and even the piled-up magazines I had left on my
desk six months earlier were still there, now covered in dust.

George, who had sent me those witty weekly missives from
the office, was the clever commissioning editor who set me to
work straight away on a 1,000-word piece. He was one of the
very few people on the paper apart from the editor who knew
that I had been unwell. With his experience of the journalist's
psyche, he knew that instantly throwing me into the swing of
things would help me to regain my confidence.

George was a journalist of the old school, proud to call
himself a hack, a man with newsprint in his veins. A journalist's son, he had risen from selling diary stories to Fleet Street's
gossip columns as an undergraduate to becoming an executive, or baron, who controlled editorial space on the paper at
an unfeasibly young age and who was now in a position to
decide the future of eager reporters like me. Luckily I hadn't
arrived the way of some of the youngsters – editor's godchil-
dren and the like – who had been foisted on him. 'I like
discovering young talent,' I once heard him say with a laugh.
'Then I can weed it out.'

While I had been ill I had discovered another side to him.
In the office he brimmed with ruthless confidence, embodied in his florid form and swaggering rounds of the newsroom
when he would alight on the desks of favoured reporters for
some banter. In his letters he had shown an uncanny ability
to tune into the moods of others and to empathise with the
vulnerable.

He invited me to lunch on my first day back. He knew

something of the last few months thanks to occasional chats with Sebastian whom he didn't know personally, but had rung to find out how I was. As we ate, he confessed that he sometimes suffered from what he called 'nerves' himself. On occasion he had thrown up before the daily editorial conference, when each section head had to set out his or her wares to the editor. I was quite sure he had never told anyone else on the paper about this. I felt privileged that my own vulnerability had allowed him to confide in me. Perhaps in his entire career he had never been so unguarded before.

Within hours of being back, it felt like I had never left. I was at home with the smell of the burnt coffee at the bottom of the filter jug and the floral tang of air freshener in the cloakroom. The reporters who had been irritable when I left were reassuringly just as bad-tempered when I returned. The letter 'K' on my keyboard was still sticking and the tap-tap-tap of journalists filing their copy all around me felt right. I belong here, I thought, as I swiped my security card and headed for home.

Here was the camaraderie of office life that I had missed. Completing my first article and looking at my byline gave me the sense of achievement I had been missing without realising it. Those fellow journalists around the water cooler were the company I desired. The ready-made, unscheduled interactions of office life fired up my social reflexes. I had to act cheerfully. Of course a few colleagues, like George, knew I had been unwell. But most didn't, and that was helpful. It's a strong social norm to be cheerful around those we don't know well, and the more I behaved cheerfully, the more I felt it. I had escaped solitary confinement.

Being back at work meant life became easier for Julie, too.

Now we returned to the deal she had signed up to. Our home life was structured around me going to work. Staying at home would have ultimately meant her leaving, and that was another decision I didn't feel well enough to make.

The children loved being with her, but sometimes George would wrap himself round my smartly stockinged leg in his efforts to stop me leaving. 'Stay, stay, stay' he would cry. Edward was even more vocal, asking why I had to go to work. I had found it easier to leave when Edward wasn't old enough to question my actions. I tried to not to think of the children as I got ready, trying instead to enjoy having a reason to get up and get dressed after the months I had spent in my nightdress. Keats apparently used to put on his best clothes before he sat down to write. I did the same. I relished slipping on tights and a suit again, even if they were somewhat damp. Like a child, I took to laying out my clothes for the next day the night before.

After one particularly traumatic morning I agreed with Julie that she would take the children out early to avoid the dreadful partings. I cowered upstairs while I heard the jolly sounds of the children getting ready to go out and Julie putting their coats and boots on. Sometimes I would watch from my bedroom window and wonder why I wasn't the person pushing the pram or holding hands with the small boy in his red wellingtons clutching a toy dinosaur. Of course, there had been a similar scene when George had gone away when I was ill. I had to silence the voice that asked why I seemed to have learnt nothing and was happy to let the children walk away from me every day.

Once I arrived at the office, the urgent need to meet newsroom deadlines helped distract me. By engaging in the world of speed-reading and trying to rapidly master different topics,

I focused on subjects other than my own worries. I was forced into an absorbing present.*

A journalist's thinking tends to be goal-focused, as opposed to ruminative: searching for solutions rather than going round in circles. I was soothing my mind, as if I had dived into a cool, clear mountain pool on a hot day. It was a return to what I knew and a way to forget what had been happening. It was, on one level, what I had been preparing for all my life. It was the aim of every educational and career milestone. To stop work would have been more frightening than to return. Once again I was part of the pattern of normal life. How flattering and energising that my editors seemed to think that I was needed in the office. Theirs were voices with which the children did not yet have the eloquence to compete.

Another less certain part of me remained permanently worried about the children, asking whether I would really be able to manage and grieving that I did not spend enough time with them. But at this stage I tried not to listen to that quiet, uncertain voice.

---

* By making your brain race on a subject other than your own anxieties, you give your mood a chemical boost, according to Emily Pronin and Daniel Wegner in an article entitled 'Manic Thinking: Independent Effects of Thought Speed and Thought Content on Mood' (*Psychological Science*, 2006). Subjects found that when they read statements quickly they felt happier, more energetic and more creative afterwards.

Early October 1997

Outwardly, no one would have known that I had been ill. I was rounder than normal but that could have been because of having had a baby. I had stabilised my dose of antidepressants. Some of the earlier side effects had begun to dissipate. My mouth was no longer dry and I was at ease with taking the drugs on my own. I had settled back into the commute and could travel with as much indifference to my fellow commuter as the next woman. My physical strength was returning and I could walk for a reasonable distance. I could now complete around twenty lengths when Sebastian and I went swimming. I no longer felt sapped and sluggish. The familiar morning tick-tock of fear had quietened to a whisper. I didn't routinely need to take sleeping pills. The antidepressants acted as a sedative at night.

I only needed extra drugs if we travelled, when I would be certain to be more anxious than usual. We largely stayed at home, but when we did go away, I began to self-medicate and would take a zopiclone to ensure a good night's sleep. I no longer always needed to consult Dr Fischer on the dosages, as we had plotted various strategies and rules in advance. This added to my sense of independent recovery.

One rule was that if, for whatever reason, I were still awake past midnight, instead of battling to fall asleep I would just take a pill. This was my emergency exit. I found it easier to have set rules than to negotiate with myself in the middle of an exhausting night. Like a child, I needed firm boundaries.

Gradually, though, I was beginning to wish to reduce my dependence on drugs. I disliked the side effects, particularly the weight-gain, though I did nothing specific to address that at this point. There was too much else to worry about. I also had a very slight sense that I was viewing life through a gauze, as if there were a thin veil over my mind. I began to wonder if the drugs were masking my true, strong feelings. Perhaps I was better anyway, and no longer needed the drugs, but for as long as I stayed on them I would never know. I wished for more self-reliance to feed into that virtuous circle of growing confidence.

Mid-October 1997

Dr Fischer was cautious at our next meeting. Now I was scrambling to combine my appointments in Harley Street and my need to be at work in Wapping. The drugs shouldn't be seen as an enemy, he said; you wouldn't be suspicious of insulin if you were diabetic, for example. He was concerned that I would reduce my dosage too quickly and relapse. There was no hurry. I had begun to forget what it had been like to be so ill, but he hadn't.

November 1997 to January 1998

In the end, coming off antidepressants took several months, as I gradually reduced my dose. Ironically, I used other drugs to ease the process, chiefly tranquillisers, which I could use as and when I needed them to reduce the fresh-minted anxiety of withdrawing from the antidepressants. Using drugs to come off other drugs clearly wasn't ideal, but it was the way I managed. My bedside table became a small pharmaceutical workshop. I would carefully cut the pills into ever smaller pieces, finding a nail-clipper the easiest way to halve the pills until there was nothing but powder, which I would suck up with a straw.

The transition was also eased by my reading of 'The Guest House' by Jalal al-Din Rumi, the thirteenth-century Persian poet and Sufi mystic. The poem says that we must welcome whatever befalls us. We are like a guest house, the narrator tells us, and we must 'treat each guest honourably' even if we are greeted by 'a crowd of sorrows'. The most seemingly unprepossessing guest 'may be clearing you out for some new delight'. Being frightened of the future, worrying whether I would manage to keep working, fearing that I might fall ill again without the drugs – all this was pointless. What would happen, would happen, and I needed to embrace that uncertainty.

This being human is a guest house.
Every morning a new arrival.

A joy, a depression, a meanness,
some momentary awareness
comes as an unexpected visitor.

Welcome and entertain them all!
Even if they are a crowd of sorrows,
who violently sweep your house
empty of its furniture,
Still, treat each guest honorably.
He may be clearing you out
for some new delight.

> *The dark thought, the shame, the malice.*
> *Meet them at the door laughing*
> *and invite them in.*
>
> *Be grateful for whatever comes,*
> *because each has been sent*
> *as a guide from beyond.*

A year later, October 1998

I took my last antidepressant a year and a half after that May evening when I fell ill. The withdrawal process had been smooth; I felt reassured that I was still taking something. The night I sucked up the last slivers of powder, my anxiety levels rose. Fortunately Dr Fischer was on hand to talk me down. He had always kept his word that he would be available when I needed him, even in the middle of the night.

October 1998 to March 1999

For the next few months my safety valve was the packet of sleeping pills in the drawer. I rarely took them, relaxed in the knowledge that they were there. By the spring of 1999, I was taking no drugs at all.

April 1999

I had now been back at work for eighteen months. I considered myself to be better and no longer thought of myself as someone with depression. The illness had been a one-off and it was over. The most visible outward sign was that I was back to my normal weight. I hadn't deliberately embarked on a weight-loss regime, but the busyness of life and coming off the antidepressants had gradually worked their magic. Thank goodness I had had lots of help with the children and, yes, they were fine, thanks, I would tell anyone who asked. Quickened with the excitement of regaining my life, I talked a little about having been sick and much more about being better. If I cried, I would disappear swiftly to the bathroom and keep the water running till I recovered. It made me feel worse to recount the unnerving bad dream of having been unwell.

Life was generally better, and there was no doubt that I loved being a journalist. I was ambitious and insecure and the job fulfilled my need for status and purpose. I had an insatiable thirst to appear in the paper, concentrating on quantity of articles rather than quality. As one colleague argued when I wondered aloud if the mad juggle made sense, we still lived in a world where a *Times* correspondent mattered (albeit far less than they once had). I was back in the world that I had spent years striving to be part of. I derived great satisfaction from trying to write as clearly as I could on subjects that I believed mattered: homelessness, the economy, the nation's heritage. I enjoyed being versatile and writing for all parts of the paper at high speed, sometimes dictating a thousand words from a phone box at an hour's notice. It was exhilarating and felt worthwhile to campaign to make better use of empty property for the homeless, for example, and I became a trustee of the charity The Empty Homes Agency. I was always amazed at how swiftly my days in the office would pass, so absorbing was the work.

But I couldn't ignore the persistent sense of unease that I wasn't spending more time at home. Producing so many articles meant time in the office. My personal best was working on six separate pieces for one issue. On that day I didn't see the children at all. The conflict was becoming unbearable. It felt like a sort of underground conversation I was having with myself but hitherto had denied was taking place.

I was now well enough to consider what I really wanted and could realistically manage, as opposed to engaging in crisis management and survival, or what I thought I should be doing in order to be liked and approved of. On the one hand, being a working mother was what my generation of women, born in the 1960s, did. Our mothers had fought for our opportunity to work. It was for us to enjoy the fruits of their struggles. Despite my reservations, there was much I still loved about my job. On the other hand, I was itching to prove my competence at home. The sense that I was missing out and had missed out in the past, especially by being so ill when George was young, would not go away. Try as I might, I couldn't stop reliving one wretched evening when the children had retreated into Julie's arms as I arrived at the front door. This time Edward lashed himself to Julie's leg to stop her leaving.

I wanted to be a *good* mother, as I wanted to be not just a journalist but a *good* journalist. My world was full of 'shoulds' and 'musts', the vocabulary of the perfectionist who constructs ideal narratives. Later, an older, less judgemental me would question this language and realise these ideals were all but impossible to attain.

Working on a newspaper turned out to be a particularly poor fit with trying to spend more time at home. It was true that when I had first gone back to work, the routine and structure had boosted my self-esteem and helped me to recover. But studies have shown that employment can also be detrimental to sufferers of depression unless it is flexible.* This is even more true when you are also trying to look after two children.

There are few workplaces less flexible than a newsroom. The news, naturally enough, doesn't coincide with a child's schedule. If a story breaks, you need to be writing away, there and then. And you never know when this will happen: quite often, it was in the evening, which was supposedly my time with the children.

I had previously found the uncertainty exhilarating. Now I was increasingly struggling. Life was wildly rushed and lived at such a pitch that I was missing deadlines both at home and at work. I had snatches of insomnia and my anxiety levels were high. It felt as if I were leading my life to please someone else, not me.

I had been drawn to a job to which in some ways I was badly suited. This was a common theme, I began to notice among certain friends, as both their careers and their characters became more established: the impatient drawn to teaching, those lacking in empathy to nursing, the cynical to politics. It was almost as if the protagonists were yearning to find what they themselves lacked, via their choice of profession. On a newspaper there is no end to how hard you can try. You could always write another story, try for another page lead, investigate another tip-off. There is no natural end to writing news stories. And I had to admit that I was writing stories I had written before. There was a predictable calendar to the newsroom year: love nests for Valentine's Day; cosy country cottages in which to celebrate a snow-bound Christmas, the regular house-price bulletins.

Even if I did manage to be promoted away from such stories, the future was likely to mean long days at my desk and

* A 2008 study from the Society of Occupational Medicine found that going back to work can help people recover from depression, but employers need to be more flexible.

office politics. The job was becoming less attractive at the same time as the draw of being at home increased.

One evening I had left slightly early to be back with the children in time to share a bath. As I swilled the warm water around me and Edward and George, a call from my editor came through on my mobile phone. As a news reporter, I was expected to be available for queries from the newsroom about stories I had written or to write fresh articles that were needed late in the day. I knew I had to answer the phone, especially as I had left the office early. Edward started trying to grab the phone. George went under the water. Either I supervised two children who might drown, or I spoke to my editor. I didn't answer.

My old enemies the fizzy head, butterfly guts and racing heart were instantly back, albeit in a muted way. I felt a profound weariness as the sheer willpower needed to keep my show on the road and answer the phone ran out. The difference was, post-breakdown, I listened to these bat squeaks announcing that depression might be lurking beneath the surface. I already knew the potential consequences of not heeding them.

I didn't just want to reduce the stress of combining work and family life. I wanted to no longer be split between work and the children but to embrace one role wholeheartedly. Sebastian pointed out that whenever I talked to him about the children, my sentences would begin, 'I'm worried about Georgie's teething/the boys preferring Julie to me/missing the news editor's call/not having enough time for the children,' while my updates on office life would begin, 'I'm worried that I've misquoted somebody/offended a colleague/ had to rewrite an introduction/been scooped by another paper.' I wanted to talk in a voice that was less anxious, both about the children when I came home, and my work when I arrived at the office.

As Sebastian and I discussed endlessly, I wanted everything. I wanted to feel calm and to sleep well. I wanted the excitement of work, and I wanted to be a good mother. Some days the desire to be more at home was in the ascendant; on other days I loved being back at the office. I also wanted something else, something which I didn't dare admit to myself or Sebastian: a third child.

Such a desire seemed reckless: we had achieved some kind of stability for a good eighteen months. Despite all my complaints, we had found some kind of compromise between the demands of work and home. Having another child might upset the delicate balance. Despite my reservations and the tug between home and work, I was holding down my job and often enjoyed it.

In the end, nature provided the solution to these dilemmas: I fell pregnant. I was delighted, I kept working through the first few months, but as the pregnancy progressed and my exhaustion increased, I began to realise that I would have to stop. Until that point, I had still imagined I could combine work and motherhood. Had I enjoyed better health and suffered less anxiety, I think I would have tried to continue even with three small children. As it was, the demands of the job and my own limitations forced the issue.

I found myself more and more pleased as I realised I would be at home full-time, able to look after Edward and George and with the prospect of time with a new baby without the immediate pressure of work. I savoured my luck that I was in the fortuanate position to be able to make that decision, thanks to Sebastian's job. On return from my last day at *The Times* after nearly a decade, Edward, George, Sebastian and I indulged in what the boys called 'jazzy dancing' to Abba's 'Greatest Hits'. It seemed as if all was set fair and we were the luckiest family in the world.

Chapter Ten

Sweet Joy Befall Thee

JUNE 1999 TO NOVEMBER 2003

June 1999

I resigned from the paper aged thirty-three. My editor seemed unsurprised; he understood that I couldn't manage the job and three children. I no longer had to quieten the voices urging me to stay at home or ask Julie to keep the children up late so I could see them on return from work. It felt compelling to do things differently this time and devote myself to being with my children.

That little word 'my' had been playing round my head. It was *my* turn, to look after *my* children. I felt a primal possessiveness, the passion of an almighty love affair that would brook no opposition, and, finally, an ability to claim my rightful place at home. I had never heard such feelings discussed by any teacher, friend or colleague and I didn't mention them to anyone now. It was much easier to confide in friends a second truth: I had also wept on the Tube when I left the office for the final time. I deliberately didn't organise a leaving party or advertise my departure, reserving the possibility that I just might return.

There was one problem with being pregnant: I might become ill again. So determined had I been to have another child that I didn't mind for myself, but I was worried that any relapse might damage Edward and George. I had previously tried to distract myself from such thoughts. Dr Fischer assured me that the boys hadn't suffered overly the first time around; so did my family. But I was dismayed when I read that rats separated from their mother and deprived of intimacy for long periods of time have a higher response to stress when older.*

The work of John Bowlby, which I sought out in this new-found spirit of enquiry, was no more reassuring. A child psychiatrist and psychoanalyst working in the 1930s and 1940s, Bowlby developed his theory of attachment. He found that a six-month-old monkey's reaction to being separated from its mother is like that of a human child. The initial screams and tears are replaced by lethargy and unresponsiveness when young, and a tendency to depression and anxiety when adult.

More recent research has tried to establish the biology behind attachment theory. The prefrontal cortex is believed to be the part of the brain that enables us to empathise, to restrain primitive emotions and to deal with stress. For it to grow properly, there needs to be close and loving contact between parent and child. This attachment causes endorphins and dopamine to be released, which in turn allows the prefrontal cortex and the rest of the brain to develop. Abandoned babies who have suffered deprivation when young, are believed to have smaller than normal prefrontal cortexes.

Sebastian was strong in my defence. I had managed to

* Professor Jane Plant and Janet Stephenson, *Beating Stress, Anxiety and Depression: Groundbreaking Ways to Help You Feel Better* (Piatkus Books, 2008).

spend time with the children when I began to feel better in the evenings, he reminded me. There had been only a few weeks when there was very little contact. The children hadn't noticed my absence. In my memory, it seemed far longer. In addition, my family were caring for the children when I couldn't.

This provided some comfort. I had read that the length of separation is crucial: the real damage comes from long periods of separation – for months at a time, not just weeks. For all Sebastian's reassurance, though, I still fretted that my earlier depression might have damaged the children and that it was rash to risk the chance of depression a second time. But neither of the boys was unresponsive or lethargic; they were cheery little chaps outwardly unmarked by my depression. Here was a chance to correct any damage I might have caused and wholeheartedly embrace motherhood. Just in case.

I delighted in my pregnancy now I was home. The gnawing seemed to have ceased, the underground conversation I had been having with myself about working versus staying at home was over. I was a full-time mother now, and seemed to be adjusting well.

July 1999

I rang Dr Fischer. He was reassuring. Yes, I was slightly more likely to experience depression in the future, having had it before, but it wasn't inevitable. Yes, I should be careful not to get overtired. But my stress levels might arguably be lower these days, as I had given up work. Congratulations, he said, as we exchanged goodbyes and good wishes.

December 1999

The ultimate Christmas present arrived in December in the shape of a baby girl. I marvelled that more love, in addition to the love we already felt for our boys, had miraculously been made available to us. I vowed I would always remember the moment I first saw her and make it jangle among my memories when I was very old. Our delight in her femininity and perfection was boundless. In the end I had to put away William Blake's 'Infant Joy', which I had stuck to our bathroom mirror, as it moved me to tears too often.

> *'I have no name;*
> *I am but two days old.'*
> *What shall I call thee?*
> *'I happy am,*
> *Joy is my name.'*
> *Sweet joy befall thee!*
>
> *Pretty joy!*
> *Sweet joy, but two days old.*
> *Sweet Joy I call thee:*
> *Thou dost smile,*
> *I sing the while;*
> *Sweet joy befall thee!*

We named our pretty joy Katherine. She stole both our hearts, instantly. She slept and fed to order and smiled within weeks rather than months. I remained well, even managing to move house shortly after her birth to a house nearby where there was room for all three children. I was very careful not to get tired and not to do too much, and I continued to practise the breathing and relaxation exercises I had learnt when I was unwell.

My mother was initially a constant presence. Everyone around me was mindful I might once again be unwell. As the months passed and my confidence grew, she would come at tea-time to read to the older children and help get all three to bed before departing: we would joke about angel's wings sprouting on her back as she returned home.

Julie decided to leave now that I was at home full-time. For all that I had found our relationship fraught when I had been ill, I could now see more clearly how challenging life had been for her when I had been utterly absorbed in the depression. It hadn't been easy for her on my return to work, either. Sebastian gently revealed that at times I had been far from the perfect boss. I was so focussed on trying to carve out enough time with the children that I had forced Julie to fit around my schedule. I required her to be flexible and fit in with my whims. Meanwhile, the strain I was under meant I could be short-tempered. Despite finding me difficult to deal with, she had never been anything other than devoted to the children. In particular she had the knack of buying them the one birthday present they really wanted, knowing them as well as she did. My choices would often be abandoned. We hugged when she left.

One friend described the life of a stay-at-home mother as being like that of a gold prospector working on a stretch of river. Much of the time your pan would contain nothing but mud and stones but sometimes there would be nuggets of gold.

Initially, all went well. The best moments happened when I

combined looking after the children with getting on with what I had to do anyway. I liked cooking while one child broke the eggs for me, or sweeping the garden while another watered plants. There were those golden nuggets: the time when Edward rushed home from school, thick with the pride of having got a delightful 'ten out of seven' in a spelling test; or Georgie's insistence on putting on his 'bowsers' himself. It felt as if I was watching a harvest ripening in front of my eyes, and that this time I would have the chance to bring it in.

But this exhilarating period after Katherine's birth gave way to a more realistic one, when the harvest could be bitter, too. As any mother knows, even with the blessing of having help at home, (we employed a series of young au pairs) unbridled domesticity can be bruising at times in its physical demands and repetitive boredom. Even a trip to the lavatory required planning.

I didn't help myself. The ambition that had once flourished in the newsroom took root at home. It wasn't enough for me to be a mother: I wanted to be a very good mother, not to mention wife, friend, daughter, hostess and homemaker. But I also craved the status and interest of a job, which none of these roles could confer on me. There were days when I felt myself to be little more than a glowing piece of livestock who had produced three prize heifers. My life was a rejection of every edict of the individualistic, adventure-hungry, intellectually curious society in which I had grown up and to which my friends belonged.

Now, with a sickening sense of familiarity, the ticker-tape in my head ran in an opposite loop. This time I leant towards missing the camaraderie and intellectual stimulus of work and hungered for life outside our cosy home. I was jealous of contemporaries who had kept working and now enjoyed stellar careers. My feminist beliefs didn't sit easily with being a kept woman. I was also troubled by the idea that Sebastian and I had begun our married life as friends and equals, but now things were different. I hated relying on him for much of my news of a world beyond motherhood. Just as I had ached for the children, now I missed the office and my friends there, in an alloy of complicated feelings.

At times I felt I was just the backdrop to other people's busy and purposeful lives, whether it was Sebastian leaving for work or the older children heading off to school. A cloak of invisibility seemed to have descended on my shoulders. I believed that I was no longer a person in my own right but somebody's mother, somebody's wife, somebody with no status in a world that values what we do, not who we are. Mine were the invisible hands that folded the bath towels; it was me who remembered to buy the washing powder. The person who once held down a job on a newspaper seemed to have vanished.

And I found the responsibility for dependent children relentless, even as I knew I was lucky to have a supportive family. One afternoon, Edward and I were in a bubble walking along the pavement hand in hand, spotting his favourite yellow cars (something to do with a fondness for Noddy and his taxi, I think). I felt his fingers slipping from mine and my heart stopped as he stepped into the road. He turned back to me in triumph, crying, 'Yellow car!' Only the screech of a driver's emergency stop and my screams halted his laughter.

A moment of carelessness on my part could mean death. I was often infected by familiar anxious symptoms and could be acutely oversensitive. Doctors call it being in a state of heightened arousal and some believe such oversensitivity to the environment may be genetic. All I knew was that the sheer vulnerability of these beings could feel terrifying. I remembered the cool calm that used to descend when my mind was focused on trying to make sense of an article at work. Maybe returning to journalism was the better path for me after all.

Sometimes my heart sank at the realisation that I was still wrestling with this seemingly intractable problem: the inescapable pull in two different directions. Gradually, though I became more optimistic that I could manage to edge back to work, at least part-time. I hoped that would provide the right life balance and the status I craved. It felt like the moment to try.

March 2002 – February 2003

For the first time in years, with the older boys now at school and my mother happy to look after two year-old Katherine on occasion, my coffee wasn't automatically cold by the time I drank it. I might not be able to rejoin the collegiate life of the newsroom, but perhaps I could once again try to establish an identity beyond being the mother of three children, as a freelance journalist, and forge anew my friendships with other women who had continued their careers.

Sebastian encouraged me to try to work. He noticed how my mood improved on the days when I had been back in touch with former colleagues. I seemed more energetic and positive, and was much nicer to him when not run ragged by domestic life, he said. Once again we would be able to swap notes on the challenges of our different professional lives, as equals. That had always been the context of our relationship and Sebastian had always passionately believed in my work.

My mother also supported a gentle return to work. She herself had happily combined writing her biographies with bringing up us three children.

Then there were the children to consider. Sebastian thought that it might actually be good for my relationship with them if I took up work again. Though I didn't want to acknowledge my own ambition, Sebastian knew I was fiercely aspirational. I had a strong work ethic, entrenched at a young age at school and university and honed over many years. If I didn't work, the danger was that all my competitiveness might be channelled into putting inappropriate pressure on the children. Far better to live out my own dreams than impose them on the children. All these were good and sensible arguments to return to work, from people who loved and cared for me.

For the next year or so, I began various writing projects, starting to produce the odd freelance piece and tentatively researching a book on London's communal gardens reflecting my own love of gardening. Returning to some kind of creative endeavour was like a rush of fresh air, blasting away any resentment I felt about being at home. I seemed at last to have found my own sense of balance.

March 2003

All would have been well, but for an inconvenient truth: another bit of me began secretly to want a fourth child, even while I acknowledged that this might be the harder course. The sensible decision, surely, would have been to stick with our three and try to continue to satisfy my ambitions with my part-time work. But the part of me that wanted to be pregnant wouldn't be silenced. It had an almost physical presence, like an itch that couldn't be soothed.

My longing for another child was in direct opposition to my desire to work again. Both were real and I just couldn't seem to find a road map to accommodate them. The problem was that I knew combining the two roles was highly stressful and might tip me again into depression. It wasn't proving easy to re-emerge into working life. In some ways freelance journalism was just as challenging as having a regular newspaper job: it required instant availability in a way that was hard to combine with small children. And to succeed as a freelancer I needed to be a self-starter, to create my own opportunities. I didn't really have the motivation; my focus was too divided, the dilemma of work versus another baby too distracting.

At least I was becoming more certain that I hoped for another child. I wanted to recreate the pleasure of looking after Katherine when she was little, a pleasure so intense that I had all but forgotten what it felt like to be unwell. She had hugely assuaged the loss I had felt for not being around more when the boys were younger. Then there was the fact that I had always considered three was a difficult number for a family: the world was set up for pairs, twin rooms with two beds, games designed for two. One child could feel left out, as I had on occasion, growing up. I didn't want to repeat my own childhood. Before long my hope became a powerful tornado of longing, overpowering any thoughts of work. At thirty-seven, it was now or never, I believed. Work could wait. By now there was nothing sweet or gentle about the strength of my maternal urge. I just knew.

March 2003

Early in 2003, I found myself pregnant again – with twins. Odd though it sounds, I hadn't discussed my hope for a bigger family either with Sebastian or my mother. Perhaps it was because I was frightened that my mother in particular might dissuade me. She naturally feared another child might prompt another depressive episode. Perhaps it was my Catholic faith and a feeling that a child was a gift from God rather than any decision we made.

So Sebastian was taken aback when I rang from the hospital to tell him that first, I was pregnant, and in the next breath that the scan had revealed two beating hearts. He came home early from work that day and had to lie down to absorb the astonishing news. Colleagues had asked him what number I was aiming for. Perhaps I could enlighten him, he said.

I too was daunted by the prospect of twins, but I could hardly admit to my fears given the circumstances. The truth was that I was also thrilled. I reassured him, full of optimism, that we would recreate the happy time I had had with Katherine. Yes, we would have five children but I wouldn't also be trying to work. I was looking forward, my thoughts echoing Wordsworth's poem 'Michael':

> *A child, more than all other gifts*
> *That earth can offer to declining man,*
> *Brings hope with it, and forward-looking thoughts,*
> *And stirrings of inquietude, when they*
> *By tendency of nature needs must fail.*

October 2003

Katherine started at the nursery school in the house next door when she was nearly three. I loved hearing the children's laughter at break time and I used to ensconce myself on our back terrace so I could see her play. She imagined the school was far away even though it was so close. I loved the joke that I could throw her over the wall to get to nursery. In fact, I was so heavily pregnant that I couldn't reach my arms around my swelling stomach, let alone touch my toes or lift a toddler. In fact, for the last few weeks of the pregnancy I could do little but sit in the wheelchair I was confined to; walking was so painful it was out of the question. The twins already weighed over six pounds each and I am only five foot two.

Arthur and Charlotte were born one Friday morning in October 2003. The only thing that can trump the joy of having one baby is having two. Arthur was pink-cheeked, fair-haired with tight blond curls and blue eyes, while Charlotte had velvety hazel eyes, olive skin and so much straight chestnut hair that I could comb a parting in it and clip it back with a butterfly clip. They both had bright lips flushed with fresh new blood. They were exactly the same weight, as if they had meticulously divided up supplies during their joint life in the womb. They shared a cot, sleeping head to toe. Somehow this apparent decision to share a life and to enter the world together seemed magical.

I had help at home and the house was full of joy, despite the challenge of caring for and feeding two infants. No infant is sent from central casting, perfectly performing its role. When I cuddled them, they didn't always stop crying. When I fed them, they didn't always nurse vigorously and well, and when they were put to bed, they didn't always fall asleep as though they were auditioning for parts as contented little babies.

But life was at first fresh like a dream, love stealing around us all, embracing the seven of us in its hold. I was so confident I wouldn't be unwell that I didn't do my relaxation or breathing exercises. By the time I had fed myself and the babies, washed myself and washed them, I told myself, I couldn't possibly have the time to be unwell. There wasn't a moment for the depression to plant its insidious roots – or so I thought.

Early November 2003

At first it crept up slowly. I didn't suddenly stay awake all night like before, but once again my mind refused to settle easily and I experienced the odd thunder-clap of fear. In addition, and much though I found it hard to admit, I was channelling the competitive spirit that had once flourished in the office into our home life. It wasn't about being good enough: it was about being the best. I desired to meet every child's need and be the best mother they could have. And it wasn't enough to triumph as a mother but to excel in multiple other roles I invented for myself, too, albeit ones that go largely unacknowledged: the other identities I had already carved out for myself as wife, daughter, friend, godmother, hostess, carer and homemaker. The problem was that we now had five children.

Whereas previously I had worried about combining work and home, now I worried about combining other roles. I worried that spending time with the twins meant neglecting the older children and Sebastian. I worried about spreading myself too thin and not being able to cope. Worst of all, I had only myself to blame for becoming pregnant again. It seemed astonishing to me that I hadn't considered the risks involved, or even thought of discussing them more fully with Sebastian. As for Wordsworth: he had never borne children himself, I reflected bitterly.

There was at first just a growing sense of unease, a draining of hope and optimism, a slow mangling of my brain, the feeling that disaster was inevitable and it was just a question of time before I would lose my footing. It was a return to the fear. I wasn't sure what the tipping point might be but I lived in dread that each day would prove my last of feeling normal, as the radiance of our little group ebbed slowly away. My usual self was hanging on by a thread. My identity seemed to be vanishing fast, as Roger McGough evokes so well in 'A Poem Just For Me', its apparent simplicity conveying the complex emotional reality:

> *Where am I now when I need me*
> *Suddenly where have I gone?*
> *I'm so alone here without me*
> *Tell me please what have I done?*

> *Once I did most things together*
> *I went for walks hand in hand*
> *I shared my life so completely*
> *I met my every demand.*

> *Tell me I'll come back tomorrow*
> *I'll keep my arms open wide*
> *Tell me that I'll never leave*
> *My place is here at my side.*

Maybe I've simply mislaid me
Like an umbrella or a key
So until the day that I come my way
Here is a poem just for me.

The evenings in particular were getting worse. One epic night the twins were crying. Another child had a temperature upstairs and while administering the ever-present Calpol my last clean shirt got covered in the pink sticky medicine. I was dropping with tiredness as I tried to read a story; I only just stopped myself from telling them to read their own bloody story. I could smell rice burning into the bottom of the saucepan downstairs as the water boiled dry. I sat on the stairs, my head in my hands, and tried to pretend that I wasn't crying as a curious Edward appeared from his room. Startled, he returned with his teddy and a handkerchief.

At that point I resolved that life at home had to change, and fast. I knew I was struggling to cope and starting to grow resentful towards Sebastian and the children, the people I loved most. I was in danger of becoming whining and self-pitying. It was time to try to regain control.

Mid-November 2003

A look that I took to be resigned exhaustion from Sebastian was the trigger for what I thought would be an inspired solution: we would go for a weekend away, just the two of us. I would at least be the good wife.

It happened when we were watching television one night. I was sitting like a cow by a milking machine as I used an electric pump to extract more milk for the night feeds ahead.

Sebastian didn't realise I was watching him, but he had his head in his hands and he was rubbing his eyes. Ever the people-pleaser, I took it as a sign that I needed to be a wife as well as a mother. The following day I put away the tracksuit bottoms and went to the hairdresser, still in pursuit of feeling normal. And I made plans for our weekend away. He was nervous, wondering if it was really a good idea to travel so soon after the twins' birth. But I was determined.

One week later, November 2003

I banged the front door shut as we headed for the Eurostar, leaving the children with my mother. A few hours later we were walking through a beautiful Parisian park gilded with autumnal light, the leaves like flowers, and then lingering over lunch. It seemed as if the sun didn't want to go down and as if we were enjoying its last smiles of the year.

All these things are true: we did walk through a park; the sun shone on us; we did savour a long lunch, and it was delicious. But for me, every pleasure was washed through with worry: that the walk would be too long and I would get too tired; that we would be late for our café booking; that I wouldn't have time for a rest after lunch if it took too long; that I wouldn't be able to sleep in a strange bed; that something had gone wrong at home with the children; that it would be too much for my mother; that something would go wrong with me abroad. The effort to be light-hearted exhausted me.

That night I tried to keep quiet as I sobbed in our bathroom, crumpled in a corner with my knees gathered tightly to my chest. I experienced a slew of familiar symptoms, as if they had been lying in wait all along. They drowned out the calm that I momentarily felt as I returned to St Theresa's prayer and recited my favourite poems. I hardly slept at all, consumed with the fear of where insomnia seemed to be leading.

As dawn broke, I had a brainwave. Listening to the hotel staff stirring in the passage outside, I formulated a plan, wonderful in its simplicity. Of course. It was obvious. As long as I didn't tell anyone, I could rescue myself. That was it. Keep quiet. Say nothing. Then there would be no proof that I wasn't normal. I would be able to keep going. I would be able to take the children to school; I would be able to make pancakes for brunch on Sundays; I would be able to discuss Thomas the Tank Engine's schedule with George; I would be able to keep breastfeeding the twins; I would be able to sing 'Hop Little Bunny' as Katherine danced in crazy circles till she fell over; I would be able to say, yes, of course Edward, you can sleep in our bed. Just as long as I kept quiet about feeling unwell.

So the next morning I shared nothing with Sebastian of my long, agonising dark night of the soul. I was up and about as usual. There were some clues, which unbeknown to me Sebastian had of course already spotted. Drained by the insomnia, I kept my head down because I knew I had started to look rather vacant-eyed. I was suspiciously quiet because I also knew I had a catch in my voice which might reveal my true state. But otherwise I ruthlessly reconstructed my defences and behaved normally, or so I thought.

Because now I was in a fight. A battle was raging between two Rachels: one who was going to pretend to herself and the world she was fine, and another who was already unwell. But I couldn't admit, not for one second, to such thoughts, or even acknowledge this unwell Rachel. Oh, no. She didn't exist. She was a bitter, stark stranger and I didn't want to know her, ever.

Here's what I had to lose. Once ill, I might never recover. That would be it, possibly for ever this time. I would no longer be able to be mother to my children or wife to my husband, daughter to my parents, or friend to my friends. I would not be able to put my children to bed. I would not be able to read Edward his stories. I would not be able to take an apple crumble out of the oven. I would not be able to test the children on their spellings. Slowly, steadily, depression would once again rob me of my functions, peeling off my roles, one by one.

I tried to enlist God on my side. Look, this time I know where this is heading, and I am sorry, but I'm not going there. Hope you are listening, God. I am not going to be unwell. I'm a believer, I promise.

No one answered.

Someone had to help. Someone had to get rid of that other ill person. Don't kill all of me, just the sick bit. Please.

But I was addressing thin air. There was no answering cry, no provision of sufficient grace. Still I kept pleading: you can't do this to me. I've got five children. I'm their mother. You must understand that. They need me to dress them in the mornings and to take them to school and to wipe their tears and read them stories, and actually no one else in the whole world can read them stories like I can.

I was sobbing now. You can't do this to them. They're young. And as for me, I've already been ill once. It's not fair that I should be ill again. It's someone else's turn. Not mine. Please.

End of November 2003

We returned to London the next day, though limped might be a better description. I hoped that a return to familiar territory might lead to some respite from the fighting, but the battle continued to rage, albeit in less exotic surroundings. One minute I was splashing my face with cold water to disguise the red blotches left by the crying, smoothing my shirt as I tottered downstairs and pretended everything was fine; the next I was clinging to my pillow, as if the bed were being tossed at sea and I would be thrown overboard if I let go. The clashing soundtracks in my head were becoming deafening: one voice violently trying to will myself to be well, versus the other who every day dragged my body deeper into sickness. I told not a soul. As long as I kept these dark forces hidden, I thought I could escape.

The effort at secrecy compounded my exhaustion. It was like being on stage, but as if I were in a show in which there was no final scene or curtain call. No actor could survive the extraordinary effort such deception demanded.

Chapter Eleven

The Sea Dried Up Like Sandpaper

DECEMBER 2003 TO MARCH 2004

Thursday, early December 2003

Every Christmas we hosted a party for our friends and neighbours. Part of me was desperate not to this year, but since I was still maintaining the fiction that everything was fine I didn't feel I could speak to Sebastian about calling it off.

Even in good health, I found the event daunting, albeit exhilarating. We always took immense trouble over the occasion, moving the furniture out of part of the house for the evening. It had become something of an annual fixture among our friends. There was always plenty to drink and plenty of guests, and I took it upon myself to try and introduce as many people to each other as possible, a habit I had learned from my socialite grandmother.

I slept badly in the lead-up to the party. I almost told Sebastian I couldn't go ahead. But I believed he wanted to, not knowing my fears, and I wanted to please him. It was one of the roles I had set myself: to be a good hostess. And I still believed that if I only kept to our familiar patterns and continued as if all were normal then I wouldn't be ill. I was like a man who carries on walking as he falls over a cliff.

In my defence, doing something had always helped. The

invitations went out, though I was only just strong enough to walk to the post box to send them. The party clothes that didn't fit covered the bed in a multi-coloured patchwork and the floor was littered with shoes that seemed wrong. Yet the mechanics of the party ground on, RSVPs trickled in (each time someone sent their regrets it felt like a well-aimed punch to my stomach) and deliveries arrived. The house was wreathed in ivy and mistletoe, while a blow-up Santa stood on the balcony waving at the street. The children were safely tucked up in bed upstairs with a babysitter on guard on the landing and their bedroom doors closed to shield them from the noise downstairs.

My parents were the first to arrive, as usual. For the first twenty minutes, I managed. The sick me was diverted. Once again it was as if I were an actress, unwillingly playing a part in a play, and the guests in their Christmas finery were the other characters. I was so absorbed in the rush of getting people drinks and introducing them to each other that I temporarily forgot that other ill Rachel. I was giddy with pleasantness, racing between familiar faces, twirling strangers together as if I were choreographing a complicated dance. Aha! Victory. I would subdue that mind of mine.

But I made one fatal error. I paused to sit down in the kitchen, piled high with crates and trays. That other Rachel who had been temporarily invisible took her chance in the moment of stillness; she reported for duty and proceeded to vent her violent fury at having been forgotten. I knew I couldn't continue.

The battle was over. There were no longer two Rachels locked in combat. Sick, corporeal Rachel had finally won. It was as if I had been engaged in a struggle to try to cut off my own dark shadow. Now the shadow and I were reunited. For all my efforts, we had never been truly parted.

No one noticed when I slipped off and walked barefoot to my parents' house a few minutes away. I let myself in with the spare key they kept in the bike shed by the front door. My feet were cold and wet. I couldn't walk in my party shoes; they symbolised the person I wasn't and the oddity of the whole situation. Here I was, feeling so ill, yet none but my family and very closest friends knew anything of the situation – principally, of course, because I hadn't told them.

I no longer clutched the possibility that perhaps I was fine after all. The party-giving Rachel was receding fast into the darkness. Soon she would be gone altogether. With every step, my confidence was haemorrhaging. I might deny my state to others, but I could no longer deny it to myself. I took my necklace off and felt a little better. Now at least the person I was and the way I was dressed dovetailed. Here was my true self, no longer adorned with a gaiety I did not feel.

Arms tightly folded across my chest, I sat in the room where I had played as a child, still with its tail-less rocking horse waiting patiently by the window. On one wall was the picture of a fox breakfasting with huntsmen, decked out in his pink coat and wielding a knife and fork, that had mesmerised me when I was a child. I buried my head into its tattered upholstery of the faded yellow sofa that had lost its springs, thirsting for its familiar scent of all the children who had sat on the cosy laps of parents, and wielded its cushions in pillow fights, just as I had craved the scent of home when I had gone to hospital. This was my last-ditch crazy attempt to stave off the sick Rachel – I yearned to somehow return to my childhood and be shielded from this pain. If I kept very,

very still, and willed myself into the past, just maybe it would all go away.

I half expected someone to come and find me in my corner; I cried louder and louder in the hope that they would come. They would rescue me, just as my mother had always done when I was a child, and again as an adult. She could decide what I should do. Of course I would be saved.

No one came. How could they, when my parents were at the party I had insisted on organising. The pantomime collapsed around me. I was in free fall now, this time ten thousand miles to the bottom of the sea and beyond. There was nothing and nobody to stop me from this dizzying and terrifying descent.

Eventually I crept back to my own house, my shoes dangling from my hand, and found the party in full swing. A waiter, not recognising me and surprised by my state, asked if I had been invited.

Sebastian helped me upstairs to our room, unfazed by my absence. He knew, and I knew, that the struggle was over: I had tried, and I had lost. I had known all along: my bargaining was an illusion. He tucked me into bed, told me he would be back as soon as he could and then returned to our guests downstairs.

I could hear the chatter of familiar voices as I lay wide awake, still in my party dress. I imagined the guests wondering where I was, what had happened to me, though nobody came to find out. Once again I was on my own, and elsewhere life carried on. I thought of W.H. Auden's beautiful poem 'Musée des Beaux Arts'. Suffering takes place 'while someone else is eating or opening a window or just walking dully along'. It was only a brief thought. Minutes later I could no longer recall Auden's words.

About suffering they were never wrong,
The Old Masters; how well they understood
Its human position; how it takes place
While someone else is eating or opening a window or
* just walking dully along;*
How, when the aged are reverently, passionately waiting
For the miraculous birth, there always must be
Children who did not specially want it to happen,
* skating*
On a pond at the edge of the wood:
They never forgot
That even the dreadful martyrdom must run its course
Anyhow in a corner, some untidy spot
Where the dogs go on with their doggy life and the
* torturer's horse*
Scratches its innocent behind on a tree.

In Breughel's Icarus, for instance: how everything turns
* away*
Quite leisurely from the disaster; the ploughman may
Have heard the splash, the forsaken cry,
But for him it was not an important failure; the sun
* shone*
As it had to on the white legs disappearing into the green
Water; and the expensive delicate ship that must have
* seen*
Something amazing, a boy falling out of the sky,
Had somewhere to get to and sailed calmly on.

Friday, early December 2003

My mother called the doctor the next morning. Summoned by Sebastian, who was by now deeply concerned, she had arrived to find her thirty-eight-year-old daughter crying into the silence of the bedroom. The agony was back. Downstairs, glasses were being collected and furniture returned, floors mopped and bottles put out for the rubbish. I was hugging one of Edward's bears.

Dr Ross had died several years before and we had transferred to a new practice. Already very ill, I was too befuddled to consider that it might make sense to talk to Dr Fischer straight away. I had had such a happy time after Katherine's birth that I hadn't kept in touch though we could easily have found his number. There was nothing to suggest to Sebastian or my mother that the new doctors might not be equally good. One of the practice's GPs visited me at home that morning and instantly prescribed citalopram, an antidepressant I hadn't tried before. It was the work of a moment as his cufflinked wrist swept across the paper and he calmly promised me I would feel better soon. 'But can't you see I'm dying!' I wanted to scream.

All my fears were transcribed onto that small piece of paper. All my symptoms were amplifying and solidifying as he wrote, my depressive illness being created, letter by letter, in his act of diagnosis, tunnelling violently towards me from the scrap of paper.

Far from feeling better after his visit, I felt much worse. This was clear proof that I was going to be ill again. Fear had grabbed me by the throat. I was being marched back to prison.

Of course, at this point, I was confused. Pills had helped

make me better in the past yet now they terrified me. Perhaps it was a memory of the ghastliness of the side effects. Anxiety muddled any logic. My head was thick with uncertainty and indecision. I couldn't see anything positive in those hateful drugs. I had fought hard to come off them. It must surely be a backwards step to start taking them again.

I have often since wondered whether if he hadn't prescribed the drugs so quickly I would have been okay. Perhaps I was already too far gone and the physical symptoms had taken full hold. Just maybe, though, I could have been righted with tremendous amounts of sympathy and a belief that there was no need to assume I would be ill. But it's a medical phenomenon that negative expectations can become self-fulfilling prophecies. This has been described as the nocebo effect: the opposite of a placebo, when the expectation that you will be better actually makes you so.

The drugs sucked me down into that familiar vortex of anxiety, leading to more symptoms, leading to more anxiety. I was literally worried sick. A single bad night once again became insomnia, tiredness a profound and insoluble fatigue.

At this point, it might seem odd that we still hadn't consulted Dr Fischer, but Sebastian and my mother trusted the GPs I was seeing to judge when I should see a psychiatrist, and who was the best expert to consult.

I tumbled back into the fear I knew so well, the repetitive, exhausting, self-consuming cycle of anxiety after anxiety. It lurked inside me, requiring to be fed with all that was good in my life. Little by little it devoured all laughter, life and love, turning goodness into a murky, noxious, vomit-inducing presence lodged inside me. I handed over my normal roles once again, like a prisoner giving up their home-washed clothes and wristwatch in a neat pile to the warder in exchange for their prison outfit, the warder in turn checking my pockets to make sure there was no trace left of my former life.

Farewell to being a mother. Goodbye to being a wife, a cook, a gardener, a journalist, a friend, a daughter, a daughter-in-law, a sister, a godparent . . . Here, take them all, all that was strong, fertile, loving about me.

I quickly became too ill to argue with those around me, both professionals and family and friends, that I didn't need the pills. One very capable friend who effortlessly managed her family asked me whether I really needed to start antidepressants. Say no, she said. If only my life were that simple, I thought bitterly. 'It's too late,' I cried back. 'Too late.' The fight had happened long ago. But then again, maybe the drugs were the answer. I didn't know. In a familiar pattern, I found I could no longer make decisions.

Late December 2003

Christmas came and went unnoticed. The feeling of ghastliness was continuous, debilitating and familiar. At least it was different for the people around me, who maintained that this time they knew what was going on. To me, their refusal to panic could seem like complacency. They might keep reassuring me that I would get better, but that didn't stop me being ill right now, and who knew for sure what the future would hold? The only certainty was that no one could pretend to me this time that the recovery would be swift.

In fact, the acute phase of this episode would prove far longer than the first one, another recognised pattern. Recovery proves more difficult each time you suffer.

Once again, I couldn't get out of bed. All my energy was consumed in trying to manage the suppurating monster inside me that kept demanding to be fed the last shreds of comfort in my life. All that was left was a single thought: how long would it be before the antidepressants started to work? 'You'll be better soon,' everyone kept reassuring me. 'Maybe even in a few days . . .' A few days turned into weeks.

Sebastian remembers the monotony of my conversations, which centred exclusively on me. I would whine like a child on a car journey who keeps asking 'Are we there yet?' 'You would talk endlessly about the drugs,' he says. 'The GP would prescribe a different dose, and you would go on and on and on about whether that would make you better and when it would happen.' It was odd, really, as on one level I didn't believe I would get better, even as I kept on asking others when I would ever escape from going round and round this maze.

In retrospect, it is painful to acknowledge the extent of my selfishness. One consolation is how commonplace such feelings are: Charles Lamb had pondered the same question two hundred years before. 'How sickness enlarges the dimensions of a man's self to himself! He is his own exclusive object,' he wrote. 'Supreme selfishness is inculcated upon him as his only duty . . . He has nothing to think of but how to get well.'*

---

* Charles Lamb's essay 'The Convalescent' appears in *Last Essays of Elia* (Edward Moxon, 1833).

January 2004

Now the GPs felt the time had come to refer me to a psychiatrist as I continued to feel worse. I was referred to a new psychiatrist who worked in a large London hospital who came highly recommended. We had an appointment to see her there, though it was obvious that I wasn't well enough to travel. I lay huddled in the back of the car as we crossed London through heavy traffic. I still associate the back of the car with extreme pain.

Sebastian helped me hobble to the doctor's room in a Portakabin adjacent to the main building. I was in such distress that I almost couldn't walk. An observer might have thought I had a broken leg, such was the extent of my moaning as we inched along the alleyway.

The new psychiatrist was young and glossy-haired, her mouth outlined by plum lipstick, but there was too much of it, and the colour seemed wrong. To me, she looked more like a film star than a doctor. She appeared to be too young. The authority she attempted to convey with a flourish of her glasses didn't work. It was as if she were trying out a gesture she had witnessed on stage, and was reading from a script. I didn't want an amateur actress. I wanted a doctor.

I asked her what might have come across as impertinent questions. Children? Thought not. Recently qualified? Thought so. Our exchanges were urgent: I had no time for small talk, formerly a speciality of mine.

She, meanwhile, had a long list of questions for me. I felt they were largely irrelevant but it was clearly the standard procedure for new patients. Did I take recreational drugs? ('You would be surprised how many people do,' she said, folding her arms tightly across her chest for emphasis.) Did I self-harm? she continued, jotting down notes. She seemed calm initially, despite the blackness of my responses. But I noticed a flicker of unease as I continued. Yes, of course I thought of suicide, and not just sometimes but all the time. Yes, of course it was because of the pain. No, no, no, she could relax. I wouldn't actually do anything, as I had the children. No, there was nothing that relieved the pain. Yes, I felt all of the symptoms she read out from a list: disturbed sleep; lack of energy; unexplained pain. In fact, there was no part of me that wasn't in agony. A tick against 'unexplained pain' didn't do justice to the full extent of it. 'I feel like a cake that has been smashed against the wall,' I ventured, hoping that might give a more accurate reflection of my physical suffering. 'It's as if I'm screaming inside,' I added.

At this point, Sebastian began to edge towards the door. He had seen what I was too ill to realise: the film star was worried, her translucent skin hiding nothing. Not just worried, but frightened. She was forgetting her lines. The longer we stayed and the more I revealed how sick I felt, the less chance we had of getting home and escaping her and her hospital's clutches. We both knew, from my highly traumatic night in hospital the first time I was ill, how bad that would be.

Sebastian was proved right. I should be admitted right there and then, she said. She couldn't take responsibility for my case if not. If need be, she said, getting up, her pointy high heels clicking too loudly on the floor, she could section me under the Mental Health Act. Sebastian looked momentarily taken aback at this. She was worried I was a danger to myself. I might accidentally take an overdose if a nurse wasn't there to care for me. There was talk of health and safety, public liability, insurance, her qualifications.

No, Sebastian argued, as he regained his composure and manoeuvred me to the door, squeezing my hand in silent communication that he would help me make the next few steps to freedom. He would care for me at home. He had done it before. He was confident I would get better. I wasn't going to hospital. He would take full responsibility for our decision to leave.

Something in his tone stilled her panic. He seemed to know what he was about. Months later, we discussed his preternatural calm and certainty. The young psychiatrist hadn't bothered him: she was just doing her job as best she could. I had imagined her as this terrifying monster, but the reality was much more prosaic. Sebastian just knew that I should be looked after within our own four walls. Our home would be not just our castle but my hospital, too.

Faced with such assurance, the consultant reluctantly agreed to let us go, but only if she could see me the next day. Somehow we managed to get back to the car.

The following day she came to visit me at home. 'It might be helpful if you listed your worries and we put them in some sort of order,' she coaxed, her suggestion echoing Sebastian's habit of asking me to list my fears, even the most trivial, so that he could dismiss them in turn.

Mid-January 2004

She would come every few days, and repeated to my mother or Sebastian at the end of the session that it would be far better for me to be in hospital where I would be under constant supervision. As it was, she had to make do with intermittent visits and updates from my mother.

My worries were so numerous it would be impossible to list them, I explained that bleak February morning. Name any aspect of my life, whether in my role as mother, wife or home-maker, and it was shot through with worry. The list would go on forever, writing it would take weeks. Anyway, I was so tired, so tired of my brain going round and round and round, fixating on nothing but worry and fear, a loop of woe. I hadn't the energy to tell her about it all.

She persisted. She needed to have a sense of my concerns.

I almost spat back at her: I worry the children will die. I worry Sebastian will die. I worry I feel so ill. I worry my head hurts. I worry my stomach hurts. I worry that I want to die but I know I can't. I worry my parents will die. I worry I will never get better. I worry I hurt so much. I worry Sebastian will be ill. I worry he will lose his job. I worry that I will never be able to work again. I worry I won't be able to look after the children. I worry that Sebastian won't be able to look after the children. I worry I have wasted my life. I worry that I am a hopeless wife. I worry that I am a bad mother. I worry I will never, ever get better.

As I paused for breath, she signalled that I had said enough.

Just as he had done before, Sebastian assured me he could work partly from home to look after me if need be. Once again his job meant that he quietly kept working both at home and in the office without burdening me with the details of his movements. I didn't resent the fact that he simply could not drop everything to care for me full time. I knew he alone had been keeping our family's ship afloat. I welcomed his stints at work: they helped keep him sane, as had the structure and sense of achievement that a job had provided when I returned to work after first being ill. The relentless sameness of life at home was enough to dissolve any feeling of progression.

Sebastian derived support and comfort from colleagues, too, some of whom had experienced depression themselves or seen others suffer. A sense of how commonplace the illness was provided some perspective. As he walked into our bedroom, he seemed to bring positive ions with him from the different air he had been breathing. He would draw the curtains even wider, throw open the window and dispense jokes till even his energy would be sapped by the vortex of gloom that greeted him. Later he told me what a strain it had been to keep life running not just at work but at home, too.

His working also helped me feel less guilty that my illness had comprehensively blown apart all semblance of normal life. At least I was at home, albeit unwell, and he was at the office. Some familiarity was preserved for the children. If Sebastian had been constantly at home, the only explanation would have been that I was days from death.

Sometimes I stayed at my parents' house, where it was easier for my mother to watch over me during the day when Sebastian was at work. By now Sebastian had employed a full-time nanny called Lucy to help look after the children, though at this point I was only dimly aware of her arrival. Somehow between Lucy, my mother, and Sebastian life continued as normal for the five. They went to school, ate their meals, wore cleanish clothes and were read to at night. Meanwhile I was back in my childhood room and hating it. I didn't want, in my late thirties, to be lying in my old bed with its iron bedposts, having surrendered any adult independence. But it was better than being in hospital.

Instinctively I had doubted the new psychiatrist from the start. But my husband reminded me that I had doubted Dr Fischer, too. We should give her a chance.

Six years after my first depressive episode in 1997, there seemed to have been little advance in terms of treatment. Drugs remained the only obvious remedy, though a doctor friend confided in Sebastian that some psychiatrists were no longer quite as enthusiastic about prescribing medication. Once it had seemed as if finally there was a spanner that fitted the nut of the problem. Now there were questions about the efficacy of antidepressants in the light of research that suggested that for some patients they were no more effective than placebos. No outstanding new drug had been developed since I was first ill, and the side effects of the old ones were just as bad. Sebastian wisely didn't share such views with me at the time; I needed to believe the medication would work.

If anything, this time my experience was worse. Once again the side effects of the antidepressants were debilitating. More drugs seemed to be the psychiatrist's only suggestion to relieve some of the physical symptoms. This is what doctors call the 'domino' effect, whereby the amount of medication a patient is taking multiplies in an attempt to control the side effects of other drugs. So on top of my antidepressants she gave me beta-blockers, which would reduce my racing heartbeat. I had other drugs to help the stomach cramps, which were a side effect of the antidepressants. Then I took a different tablet to manage the anxiety: this one was less addictive than tranquillisers. Some of the pills had to be taken three times a day. Every night I needed to take a sleeping pill. Some patients found that the antidepressant I was taking reduced their anxiety to the extent that they were able to sleep at night, but it didn't work for me.

Taking the pills was a full-time job. Even as I felt ever more ghastly, at least it was something to do. Sebastian set up a whiteboard in my room where he wrote down the timings and quantities of the various drugs in different-coloured marker pens. It was an attempt to make light of the whole thing. Naturally, the more pills I popped, the more anxious I felt, marker pens or not.

By March, I could think of only one person who might be able to rescue me.

March 2004

An inexorable march of other experts had taken over my care and I hadn't been well enough to protest. It was impossible to know if I would have responded any differently if I had been treated by a different psychiatrist.

Now I felt wistful for Dr Fischer. He, after all, had got me well once before. I liked him. I wanted to hear his voice and see him flourish his fountain pen. Awash with hopelessness, I needed a full-bore infusion of his confidence that I would get better again.

By now I was being seen by one particular GP from the practice, a different one to the doctor who had first visited me and written out a prescription for antidepressants. Dr Smith was a highly experienced man of deep compassion who had a long-standing interest in depressive illnesses. He would pop in regularly, bringing an extraordinary combination of fresh vitality and deep calm with him. Our conversations ranged from the local fruit and vegetable market – he confided he liked to wander around during his lunch break for an infusion of *joie de vivre* – to the photographs of the children that lined every wall of our house, testament to Sebastian's love of photography married to his devotion to our offspring. Just as Dr Fischer had judged my mood by how I responded to him, so did Dr Smith.

We talked about me returning to Dr Fischer. Dr Smith was entirely supportive, recognising the need for a connection between psychiatrist and patient. He kindly rang Dr Fischer on my behalf.

Impatient as ever, I thought changing psychiatrists would have instant results. I imagined Dr Fischer would automatically switch my medication and put me on dosulepin, which had helped me to recover before.

Mid-March 2004

Seven years seemed to vanish when Dr Fischer reappeared in our lives one spring morning. It was as if there were seamless continuity between the last episode and this one and nothing had happened in between, even though Katherine and the twins had been born since then.

But of course there were differences: the drugs I was taking, for a start. There were no social niceties as we talked, only an urgent discussion of essentials. He told me I couldn't just suddenly swap drugs. Antidepressants always take time to work. It would waste precious weeks to start again. So we would stick with citalopram and the sleeping pills but I would give up all the other drugs.

He told me that I, like around a third of his patients, didn't respond immediately to the drugs. For another lucky third of patients, antidepressants can start to work within ten days.

Dr Fischer was tweaking the doses, just as he had during the first episode, until I was more stable. I simply had to wait.

Late March 2004

My inertia continued as the spring ground on. Nothing could penetrate the thick layer of my misery: not prayer, not breathing techniques, not poetry. Once again, 'God had gone out of me as if the sea had dried up like sandpaper'. Nothing helped. Nothing improved. Nor did my conversation. It was all very well saying I was going to get better but the ongoing agony was no less painful just because one day, theoretically, it would end. Perhaps it wouldn't. If I bored everyone else, I certainly bored myself.

'So will I be better by George's birthday?' I would ask.

'Yes, by George's birthday,' Sebastian would reply. But I wasn't.

'So will I be better by Easter?'

'Yes, by Easter.' But I wasn't.

I felt bitter at the unfairness of it all. All other people in the entire world were allowed to sip their tea or stroll through the park, to meet a friend or amble to a movie, or even just to walk around the block. Not me. It was the ordinary I longed for, not some divine revelation, just to be handed back my normal clothes, to refasten my wristwatch and reinhabit the world outside this prison. I wished desperately to achieve the simplest task, to hold one of the children in my arms, to engage with any of the people in my life. I wanted my life back.

The weeks rolled on and I felt just as sick, my being shrunk to fit the prison. I had been bludgeoned into submission and was stuck in this unbearable present. It was always the same. The room the same, the duvet the same, the view from the window the same, and always the same grinding pain. I abhorred the sameness. I would never step back into the wider world.

Whether it was night or day, hot or cold, wherever I went, the pain always came with me. That was what I had been left with; that was the deal. It could butcher any defence, distort any thought. It would always win, even if for a second I managed to edge back to normality and enjoy that first sip of tea, or the glimpse of a flower in bud; minutes later the pain would be back, triumphant, a mocking beast that laughed at the idea I could even imagine life without it.

I no longer believed I would ever recover. Depression had won, Dr Fischer or no Dr Fischer. I didn't know if it was worth going on living.

Sebastian and my mother kept their faith. I had lost mine, it seemed. The power of prayer, which had been so magical on occasion before, no longer reached me. People kept saying there must be good things about being ill, a new perspective. No, there wasn't one good thing, not one, and certainly not my sense of faith. I hadn't the energy even to be angry with God. But my family kept praying. They were confident I would improve, given that I had recovered before.

End of March 2004

I tried to soothe the beast within me. Most frightening for my mother was my habit, acquired during my first breakdown, of trying to relieve the pain with burning-hot baths. Locked in the bathroom in an effort to preserve some adult dignity, I would once again slip beneath the water, seeking to unclench my tensed muscles.

One March day, I was locked in the bathroom. Unbeknown to me, my mother was outside. I finally heard her cries as I came up for air, gagging as the water flooded my nose. 'Unlock the door!' she yelled. For all she knew, I might have accidentally drowned, or even done so intentionally. I hobbled to the door and let her in before shrinking back into the heat of the bath water, my arm crooked over my head and my back curved to her frightened gaze.

Eventually I allowed her to offer me a towel and help me out of the bath. Henceforth, there were no locked doors. I had to accept being dependent.

This time there were five children to care for, not two. Someone had to be in charge, and I had handed over that role long ago. I might loathe having to rely on Sebastian and my mother to make decisions, to get me out of the bath, but there were mouths to feed, children who needed to go to school, washing machines to load, dishwashers to empty. Someone had to decide what we were all going to have for lunch.

At first, this dependence seemed a horrid, passive thing. I was beholden to others, relying on their charity, burdening them. The whole point of my life had hitherto been to become independent. It was the mantra of my generation: women could and did multitask, both at home and at work.

I had to set aside such notions. I had no choice. I was being forced to learn new lessons: that dependence could mean a closeness, a new way of receiving love. It meant tearing up old timetables and assumptions. I might be in my thirties but the lessons that were being forced on me were lifelong.

Slowly I came to understand that this was a new way to look at the illness: somehow it was teaching me what I needed to learn and presenting new truths to which I had to adjust. For the first time in months, I found comfort in God once again. He was demanding of me. As I surrendered to Him, it felt as though I had been struggling to open the lid of a jar, only to hand it over to someone else who managed it at the first twist. My mother helped this nascent recovery by trying to coax me to do something, anything, just as my family had done the previous time I was unwell.

Looking after someone with depression is bleak for the carers. It was not just the mind-numbing boredom but also the constant feeling my mother and Sebastian both experienced that somehow they were to blame. But though their spirits occasionally, inevitably dipped, mine were beginning to rise. I now knew that I would be better when my existence wasn't dominated by what seemed like self-obsession and the absence of any desire.

Chapter Twelve

Cure Me with Quietness

APRIL TO AUGUST 2004

Mid-April 2004

The annual miracle of spring largely passed me by but it was accompanied by the first snatches of calm, when the pain eased in my over-wound body, just as it had done after my first breakdown, and hope moved in. Some of the skills I had learned first time round again proved helpful. This time I clung especially to a poem by Ruth Pitter, with its wonderful title 'Cure Me with Quietness', which I slowly learnt by heart. At first I could only remember a couplet, then three lines, then four. But after a week or so I had mastered the whole poem, infusing me with a sense of achievement as well as a sort of warm feeling that I now knew the words by heart and they were literally inside me, never to be lost and to be drawn on at will.

> Cure me with quietness,
> Bless me with peace;
> Comfort my heaviness,
> Stay me with ease.
> Stillness in solitude
> Send down like dew;

Mine armour of fortitude
Piece and make new:
That when I rise again
I may shine bright
As the sky after rain,
Day after night.

I would rise again, I promised myself and, very slowly, I did. The prayers now came like friends, then the poetry, then the deep breathing and the relaxation exercises. Once more, for a few moments each day, I was able to smell the dew and the rain, once more I could turn to nature as the greatest consolation. As Matthew Arnold writes:*

Soon will the high Midsummer pomps come on,
Soon will the musk carnations break and swell,
Soon shall we have gold-dusted snapdragon,
Sweet-William with his homely cottage-smell,
And stocks in fragrant blow;
Roses that down the alleys shine afar,
And open, jasmine-muffled lattices,
And groups under the dreaming garden-trees,
And the full moon, and the white evening-star.

Late April 2004

Most days it was a case of plodding rather than pressing on. In the mornings I was shy of coming downstairs. I felt

* In 'Thyris', written in commemoration of Arnold's close friend Arthur Hugh Clough.

intimidated by anyone outside my immediate circle and a pressure to appear better than I felt. The only people I didn't feel embarrassed to be with were my doctor, mother and husband.

Sebastian's skill was to lead me gently back to normal life by way of the nursery. He realised I needed some kind of structure and a reason to get out of bed. Otherwise it would be impossible to find the courage that getting up still entailed. Yes, I felt better, but either side of my bed still felt like a cliff-face and it was terrifying to leave the warmth of my duvet. Moreover, I often threw up when I first got up, usually at about eleven. It was a daunting way to begin the day.

End of April 2004

I had been leaning on two constructs, like handrails on either side of me. The first was that the children needed me to get up. They hated what they called my 'lions' (lie-ins). This had to be delicately managed, though. If Sebastian overemphasised that I was in demand it might defeat me. But equally he needed to galvanise me.

The second helpful idea was that if I did manage to get up, thereafter I wouldn't have to worry about what to do next. There was an obvious timetable in the house to which I could hold fast: the children's routine.

That their lives were continuing more or less as normal was largely thanks to Lucy, the new nanny who had arrived in January to help during the crisis. A blue-eyed blonde from Perth in Western Australia, she held the fort with a confidence that belied the fact that she was just eighteen. Lucy was to stay with us for a year before going to university. My mother was still enormously involved as well, but she was older now and also needed to look after my father.

In the end it was George who managed to help me come downstairs for the first time. One morning, shortly before his school was breaking up for the holidays, he crumpled into my arms, a universe of fear in his eyes. He confided that he had been scared of getting up. He didn't want to go on a play date after school at his friend's house. He didn't like the food there, and the other mummy made him eat it.

We snuggled into each other in my bed, him scrubbed in his uniform, hair combed and parted ready for the day, me still thick with the smell of sleep and in my nightclothes. I found myself reassuring him that it would be fine at his friend's house, and that I too found it hard to get up. Somehow, the two of us would manage together.

As I lay there, his beating warmth pressed against mine, I doubted my words. But I willed myself to gather him up and wheel my own body out of bed. Hand in hand, the two of us walked downstairs.

Early May 2004

For the next few months, on the ever-increasing number of days when I felt better, my life was no different from that of the children. When they had their mid-morning milk and snack, so did I. When they went to the park to feed the ducks, so did I. When they had their tea and bath, so did I.

They were old enough now to have a clearer sense of what was happening. When I was ill before, Edward was just a toddler and George a babe in arms. If they were affected by my illness, they couldn't express it. There was no buffer protecting me this time from their concerns, even if my mother and Sebastian tried to shield me from any conversation that would worry me, chiefly by never leaving me alone with the children. In turn, I wasn't well enough to hide my own fears, much as I wished for the energy to disguise them. It is one of the regrets that gnaws at me the most, that I couldn't shield them from the reality.

One evening Edward sneaked into my bed, his eyes shiny with tears. Why was he suddenly no longer allowed in my room, he demanded? 'Mummy,' he went on, his head pillowed on my chest. 'You always make it nice and now it's not. Secondly, no one knows the things I like. Secondly, it's always annoying. And secondly, I don't like school.'

I managed to hug him, suggesting we sing some of our favourite songs from *The Wizard of Oz*. At the end of 'Over the Rainbow', I turned to him and began to try to explain that the last few months had been a bit like a rainbow, but one that had been hidden behind black clouds.

'But rainbows are always colourful,' he replied. 'They never have black in them.'

Our rainbow would be colourful very soon, I reassured him.

Meanwhile, somehow we had to make the best of things. I could not improve on Charles Mackay's poem.

Oh, you tears,
I'm thankful that you run.
Though you trickle in the darkness,
You shall glitter in the sun.
The rainbow could not shine if the rain refused to fall;

And the eyes that cannot weep are the saddest eyes of all.

Each child responded differently. Edward generally focused on the consequences of me being unwell, noting that he was no longer allowed in our room, or I wasn't available for the school run. At other times he tried to provide solutions, chiefly through comforting words and actions. 'You're being very brave,' he would tell me. 'It won't go on much longer. Shall I kiss it better?' Once he confided in me his own theory of why I need not worry about the children. I was like a star, he explained, or rather, one big star that had turned into five smaller ones. Each of the children had already swallowed their own star and had me inside them. I was part of them, even if I wasn't well enough to get up and play with them. I need not worry.

More often than not I wasn't even well enough to talk, so I just listened. He understood when I was not up to conversation and would give me a foot rub instead. Sometimes he would produce his favourite giraffe and tuck it under my arm. One day he gave me a picture of stick figures with a large heart and the text 'Dair mummy I hope you Get well I'am sad you air sick love Edward'. Another note read 'Dear Mumy, the oul family love's you. I am also a bit worid. Love Edward.'

At other times he would arrive upstairs with a hot lemon and honey, which was offered as the answer to most ailments he had hitherto suffered himself. When I hugged him to say thank you, it felt as if the two of us had completed an electric circuit that had been waiting to be connected. I was so grateful that I found I could say nothing at all.

I worried that the children were counting the weeks I spent

in bed but their perception of time was more accepting. 'What's happening?' George asked one morning when Dr Fischer came to visit after a bad patch. 'Mummy's not well,' said Sebastian. 'You know you can break your arm? Well, Mummy's head is a bit broken, but it's getting better. So the doctor's coming,' Sebastian explained. 'Again?' was all that George replied.

I had much to learn from their patient acceptance and forbearance. One afternoon I found George at the kitchen table weeping over his spelling list of words containing the letters 'ai'. He had copied out 'rain', 'gain' and 'obtain' but had abandoned his efforts at 'snail'. His red face was squashed flat on the table, his hair flopping over eyes pooling with tears.

I scooped him up into a hug and chatted about the horrors of spelling. All he would say between the sobs he was trying to silence was, 'Doesn't matter.' Ten minutes later he had found both his courage and his pencil. I watched his unveined hand, a miniature arc of dirt underneath each nail, as he slowly filled the page.

While I learnt from the children's perseverance, there was one other person who taught me how to recover: Lucy, an exceptional young woman who did much to prise me from my shell.

Mid-May 2004

Though she had arrived in January, it was only now that I began to be well enough to engage with our new nanny. Lucy had a fresh, easy laugh and gave the room a charge as soon as she entered. All I could think when I first saw her was what a fabulous smile she had. Nothing seemed to dim her sunny ways and the almost celestial light that floated around her. Her manner was so inviting that within minutes of arrival the children were trying to sit on her lap and competing with each other to play with her. Edward's first words to her were, 'I say, would you like a game of Jenga? I'm rather in the mood.'

She had all the chutzpah of an eighteen-year-old who had just crossed the globe, a sort of toughness that suggested she would weather whatever might lie ahead and an ability to live in, and participate in, the richness of the moment.

Whereas Julie as a trained sole-charge nanny specialised in whisking the children away, Lucy's skill was to gently allow me to care for them once again as I recovered. She instinctively knew that the more the children needed me, the more it would shore me up. There was nothing overt about it. But she would give me one of the babies at the exact point when I was able to change their nappy and to feel triumphant having done so. She seemed to be able to judge my mood as expertly as a greengrocer could sense the ripeness of a melon or how easily a peach might bruise. Lucy thereby rescued me from being boxed into the role of 'Officially Ill Person'. It wasn't that anyone was forcing me to stay upstairs, or wished me to stay unwell. The danger was that I would banish myself thanks to a mix of shame and fear, which meant that before long it was simply easier for me not to emerge from my den.

The feelings of shame arose because, in spite of undeniably being unwell, there was still a part of me that was embarrassed to be so – in a strange way, I felt this all the more now that I was getting better. If I was able to get better, then I should have been able to stop myself getting ill. And I felt fear because it takes courage to change. I had got used to my role, and familiarity was soothing.

Lucy knew how difficult I found it to re-engage with life. She knew that technically there wasn't actually anything for me to do, as the household had been reconfigured to manage without me. Her skill was to make me believe that even if everyone *could* manage without me, they would much rather manage *with* me. She let me gather myself together.

For the next six months I spent more time with Lucy than anyone else outside our family. She became as much my nurse and friend as the children's nanny. Her nature was so engaging that I fell in love with her. Our whole family did. She was also comfortably in charge of decision-making, which was still beyond me. Lucy decided when we were going out and coming in, when it was time to have a bath or to get ready for bed. I followed her lead.

'It was this extraordinary piece of luck that she came into your life,' my mother later said. 'She gave herself utterly to the family.'

During the day we often teamed up with my younger cousin Mary. In her twenties, she was all poised elegance, with a career as an osteopath under her stylish belt. But for all her success, she too had been felled by ill-health; she walked with the bent gait of someone much older, having undergone a back operation. She was off work, needed to exercise to recover, and she lived nearby.

Mary's presence gave added and necessary purpose to our trips outside. She became fast friends with Lucy, later making her godmother to her first child. Meanwhile, we provided Mary with company: most of her friends were unavailable for daytime strolls.

One May afternoon our trio was walking slowly up the hill near our house, Lucy pushing the twins in their double buggy. A young cyclist was straining every sinew as he edged up the hill, his face tense with the effort and concentration involved. 'Keep going,' I shouted, as much to myself as to him. The smile he flashed back illumined the rest of the day. There was truth to be found outside our front door and all it took was one small step onto the pavement.

I never talked about my depression with Lucy, though Sebastian had briefed her about the nature of the illness. She didn't question that I was unwell. I didn't feel I needed to be better on her behalf. We just accepted each other and the oddness of our joined lives.

In a way, she met the need that had been fulfilled by Felicity during my first breakdown. Felicity had since become ill herself. I had stayed in touch and visited her, though not as much as I would have liked once we no longer lived in the same street. I was aware that I failed to match her own exceptional gifts of looking after others in need.

While I did see others briefly, the ever-changing nature of my moods meant that, really, only one friend could truly keep abreast of my ups and downs, and this time round, for me at least, that friend was Lucy. Later I considered that she was experiencing life very differently. She may have liked me, but she was primarily working exceptionally hard, looking after our children and effectively also being a nurse. Quite rightly her real friends were her own contemporaries, but she was too kind and gentle to disillusion me at the time.

She patrolled anything that might throw me – gloomy music, for example, or the violent front-page story of a newspaper. 'We listened to an awful lot of Beatles and Dido, which

I introduced you to,' she recalls. 'Nothing downbeat. All your interactions were very heightened. Things could set you off – a sharp word, for example. You were most settled when you were planting bulbs.'

She remembers the peculiarity of the situation. 'It was very hard. I remember lying down with the babies on top of me one afternoon and thinking, "What the hell is going on?" It was bearable because of the kids. But I absorbed your anxiety. I would have to go and have very long decompression baths at the end of a day's work, with all the lights off and candles. You didn't recognise other people's needs. It was a bit like living with a drug addict, not least because you were obsessed by the medication. I thought, "Oh my God, can't you stop talking about the drugs, be a bit interested in people's lives, in my life?" I couldn't talk to you about the drugs as I didn't believe in them.'

It was still the case that at times I would be ill upstairs for days. Then Lucy would be left in charge of the household. Life would continue as before; I just wasn't there. Dr Fischer would visit regularly. He always came in the evenings, after his rounds elsewhere, and would see me upstairs in our bedroom. 'Through the day the house was full of women and children,' Lucy says. 'Then at night the men in suits would return, Sebastian from work and Dr Fischer to see you. The energy completely changed.'

Dr Fischer's visits sometimes disturbed the children. Katherine in particular would ask in a matter-of-fact manner if I were going to die. Lucy would put the kettle on as she reassured Katherine that this wasn't going to happen.

June 2004

I timed the illness by the number of weeks that passed during which I remained unable to drop the children at school: the older two to their prep school, Katherine to her nursery school. To be able to manage the school run again became something of an obsession. It would mark the return of purpose to my life. I might be better in the afternoons, but if I could return to my usual start to the day, I would be better full stop.

I needed to force myself out of bed, I would tell myself from the moment I woke up. I must get up, otherwise the children wouldn't get to school. It was a hard target to set myself, as I was at my worst in the mornings. All I wanted to do was to gather my entire family under the duvet, engage in a mass hug and stay there all day.

The easiest prospect was to manage to drop Katherine at her nursery school which was immediately next door to our house so the logistics were not complicated, but the fact was that even when well, I had found dropping her off challenging because of the multiple social interactions involved.

On the surface, it was all about the lightness and sweetness of parents engaging with little children; yet often it was crushingly unpleasant. Mothers excluded other mothers with a flick of their long, highlighted hair and a swivel of tiny waists that bore no trace of having given birth. In contrast I sometimes felt as fat as a Christmas pudding. Parents would come deliberately early to take advantage of the networking possibilities offered by the queue. They would time their exit from their cars to accidentally-on-purpose bump into other Queen Bee mothers emerging from their hives, all wearing uniforms of skinny jeans and slouchy handbags. Woe betide anyone who needed to wear a suit to work, betraying their humdrum existence. This was a neighbourhood where people were hard-working, competitive and insecure, and you should be trying to get your script made or complete your novel.

I felt that being a stay-at-home mother made me invisible. Most days it seemed that my waggy-dog smiles were met with looks that said, 'Who are you again?' This despite months of standing side by side in line waiting for the children to emerge. It was shaming how pleased I was when someone I thought was glamorous acknowledged my 'hello'. Over time I learnt to watch the carefully choreographed dance from our kitchen window and only arrive at the last minute, thereby avoiding this ritual humiliation.

Gradually, I found gentler souls and true friends among those who lived nearby. But in general, perhaps like a lot of London, our neighbourhood was not a place for the old or sick. Though there were honourable exceptions, many of its occupants were obsessed with their health and good looks; the plethora of Pilates studios and beauty salons was testament to that. London stood for competition, engagement in the world, go-getting husbands and their pretty wives attuned to success as finely as a mother to the sound of her child's cry. I once asked a successful local writer why she worked so hard. Otherwise nobody would like her, she replied. It could feel like an enormous trundling juggernaut, surging forward, with no time for those flung into the gutter. After I fell ill again, it got worse. People behaved as if depression might be catching.

Lucy says she was struck by how little compassion there seemed to be locally. 'Of course, you had friends who weren't like that. But generally there was no sense of community, not even a token one. The attitude seemed to be, "everyone is okay behind their front doors; there's no need to interfere; there must be enough resources to sort these things out." I thought that no one could really be crazy if they felt included and loved. But inclusion and love were not part of the story.'

I was not as negative as Lucy: the area offered proximity to my parents and I was attached to the place where Sebastian and I had both grown up and now enjoyed some devoted local friends, some of whom I had known since childhood. But there was no doubt I could find the wider dynamics of the neighbourhood challenging.

In the end I missed a year's worth of school runs. Every day started with failure, as someone else would drop the children off.

After my first breakdown, going back to work had been a clear declaration that I was well, a sharp therapeutic shock. After this second bout of illness, returning to looking after the children was a far more nebulous affair. In some ways the vagueness suited me better. It meant that I could pick up the reins of life more slowly, gradually upping the challenges in the comfort of my own home. I could control who came and went and what I did.

But equally, there was no binary moment when I could say that yes, I was better, I was back to work. Doing the school run was my work now, the closest thing to returning to the office in terms of re-engaging with the adult world of parents and teachers, the sort of social experience that required a thicker hide than I had yet grown.

Mid-June 2004

One June morning I made it all the way to the school's front door. I was elated but also deeply anxious. Then I spotted some familiar parents with their charges as they queued in line to be welcomed by the teacher. The first parent I saw was someone I knew a little. She had once said hello.

'Oh,' I cried, tears suddenly leaking down. 'I can't believe I managed it; I've been so ill . . .'

I'm not sure what I wanted from her – a hug, or some super-human understanding that I wasn't leading the life she had imagined?

Her reaction was rather different. Worried by the effect I was having on her three-year-old, she instinctively shielded her child as if I might be violent or possibly contagious.

'You shouldn't be here. You're not well,' she said, loud enough, it seemed to me, for all the other mothers to hear. 'Go home.'

I shielded my own head as if she might be about to beat me, at once shamed, furious and frightened, and utterly surprised. She might as well have punched me, so violent did her verbal assault seem to me, though I later learnt that she hadn't shouted, only spoken normally. My own heightened sensitivity meant I retreated indoors for another two weeks, all confidence annihilated and joy dimmed. I was terrified of meeting her again.

Once again, a poem provided inspiration and gave me the words needed for the courage and perseverance to keep going. This time it was Arthur Hugh Clough's 'Say Not the Struggle Naught Availeth', which I added to my collection of favourites, stuck to my mirror.

While Clough addresses a soldier striving to keep battling on, his description seemed to fit my own struggle to take the children to school. Many was the morning when I mumbled his lines as I came downstairs, steadying myself on the banister. I would repeat to myself, 'Westward, look, the land is bright!' Despite occasional appearances to the contrary, I knew I was improving, gaining 'painful inches'.

Say not the struggle naught availeth,
The labour and the wounds are vain,
The enemy faints not, nor faileth,
And as things have been, things remain.

If hopes were dupes, fears may be liars;
It may be, in yon smoke concealed,
Your comrades chase e'en now the fliers,
And, but for you, possess the field.

For while the tired waves, vainly breaking,
Seem here no painful inch to gain,
Far back through creeks and inlets making
Come, silent, flooding in, the main,

And not by eastern windows only,
When daylight comes, comes in the light;
In front the sun climbs slow, how slowly,
But westward, look, the land is bright.

Two weeks later, July 2004

The next time I attempted the school run, I went with Lucy and a copy of Clough's poem photocopied from my poetry book scrunched into a ball in my pocket. I found it best to hold one of the twins in my arms, trying to imagine their warmth and solidity as a shield against the outside world.

I still found the experience frightening, but the sheer number of children meant at least a bit of me had been liberated. I had less time to worry about the scary mothers, and I knew I didn't have the strength to take on too much. It was a relief to realise my limitations. My new challenge was to try to cope with the ongoing reality of being a mother of five children, and as someone who had a tendency to depression. Everything else, including my fellow parents and the social anxieties they induced in me, had to be relegated to a place where it would not distract me from that main goal.

Mid-July 2004

Up until now I had survived by putting myself firmly in the children's camp. I only felt safe around their spontaneity and openness, both in good moods and bad. Their love was unconditional and they didn't judge me. With almost anybody else my breathing would speed up and my chest tighten. Yet I knew that at some point I wanted to edge out from under the umbrella of the children's timetable and reconnect with adult social life. Frightening though it might be, it was also part of getting better. For me, achieving that meant continuing, for the time being, to be bound by my beloved rules.

Sebastian had always exhibited remarkable discipline and

organisation in his own life. A peripatetic childhood had instilled early habits of looking after himself. I remember him at Oxford breakfasting on poached eggs on brown toast before his final exams. His shirts were always clean and his room tidy, just as his handwriting was meticulously neat in his notebook.

Now, as then, his discipline was as much mental as practical. He had an ability to switch off and he had rules to help him do so. There were to be no difficult conversations after eight o'clock at night.

Lucy remembers how much I relied on him.

'He was very much in control. Your conversations were always along the same lines. He'd keep telling you that you would be fine, that people have had this illness before and they get better. He'd reassure you all the time, especially if he had to go out, when you would get panicky. If you were even slightly rattled by anything, you would immediately ring him for more reassurance and be absolutely panicked if you couldn't get through.'

Sebastian was in charge of dealing with visitors. Being ill for so long meant that a fresh crop of family and friends who hadn't seen me the first time I was depressed were shocked this time around. Sebastian allowed more people to come to the house than before, almost keen that others should see me unwell, and also in the certainty that I would get better.

'It was different the second time,' he says now. 'I wasn't frightened in the way I had been when you were first ill and none of us knew what was going on. That was what was so incredible, that none of us, not even your mother, had come across this kind of depression before. This time I knew you would get better and that's why I was okay with visitors.'

He kept the length of visits to a minimum, always setting an end time and limiting numbers to one or two. Any more was too much, especially as I had a tendency to try to offer visitors 'silver service', in Sebastian's phrase. I would try to get up and make them tea or enquire exactly how they were feeling – a reaching-out that I was not yet well enough to deliver.

For some of my friends, actually seeing me lying in bed was what it took to believe in the illness. I almost felt relieved by this. After the first recovery I had deliberately erased all memories of being unwell and had been left with the vaguest sense that I had made it all up. No one wants to think of themselves as being mentally ill. I had tried to pretend it hadn't happened, or if I did admit to depression, it was very much as a minor one-off thing.

The second time, I could not help but reflect on some unpalatable truths. I had been seriously ill, not once but twice, with terrible moments in between. That fact demanded more analysis. The overriding question was why.

There is still no simple, catch-all physical explanation for this complex illness. I have come to believe depression is partly biological, but only partly. In my opinion the tendency of many women to succumb to mental illness has been exacerbated by the demands that women put on themselves to fulfil so many different roles as carers, homemakers and breadwinners. In my case, my character didn't help: I had to accept that on some level my very being and identity, in particular my anxious, striving character and desire to achieve, whether at home or at work, had in part caused the illness.

I think that's why mental illness remains so challenging for sufferers and witnesses to accept: it's because we feel it's partly the fault of the individual. We can't simply say we are victims of depression, as we can say we are victims of cancer or diabetes, thereby relieving us of any responsibility. A victim must have an attacker, some angry rogue cells or dodgy insulin suppliers. Depression is different. It is our fault. We should be better able to control ourselves, and all those feelings that accompany searing anxiety and depression. But we can't. And we feel shame and a sense of failure because of it and because of the self-absorption that ensues.

Chapter Thirteen

Happiness – It Comes On Unexpectedly

JULY TO DECEMBER 2004

Mid-July 2004

Out of the blue, my friend Tony came to see me. He was look-ing for a job, any job, right now. I felt just as ill as before, but, miraculously, I was needed. This unexpected sensation pierced my gloom. I got up, got dressed and opened our frightening front door. I knew the shops in our neighbour-hood well, the result of my village-like existence. My friend wanted me to introduce him, as a help in his efforts to get work as a waiter or shop assistant. Of course the twins could come, too.

So our odd quartet set off, despite the light cold rain, in search of employment, me wearing a hat and holding onto the twins' buggy to steady me. With each shop and café we stopped at, I felt better. I relished the sense of competence that I was doing something helpful and even quite surprised myself at how fluent a saleswoman I could be on someone else's behalf. By the end of our rounds of the area we had secured him a job in a café. I felt well for the first time in months, once again familiar to myself, as he hugged me to say thank you.

As soon as I got home, though, I felt a rising pressure between my ears and a familiar jitteriness. I lost my nerve and returned to the safety of my bed. My symptoms returned. I learnt that such a pattern is common. I heard of another patient who, despite her illness, managed to keep working as a counsellor with her clients. She would freak out before and after, but during the sessions, the illness lifted. It was less one continuous break-down than a series of recoveries and collapses.

Late July 2004

Picking up our social life was carefully managed by Sebastian, as the days lengthened and grew warmer. I had always been sociable, especially since I had been based at home, but the danger was that I would take on too much.

One summer's day I felt well enough for all seven of us to set off to the local park for a picnic. A flawless sky seemed to bless the outing. The twins wore matching his and hers blue and pink sunhats, which I had miraculously found in time, and the three other children were standing in a circle throw-ing a ball to each other. To their delight, they had each managed to catch it consecutively for several rounds and were widening the circle each time.

Really, I was better, I thought. It was my turn to enjoy the fluttering of the wind in the trees and the smell of the sun-warmed grass. All the joys of every previous trip we had ever been on merged into one supreme expedition. We relaxed into happiness, great scoops of laughter rising from the rug.

Yet the idyll began to unravel seconds later. Tania, a neigh-bour, who unsurprisingly I hadn't seen for months, approached. My old social reflexes kicked in. I leapt up to say hello.

'Don't you all look like the perfect family,' she said.

As I caught up with Tania's news, I heard Sebastian tell the children, 'We'll start our picnic later,' which I took to mean: 'I'm not starting the picnic as Mummy's gone off with her friend.' The children's play turned to bickering, which I felt was my fault as I had stopped watching them. 'We're hungry,' I heard one of the boys moan as another child began to wail over their spilt juice. I felt the first prick of anxiety. It was a twitch but it was enough. The picnic was drained of all charm, the happiness curdled. I saw then that the strawberries were over-ripe.

'Oh no, please don't let me hold you up . . .' Tania said, our chat evaporating on the summer breeze as quickly as my sense of wellbeing. My heart began its familiar pounding as my face coloured with a rush of anxious blood. My body clenched up.

To anyone else, the sight of pools of spilt lemonade and Sebastian's face as he attempted to restrain a twin from falling head first into the strawberries might have been comic, a bit of a charming mess. For me, it was a trigger for desperation. In my perception, Sebastian disapproved of my stopping to chat, the children were running riot. The picnic had been so fresh, now the dew was off it; everything was ruined. And it was all my fault. If I had been the perfect mother and wife, I wouldn't have been distracted and all would have been well.

I wanted to be back in bed. To the surprise of the children, I retreated under the picnic rug as if it were my duvet. I felt as if I had been standing on the deck of a ship, enjoying the crispness of the spray, only to have been knocked over by a malevolent wave. Now I was clinging by my fingertips to the railings.

As I lay shrinking under the picnic rug, I felt Edward snuggling up beside me. 'I want to go and be sad with Mummy. What Mummy needs is a big hug.'

Later that day I talked to Sebastian as he smoothed my hair. I crumpled into his arms. The expedition had been freighted with impossible expectations, he said. I was still ill, even if I was recovering. As a practical, unemotional matter of fact, I was fragile. I needed to stop trying to be all things to all people. Either we engaged with a family picnic and properly looked after the children and each other, or we talked to friends. At that time, I, we, and us as a family couldn't manage both. When I looked up at him, I realised his own eyes were damp, for all the reasonableness of his voice.

End of July 2004

One of our first sorties as a couple after my second bout of depression was an attempt to combine not one but two evening functions. It seems unbelievable to me in retrospect, especially when I consider that merely chatting to Tania in the park a few days before had caused such panic, but I felt I needed to put my party hat back on. Being a party-goer was one of the roles I had adopted as a full-time mother: I still craved approval and acceptance from our high-achieving neighbours, for all my ambivalence about Queen Bee mothers at the school gates. Sometimes Sebastian would count how many people I greeted when we went out together locally. My record was eight.

The first event was the showing of a friend's film, the second a party. I still found it impossible to choose between things, and Sebastian had indulged my indecision and said we would manage both. At the time it seemed the simplest way to keep me calm.

My hands fumbled as I tried to do up the pearl buttons of

my shirt. My heart was knocking like a shoe trapped in a tumble-dryer. Nor could I put on my high heels: I tried to stab new holes into the leather straps with one of the children's compasses so I could tighten them around my ankles. My mind might be rattling loose but somehow my shoes and clothes could help contain me. My coat had never been so tightly wrapped around my body.

I tried to calm myself by chatting furiously to Sebastian as if engaging with him would siphon off the top layer of worry. It didn't work. As we clambered out of the car and arrived at the cinema, my stomach lurched in the same way that it had done when Edward had run into a road in pursuit of the yellow car. I clutched Sebastian's hand tighter, feeling utterly undefended despite the supposed armour of my clothes.

The sickness briefly eased as we sat entombed in the dark at the back of the cinema. At least now no one could see me or my outfit, which not only was failing to act as a shield, but was in addition positively wrong. The others were supremely casual and my dressy clothes seemed ridiculous.

Almost as quickly, the worry started up again: I worried that we were going to be late for the other party. As soon as the opening titles had finished, I crept along the row, bent double to avoid the disapproving glances of the other guests, and clunked open the security door at the back of the cinema to wait outside for a bemused Sebastian.

His bemusement turned to resentment as he realised that only minutes after arriving I now planned to drag us to the other party. We trudged along in the rain in silence, our hands now limp by our separate sides. The gloom of the weather seeped right through to my fingertips and mirrored my worsening mood.

We arrived dishevelled at the reception, my sticky hair clamped to my head and making me feel even more wrongly fitted-out than before. Guilt that I wasn't at the cinema mingled with the familiar nausea. Blood pounded in my ears. My heart quickened. With each step up to the front door I felt as if I were changing lanes on a motorway, the cars speeding around me, my judgement of distance less and less assured, the only possible ending a crash. At least then all would be still again. In the end, we turned around and retraced our steps without ever ringing the bell.

A fat slab of tension sat between us as we went home. There was a kind of tautness about Sebastian, a familiar response when he was stressed. We had both withdrawn into our private worlds, our joint endeavour over. We were no longer even walking in parallel.

There was nothing else to be done but to once again submerge myself in yet another hot bath. Defeated, my eyes puckering with tears and all my spirits sagging, I took a sleeping pill. I knew from bitter experience that I would need hours to fall asleep otherwise. I didn't want to be reminded of any of it, not the vain attempts to please, the utter dejection and sense of distance from Sebastian. I had no more resources left. I just wanted oblivion. The idea that tomorrow was another day was no comfort.

Early August 2004

There was no obvious reason why the second episode lasted so long. Perhaps it was being on a different drug. Perhaps we should have tried a different treatment: psychotherapy is far more commonly prescribed now than when I was first ill and arguably I should have turned to it sooner. Perhaps electro-convulsive therapy (ECT), which sends an electrical current through the brain to trigger a seizure similar to an epileptic fit, might have worked for me. Perhaps the second period of illness lasted longer precisely and simply because it was my second bout. Sometimes I wonder if the lack of any deadline to get back to work let it linger on: for all that I felt an urgency to look after my young children, the family was clearly coping without me, and there was no concrete imperative to be well. It proved harder to re-engage with domestic rather than professional life. But in the end, depression doesn't follow rules: it is a devil that comes in many guises.

One month rolled into another with little change. The illness was well settled in, a weighty presence inside me that had made itself comfortable and didn't shift. I read the papers differently now. It was not news of atrocities and the cruelty of the perpetrators that struck me. It was what the sufferers could endure: our capacity to live with ongoing, relentless pain that could strike anyone at any time and from which there was no hope of escape.

Even if I did get better, there was nothing to stop me becoming unwell again, even more unwell than this time, and for even longer. I feared that what I had thought of as a one-off episode had become a pattern – my pattern. I would just go on suffering. How ludicrous to imagine I was different from anyone else. This was the human lot. I sunk into a profound gloom separated from all hope.

And yet that August, for the first time in nearly a year, one day I got up and managed to stay up all day. Nothing about the recovery was straightforward, though. The next day I was back in bed. Matters were further confused by trying to please all the well-wishers and resume all my multiple roles. So many friends had so much well-meaning advice about what to do that the danger was trying to do it all to please them. Sometimes I even felt as if I had to be ill to satisfy friends, who actually enjoyed playing nurse.

Mid-August 2004

A friend visited one hot, peppery morning. The younger children were running around without any clothes on. Oddly, I felt cold despite the warmth. I was sitting with a rug wrapped around me. Perhaps it was just the extra layer of protection I sought.

We talked. I wasn't feeling well, I told her. But actually that wasn't quite true. I did feel better. Somehow it was easier to deliver a single, simple message. Perhaps it was because of the rug and my own self-image of a patient sitting wrapped up as if I were in a nursing home. Perhaps it was because I also believed, probably wrongly, that I was pleasing her by allowing her to reveal her true compassion. She had come all that way to see me. I would act my part, she hers. It was frightening to change states from ill to well, as all change was terrifying, even if it was an improvement. Anyway, even if I was feeling better it might not last, and it would be impossible to convey the start-stop process to an outsider. Better play safe and remain ill. So even though was I feeling better, sufficiently well to go shopping, I remained glued to my pillow and found my stutter returned with ease. By the end of her visit, I had almost convinced myself I was ill again, and had to examine myself in the mirror out of interest to try and work out if I was sickening or not. I did look a bit pale, I thought.

That afternoon I was up and about. I wanted to go to a disused theatre nearby that was now used by retailers selling off old stock at a discount. Ever the bargain hunter, I had a sudden urge to shop, partly because I hadn't done so for months and I knew that such a trip could be morale-boosting after months in shapeless dark clothes. I fancied something pink and cheery.

My hopes were dashed when I had to hide behind the changing-room curtain: I had spotted my friend inspecting the same rails. It would have been impossible to explain my miraculous transformation, or the extent of my exhausting mood swings. Annoyed that I had mucked up my own chance to go shopping, I slunk home. I began to realise there was a cost to not being honest about how I was feeling.

Late August 2004

Very gradually, the days I was bedridden became more unusual than the days I got up. It coincided with trying a new treatment: acupuncture. The sharp shocks of the needle seemed to help jolt me back into existence. Known as the white witch of the neighbourhood though she looked more like an angel, Maria was blonde, with a beatific smile. Radiance poured off her and her own glowing good health could not but inspire confidence. She combined using needles with wise counsel and a deep-seated curiosity and concern about every aspect of my life. I liked her very much. No one else had suggested such a comprehensive approach to getting better. She advised on nutrition, meditation and herbs. She recommended various vitamin supplements, Pilates to stretch tensed muscles and homeopathic remedies. She suggested ways of making the house cosier by closing up spaces and adding rugs and blankets in earthy colours: the space you live in cannot heal, but it can be more conducive to healing. Such was the volume of her various prescriptions that I couldn't help but believe she cared, and that mattered hugely.

For difficult situations, she set out a three-point mantra: don't react; find the strength within; and do whatever it takes to make life easier in the circumstances. I had broken down. She wanted to build me up again, like a mobile phone that needs to sit on a charger for a long time. Perhaps the most visible sign of her involvement was the quantity of bottles of drinking water around the house. She told me that our bodies are often so used to surviving on not enough water that we no longer even feel thirsty, in contrast to children who often are desperate for water, she told me. Dehydration means lethargy. Water restores energy levels, never more pressingly than in the morning when we first wake up and are naturally dehydrated after the night. Depressives, as I had come to understand only too well, need extra help in the morning.

Lucy and I printed a page of labels saying 'DRINK ME: YOU ARE DEHYDRATED' and stuck them on water bottles distributed round the house. The odd thing was the more I drank, the more thirsty I became – a common response, the acupuncturist said, because our bodies adapt to being allowed to be properly thirsty as water supplies return to normal levels. I am sure the water was a good idea but in retrospect, it was particularly about doing something positive and doing it for myself. I loved sticking on those labels.

It was hard to untangle the different approaches and decide what was helping. Perhaps the drugs were beginning to work at precisely the same moment as the acupuncture. I do believe it was, in part, the special blend of love and expertise dispensed by the white witch. In her room I could be fully myself, safe in the knowledge that she accepted completely all my worst and best elements. It seemed as if we were on a journey together, not as if I were draining her of her healing wisdom. Some of her philosophy became mine: the idea that although I wouldn't find a quick fix for the depression and it would be a lifelong journey, she would be at my side. In my case, she believed the illness was partly a result of my doing too much. Other women expressed their stress in other ways and through other illnesses: mine had come out as depression.

'You're typical of a whole generation of women,' she said. 'Women who are at the mercy of their "to-do" lists, and they never get to the end of them. It is the curse of your generation, who for the first time have had so many choices – they can work, they can have children, they can work and have children, they can control when they have children. With all these choices comes anxiety, as there's no obvious road map. Many women just don't have the necessary bandwidth for all these worries and responsibilities. And women in general have a sense that they're not good enough. Ask a woman why something has gone right and she will attribute praise to outside circumstances. Ask a man and he will credit himself.'

One way of looking at the depression was that it was partly an expression of regret about choices I made in the past and fear of what roles I might or might not be able to manage in the future. The acupuncturist would help me to try to live more in the present.

Sceptics attribute acupuncture's apparent efficacy to the placebo effect: patients benefit from the idea of receiving the therapy, rather than the needles themselves. One expects to get healed, therefore certain symptoms disappear. In addition, the extra time taken to listen to the client enhances this placebo effect, in the same way that the time a psychiatrist spends with their patient may enhance the effect of antidepressants.

I didn't really care about the scientific proof of whether or not acupuncture worked, or that others thought it was all nonsense. It helped me. It might have been due to the placebo effect, but it seemed to me to be very powerful.

September 2004

By the onset of winter 2004, almost a year after the second serious depressive episode began, most of the physical symptoms had lifted. In the words of the Leonard Cohen song, cheerfulness kept breaking through. The better I got, the better I got and the more my heart laughed.

There were days when the sheer pleasure of being alive was breathtaking. I felt an elation in every encountered detail, the more pedestrian and otherwise inconsequential the better, be it the diamond brightness of an illuminated raindrop or the waxy creaminess of a new magnolia petal so delicious-looking you wanted to eat it. There seemed to be no past or future, just a powerful and vivid present: the most delectable waking dream of everyday sublimity. Flushed with this newfound joy, my palate was sharper and the children's smiles were more delicious. Every sense was heightened, not in a frightening way as before but in a way that was normal and true. Raymond Carver captures such a feeling in his poem 'Happiness': the way it creeps up, without any need for over-examination and is about a kind of simplicity.

So early it's still almost dark out.
I'm near the window with coffee,
and the usual early morning stuff
that passes for thought.
When I see the boy and his friend
walking up the road
to deliver the newspaper.
They wear caps and sweaters,
and one boy has a bag over his shoulder.
They are so happy
they aren't saying anything, these boys.
I think if they could, they would take
each other's arm.
It's early in the morning,
and they are doing this thing together.
They come on, slowly.
The sky is taking on light,
though the moon still hangs pale over the water.
Such beauty that for a minute
death and ambition, even love,
doesn't enter into this.
Happiness. It comes on
unexpectedly. And goes beyond, really,
any early morning talk about it.

The only time to which I could liken this period was the miracle second directly after giving birth, when the world seemed profoundly new and touched with the divine.

This positive experience of heightened senses proved to be a fleeting blessing of the illness. For so long, the world had been monochrome. It was as if my senses of sight, taste, touch, smell and sound had all been cloaked in a sickly grey and bitter dust, blurring vision, destroying taste buds, obliterating all sensuality. No wonder being able to feel sharp sensations again was more pleasurable than it had ever been before, having been denied to me for so long.

It was not just my senses that I had missed. This fresh awareness reflected a change of pace in how I experienced the everyday. I had learnt the cost of constant busyness. A friend reminded me that one definition of 'busyness' is being 'cluttered with detail to the point of being distancing.' My new awareness was about closing that distance.

Mid-November 2004

I still had one concrete reminder of the illness: my pack of antidepressants. Just as before, I didn't want to be stuck on the drugs for ever. But this time I was less confident that I could stop taking the drugs, or even that it was the right thing to aim for.

I knew that having a history of depression made you more likely to have another bout. The pattern is that the subsequent depressive episodes tend to be worse, not better, and harder to recover from, like the layers of paint on a watercolour that darken slightly with each successive wash.

It was time to talk to Dr Fischer about such matters. For several months now I had been going to his Harley Street room for my weekly appointment. Every time I saw him, the previous week seemed to evaporate as we picked up where we had left off in what felt like one continuous conversation.

We discussed my physical state, sleeping patterns, eating, how things were going with Sebastian, my mother and the children. Sometimes we even ventured into a wider chat about something in the news. There was nothing in our exchanges that would have embarrassed either of us had it been broadcast. What was striking was Dr Fischer's focus while I was with him. I once popped back after our appointment was over and he was already busy with another patient. When we spoke, very briefly, it was almost as if he didn't know who I was, so involved was he with another case. While he loomed exceptionally large in my life, I was only one of his many patients.

At my next visit Dr Fischer told me he couldn't promise I wouldn't be unwell again. As we had already discussed, the reasons for depression are complex and another major upset could once again tip me into the illness. I was inevitably more vulnerable and fragile, having been so ill for so long. My case wasn't simple: I had become sick when working, and sick when not working. The common thread was that I drove myself very hard. Whatever choice I made, I worried about it and always had a sense of the other decisions I might have made. I needed to be careful not to take on too much, to be aware this was my particular pattern. I still had our children to bring up, with all the sapping anxiety that could bring, as well as the many joys.

The Royal College of Psychiatrists lists seven factors that may predispose someone to depression: things that happen in our lives; our current circumstances; physical illness; personality; alcohol; gender (women are more likely to have depression); and genes.* There is a constant supply of research

---

* Despite the work of the human genome project, research has yet to identify a genetic cause for depression.

adding to our understanding of the multiple causes of this complex illness.

Some doctors describe depression as a slot-machine disease. Getting one strawberry, or even two in a row, is uneventful. But with three strawberries, you have enough factors to hit the jackpot. As with cancer, depression happens when several risk factors line up at once.

The stress of giving birth to the twins may have triggered several factors. I hadn't suffered a physical illness, but the strain on my small frame of carrying two seven-pound babies had been huge. I had spent the last three months of my pregnancy in a wheelchair as I couldn't walk: the weight of two babies pressing down on the joint at the front of my pelvis made it agony to move. Perhaps more relevant was that I ticked other boxes, too: I was an anxious striver and perfectionist attempting to combine multiple roles. A member of my family had also suffered from depression. I hadn't thought about this before, partly because only now did I spot that her symptoms were those of a depressive illness. My relative had never been diagnosed, being from an earlier generation. Her insomnia, anxiety and mood swings all now made sense.

Once several factors line up, one particular episode may trigger the illness. Someone with a predisposition to depression is like a pile of twigs. Any one of a number of things might cause the wood to go up in flames, or there may even be no obvious spark at all: the onset of depression can be spontaneous.

Sometimes depression felt like being back on the crashing plane. Sometimes it felt as if all colour had drained from my existence – the rainbow turned black. Sometimes it felt like being at the mercy of a river that has burst its banks, a torrent of water sweeping right through me.

There seems to be a switch in the brain when the banks of the river collapse. For all the recent advances in MRI scans and neuroscience, doctors are still uncertain how this switch operates, or which (if any) environmental factor or combination of factors turn it on. Of all the organs, we know the least about the largest and most complex one, the brain.

Even the precise links between mind and body are unclear. It is true that strong emotional states have an effect on our body. It is harder to establish whether a distressed emotional state produces a faulty brain, or whether a faulty brain produces a distressed emotional state. Such a dilemma is falsely simple: the reality is likely to be a messy and ill-understood dance between the two.

I was a case in point. I had been ill a while after giving birth the second time and again after the fourth pregnancy, but not the first and third. The next breakdown could coincide with something completely different: possibly something overwhelming like losing a parent; perhaps something that superficially might seem unimportant. The true causes of depression remain complicated and there is a danger of oversimplification. Even knowing exactly what caused a particular case doesn't stop the illness being extraordinarily painful.

Setting aside my quest to evaluate the risk of another major depressive episode, there were certainly ways my everyday life might be improved. Had I thought of therapy? Dr Fischer asked. It might not elucidate why the breakdowns had happened, but it could perhaps help me manage myself better to avoid another recurrence, especially my tendency to do too much and pile pressure on myself. Now was the moment to embrace therapy, as I was well enough to do so.

The second breakdown could be seen as a positive opportunity to change. This was about creating better mental health, rather than simply focusing on the problem when things had already gone wrong.* There is evidence that Cognitive Behavioural Therapy (CBT), in particular, can help those with depression, Dr Fischer told me.

Two episodes of depression had left their mark on me, and I found Dr Fischer's message of self-empowerment chimed with the predominant cultural message of my generation: that with willing, know-how and effort, we could solve problems. In confident moments, I believed I could rid myself of my anxieties and therapy would be the first step. At other less robust times, I wondered if I would ever recover from depression's deep wounds. It was as if my nerve endings were now on the outside rather than the inside, as though I were dancing in bare feet when most of the world wore shoes.

---

* Martin Seligman, a professor at the University of Pennsylvania, talks of 'learned optimism' rather than 'learned helplessness'. When in 1998 he was elected president of the American Psychological Association, he used his presidency to shift the discipline from its historical focus on mental illness to a focus on mental health.

Chapter Fourteen

Balm of Hurt Minds

2005 TO 2006

I hadn't been able to consider therapy as an option before now. Like others in the grip of a serious depressive episode, I was too ill, the problem too acute. I needed medication. At that stage, my family had been the best therapists. They had provided a safe, calm haven.

But I couldn't go on putting such a strain on those closest to me forever, as they themselves pointed out in a nicely understated way. Recurrent depression places a burden on the family, and on marriages too. Your partner suffers not only the strain of looking after you but also the sense that they are somehow implicated in what happened. Sebastian worried that our pressured lifestyle, for which we were both responsible, had contributed to me being unwell. It was equally certain I wouldn't have recovered without him.

The sympathy of friends had limits, too. Friends were unlikely to point out uncomfortable truths, especially as I had been so ill. As one confessed to me, she worried that too much straight-talking might tip me over the edge again. It made sense to shift some of that burden onto a therapist, who could help me foster good mental health.

Having therapy would also be about my changing

perception of depression itself. The first time round I saw the illness as largely physical, or biological. I had been amazed and appalled by how unpleasant the symptoms were. Equally, the cure was physical, concrete: swallowing small pills. But after a second breakdown, I began to view depression as both a physical and mental illness that happens in the context of your whole life. I was more prepared to face up to the personality traits that possibly predisposed me to depression.

This first flicker of responsibility is a significant moment for anyone going through a depressive illness: I can remember the exact second it happened, right down to the pattern on the plates I was unloading from the dishwasher. Perhaps it was time to accept that the psychological reasons for the illness might be helped by the 'talking cure', as Freud called it. A person, unlike a drug, can listen to your story when you are well enough to tell it and provide a new perspective. This was something I could now do for myself. As I came off the drugs, therapy would allow me to judge carefully any improvement. It might prove empowering.

A rough straw poll of others who had undergone therapy revealed that several had struggled to find the right therapist. There was always the danger of people preying on the vulnerable in a largely unregulated profession, which is also a risk with alternative health practitioners. But most of the people I consulted were enthusiastic. If you broke your arm, after you had the bones set and the plaster removed, you would then do some physiotherapy, they argued, and a depressive episode was no different. 'Go on,' said one therapy enthusiast. 'Treat yourself and everyone who loves you to being a better and a calmer person.'

I realised that I was prejudiced about therapy, just as I had been ignorant about depression. There had always seemed to me to be something shameful about it. If only therapists had offices on the high street, rather than being out of sight as if they had something to hide. If only therapy was marketed more as something for everyone and not just for the supposedly 'unbalanced'; if only it would be odd if you didn't have therapy; if only it was easily accessible for all of us. If only therapy was regulated in such a way that not just anybody could claim to be a counsellor.

Some of this undoubtedly had to do with my background. My parents had both grown up in the shadow of the war, and in turn their parents had rarely mentioned the privations they had experienced and the dreadful things they had seen. It was a particular axiom that my grandfather never talked about his experience of the war. When he arrived back from Dunkirk, having just survived impossible odds, family legend had it that my grandmother greeted him with the words, 'Come on, Ronnie, we can just make the 4.42 to Basingstoke if you hurry.' Somehow the idea of talking to a therapist was conflated in my mind with complaining about my lot. And who was I to complain when my forebears had shown such heroism?

The problem was that I had now had two serious depressive episodes; I might have been able to brush off being ill once, but I couldn't dismiss it after the second bout. Despite feeling competitive with contemporaries who had become high achievers, I didn't think of myself as a failure, as many do who suffer from depression. My former employer's attitude had helped; the depression had never been held against me when I returned to work after the first episode.

But for all the arguments in favour of therapy, I still held back, see-sawing wildly between opposing views. Therapy is one of those situations where the customer is always wrong, one inner voice said. It is the resort of life's losers, taunted another. In my mind, those who had therapy still stood for slippery New-Age nonsense in a world where others were struggling just to stay alive or find clean water. Many people I admired would mock therapy enthusiasts in the public eye for their talk of journeys and self-discovery and 'how I learned to love myself'.

I was anxious about what I might reveal of the darker recesses of my mind, fearful of being psychologically violated by someone else or even myself. Too much unpicking might make things worse. I was surviving. Wasn't that enough?

I doubted therapy could reveal much about my particular type of depression, when it seemed as if my body took over in such a dramatic and forceful way for no apparent reason. I tacked back to the safety of the position that my depression was purely physical. And if I admitted it might be slightly more complicated than that, I doubted mere conversation could possibly elucidate the mysteries of the relationship between mind and body, nor did I wish to discuss the shameful possibility that it was all my fault. That would be indulging the very narcissism that lay at the heart of the illness, the selfishness that I was trying to avoid.

November 2005

The months galloped away. Each signpost of our family's year – the children's birthdays, the Easter-egg hunt, our summer holiday in the Lake District – whizzed past as if in a rear-view mirror on a motorway. We even hosted our Christmas party the following month, albeit on a slightly smaller scale and despite the dramas of the earlier debacle. Having the party was what we did; I wanted to get back to normal.

There was always a doctor's appointment, school visit or play date to ensure that finding a therapist failed to take priority. But a comment from Dr Fischer at one of our sessions made a deep impact on me. To embark on therapy wasn't indulging my narcissism, he said. It was an attempt to try and remove it. The happier we are, the more we are able to put ourselves in the shoes of others. Think of it as having a better working relationship with yourself.

While the sense of not being in control of the illness is real, he explained, it is only by taking responsibility that we can try to change. I had a choice. I could continue to attempt to control the illness from without, as it were, chiefly with pills. Or I could heed the call to change and attempt to control the illness from within.

We settled on a compromise: therapy-lite, as it were. I would start to pursue Cognitive Behavioural Therapy, which concentrates on changing patterns of thought rather than any Freudian sleuthing around the unconscious. But for now, I would do so with one of the many self-help books on the subject rather than a real live therapist as – unbelievably, in retrospect – I believed myself to be the sort of competent person who could sort myself out on my own. I didn't want someone else telling me what to do or think.

I would also come off the pills in an even more gradual process than the first time. This would take about eighteen months. While still protected by the drugs, I would adopt other approaches to manage my tendency to depression and anxiety. Dr Fischer suggested that alongside CBT, exercise and diet should also play a big part in making another episode less likely. These were things I had already begun to investigate for myself, but now I was ready to prioritise them.

Perhaps the most important thing was that I was willing and able to take steps to help myself. Now that the worst of the breakdown was over, I didn't want small white pills controlling my brain long-term if I could possibly control it myself. This was a different stage of the illness, which could be approached with different strategies. While the drugs might make for a life less anxious, it could also prove a life less exciting. I had accepted this compromise earlier on, when I was worn down by physical agony, but now I was better I didn't want to be robbed of the full range of experience. The best of times could only be truly known in contrast to the worst. That's not to say I wouldn't return to medication if faced with a full-blown breakdown.

Another factor was that I was no longer inclined to endure the drugs' physical side effects if I could possibly avoid them. Some people experience no secondary problems at all on antidepressants, but the citalopram I had been prescribed for this second breakdown had left me about a stone heavier than normal. Some patients report that the side effects they experience can be worse than their initial depression.

January 2006

It was a photograph that gave me the final push to start reducing my dose. After six months of stability and a life that had returned to normal, I went out with Lucy for a farewell celebration. She was due to return home to go to university and train to be an architect. Later I was shamed to learn that on her return to her mother's arms she collapsed for several days in bed, worn out by a year of such exceptional hard work. She returned to London seven years later, partly, she told me, because she wanted to see what I would be like when well. 'I always used to wonder what you would be like as a normal person.'

That New Year we were photographed in our finery, Lucy svelte in a tailored dress. When I saw the picture I didn't at first recognise the swollen stomach and enormous breasts of the otherwise small figure standing next to her. I carefully covered the face on the photo with my hand and looked at the headless figure. I didn't want to be that person. I knew I wasn't that person when I was properly myself. It might seem a sideshow to care about my weight when the key issue was how to live without the drugs. But the less than profound truth was that I did care.

This time I had to work much harder to lose weight. I ate carefully, with as much focus on eating to reduce my anxiety levels as to slim down. I carried on swimming, as I had done after the first breakdown, as well as my Pilates. This particularly appealed to me because of its focus on breathing in addition to stretching; I was back to using breathing techniques to help me calm down. We should keep returning to the breath as an anchor, our teacher told us. Our minds would wander, as that was what minds did, but we could keep returning to the safety of the breath.*

I once again used other drugs to ease the process of withdrawal from my medication. I continued to take small amounts of sleeping pills if I couldn't sleep or when we travelled. I used tranquillisers as well, though I wanted to eventually wean myself off these, too. I knew Dr Fischer couldn't go on prescribing large quantities forever. Doctors are rightly wary of letting their patients get addicted to the tranquillisers known as benzodiazepines. In the 1970s and early 1980s they were among the most commonly prescribed drugs; now doctors view them with far more caution. They can ease agitation and stress and help patients sleep, by decreasing the amount of chemical activity in the amygdala, the brain's fear centre. They also increase levels of chemicals that contribute to tranquillity. But if you stay on them for too long, withdrawal symptoms can include insomnia, anxiety, panic attacks and in some cases, suicidal thoughts. Ironically, the most frequent symptoms of benzodiazepine withdrawal are almost impossible to distinguish from the typical symptoms of anxiety.

Nor are sleeping pills ideal. They trigger uncertainty, even if you do try to make rules for yourself, as I had. It is hard to know if you should take an extra pill if they seem not to be working, and if you do, there is a danger you will sleep through your alarm clock. Nor is it easy to decide at what point in the night it is too close to daylight to take a pill. The questions multiply, as the more you use sleeping pills the more their sedative capacity wears off.

---

* For more details on my approach to exercise and diet and how they helped me recover, please see appendices at the back of the book.

Sleeping pills also have side effects. They can result in feelings of grogginess in the mornings and an unpleasant aftertaste in your mouth. They can also leave you with a feeling of failure, however much you rationalise their use. You feel you should be able to sleep on your own; after all, even children can manage that.

I wanted to come off the drugs, and to be slim. I also wanted to be well for the children, though chiefly to benefit me rather than them. I now had a strong sense that they were going to be fine and would turn into the people they were always going to be, as long as they were well looked after by someone – even if that someone was not me.

But whether it was crucial to them or not, trying to be a fit mother in every sense certainly gave me the motive I needed to get better. Everyone suffering from depression needs a good reason to be well. Trying to be well for the children had already helped me by providing a focus beyond myself. Feeling that others depended on me meant I had to learn to depend on myself. I was longing to rid myself of my self-absorption. In the safety instructions in a plane you are told to fix on your own oxygen mask before you attend to those of your children. I had to fix on the mask.

A line from *The Prophet* by Khalil Gibran inspired me. He talks of being a 'bow that was stable' from which your children could shoot forth like arrows. It was time to try and become a bit more stable.

Your children are not your children.
They are the sons and daughters of Life's longing for itself.
They come through you but not from you,
And though they are with you yet they belong not to you.

You may give them your love but not your thoughts,
For they have their own thoughts.
You may house their bodies but not their souls,
For their souls dwell in the house of tomorrow,
which you cannot visit, not even in your dreams.
You may strive to be like them,
but seek not to make them like you.
For life goes not backward nor tarries with yesterday.

You are the bows from which your children
as living arrows are sent forth.
The archer seeks the mark upon the path of the infinite,
and He bends you with His might
that His arrows may go swift and far.
Let our bending in the archer's hand be for gladness;
For even as He loves the arrow that flies,
So He loves also the bow that is stable.

February, 2006

The most important step to becoming stable was relearning how to sleep. Everything else would follow, I argued to myself. Once I was sufficiently rested, I would have more energy for exercise and be able resist the quick high-sugar fixes I turned to because I was exhausted.

Insomnia was the way the illness had started for me and insomnia needed to be dealt with if the illness was to end. I had trouble getting to sleep, trouble with waking in the night, trouble waking up too early. I craved the deep, healing, oblivious sleep that would underpin my recovery, the kind of rejuvenating sleep that Shakespeare described so well in *Macbeth*, the sleep that 'knits up the ravell'd sleeve of care/The death of each day's life, sore labour's bath/Balm of hurt minds! Great nature's second course/Chief nourisher in life's feast.'

When we don't get enough sleep, the emotional centre of the brain becomes more active. This is particularly unfortunate if you suffer from anxiety and depression. Manageable fears become terrifying obsessions.*

The reassuring news is that learning to sleep is a skill like any other. But it's a skill you can probably only acquire as you start to get better. When I was in the grip of acute depression, there was nothing for it but to take sleeping pills.

The first breakthrough was once again a conversation with Dr Fischer. He believed I had to change the way I looked at the problem altogether and understand what was happening. Our most troubling sensations are those we don't understand.

Not sleeping very much is not the problem. The danger is worrying about it. That is what can stop you from sleeping and make you ill. Our bodies are cleverer than our minds. When we are truly tired, we will fall asleep. Sleeping is a natural action. You don't have to do anything to get to sleep. It is not humanly possible to stay awake forever. The one topic that

---

* In one study a set of increasingly disturbing images were shown to people who had slept normally, and to others who had been deprived of sleep for thirty-five hours. It found that the emotional centre of the brain, the amygdala, was about 60 per cent more active in people who had been sleep-deprived. The study also found that the connection between the amygdala and the frontal lobe of the brain had been disrupted by lack of sleep. The frontal lobe slows down the brain's emotional centre. When you are sleep-deprived, you lose control over your emotions. ('The Human Emotional Brain Without Sleep: A Prefrontal-Amygdala Disconnect,' *Current Biology*, 2007).

mustn't be on one's list of worries is sleep itself. It is the ulti-mate paradox: to achieve sleep, you have to abandon the imperative to achieve it.

Lying awake in the dark, we are robbed of normal cues. We feel hopeless. We cannot see the reassuring prompts of our familiar surroundings. We are fearful as we feel we are alone: even if we share a bed with someone, when they are asleep, we are alone with our insomnia.

Step one, then, is to stop being anxious about sleep itself. I had to start believing that in due course I would get the sleep I needed, though it might not always be conveniently at night, and I needed to arrange my life as far as I could to make this possible. Even twenty-five minutes' napping makes a differ-ence, a finding backed up by the fact that the first twenty minutes of sleep is usually rich in slow-wave sleep and there-fore deeply relaxing.

Meanwhile, if I was awake at night, I needed to make it feel normal as opposed to frightening. One obvious resource for me was to remind myself that I wasn't alone. Poetry could be with me, and so could prayer.

I now try to enjoy lying awake in the dark with my feelings, even going a step further and contemplating that I am awake for a reason and it is safe to be so. I practise breathing tech-niques: every outbreath should contain a negative thought, every inbreath a positive one. I try to meet my own needs for reassurance and calm, to have a conversation with the scared person who is sweating at four o'clock in the morning. I imag-ine that I am soothing a frightened child. Odd and embarrassing as this sounds, it means giving myself a hug, being a mother to the nervous three-year-old inside me who has surfaced in the middle of the night, not blaming her but trying to be compassionate and accepting of all the feelings that are raging away. What would I say to Charlotte or Arthur? I wouldn't chastise them for their worries or deny their anger or fear; I would try to answer their needs.

Being compassionate to myself is sometimes enough. When I am sufficiently calm, I can then try to change the narrative of my thoughts. Every time the worries return, with steady will-power I force my skittish mind elsewhere, as if I am on a train and have to move along the carriages until I find a comfortable berth. I then try to anchor my thoughts to something more positive and pleasant, something complex enough to hold them for a long time.

At these moments, I often revisit in my mind my grandparents' home. The mock-Tudor house where my mother grew up was a place I knew and loved as a child; its memories induce a rare nocturnal calm. I retrace my steps, remembering the hall table upon which were invariably a few small envelopes, addressed in my grandmother's purple ink, and bearing a second-class stamp. I can smell the coat cupboard with its navy cashmere greatcoats, their pockets full of mothballs, and the scent of beeswax from the polished wood floors. I can taste the thinly sliced and buttered bread for tea and hear the heavy tread of my grandfather as he went around the house rewinding the clocks. Room by room, I travel back in time and recollect the peace of a happy childhood.

There was the pond in the garden from which we scooped frogspawn into jam jars and watched as they turned into tadpoles. And the greenhouse with its broken panes, scented with tomatoes and peaches and grapes. Every spot in the house and garden had a memory that might be capable of soothing me to sleep.

Alternatively, poetry might once again be my friend, especially a transporting poem such as 'The Lake Isle of Innisfree' by W.B. Yeats. Its soothing cadences and evocation of quiet would often work their magic, my unconscious mind not distinguishing between real or imagined experience as I listened to the lake water lapping and gradually fell asleep. If I was awake for long periods, I would get up, put the light on and try to learn a new poem by heart. Yeats's words recharged the spent batteries of my own language. The concentration required would fix me in the moment, forcing me to abandon past and future worries and leave me yawning and finally ready for sleep.

I will arise and go now, and go to Innisfree,
And a small cabin build there, of clay and wattles made:
Nine bean-rows will I have there, a hive for the
*   honey-bee,*
And live alone in the bee-loud glade.

And I shall have some peace there, for peace comes
*   dropping slow,*
Dropping from the veils of the morning to where the
*   cricket sings;*
There midnight's all a glimmer, and noon a purple glow,
And evening full of the linnet's wings.

I will arise and go now, for always night and day
I hear lake water lapping with low sounds by the shore;
While I stand on the roadway, or on the pavements grey,
I hear it in the deep heart's core.

So my dual approach to tempering my fears was partly to accept them, and partly to change the story running in my head. As I recovered, I could also take more practical steps and practise what doctors now call good 'sleep hygiene'. All the clichéd approaches helped: a completely dark room (I put up blinds); a milky drink (dairy products are rich in tryptophan, an amino acid that also acts as a hypnotic); doing nothing too stimulating before bed (a wind-down routine); and going to bed at roughly the same time every night. It wasn't as though I didn't know about such approaches. The difference was that now I rigorously put them into action.

Dealing with insomnia by trying to retrain my brain was the natural precursor to beginning the therapy that I had hitherto ducked. Now I had started to reduce my anxiety at night, I could try to change my way of thinking in the day.

I had already agreed with Dr Fischer that CBT was the right approach for me. One estimate suggests there are around four hundred different schools of psychotherapy*, and such an array of choice would usually have put me in a tailspin of uncertainty. I relaxed when I realised that evidence suggests similar results for all the main models when dealing with depression, with probably the most detailed studies in favour of CBT. I also favoured CBT as it only required one weekly session, compared to Freudian analysis which needs clients to commit to four or five sessions of psychoanalysis a week, and as a result very few therapists now work this way.

A CBT therapist will initially work with a patient for an hour long weekly session for perhaps twelve to sixteen weeks,

---

* Joe Griffin and Ivan Tyrrell, *Human Givens* (HG Publishing, 2004).

focusing on a particular goal. Other therapeutic approaches tend to take far longer. I naturally gravitated towards an approach that was supposed to deliver quick results. I believed I would be able to sort myself out even more quickly working on my own, from a book.

Chapter Fifteen

I Would Be Sillier Than I Have Been

2006 TO 2007

February 2006

The basic premise of CBT is not new. I read as much in what was to become a very well-thumbed book: *Mind Over Mood: Change How You Feel by Changing the Way You Think.** The maxim that underpins CBT thinking, 'Men are disturbed not by things, but by the view which they take on them', was coined some 2,000 years ago.** Trite as it may sound, it is true: events don't upset us; it is the meaning we attach to those events that does. CBT aims to help us become more flexible and realistic about our responses, however bleak those events are. Over time, constant practice at altering our responses can create new neural pathways and actually change our brain chemistry. More positive thoughts in turn become habitual, our view of the world and ourselves shifts and eventually, we are no longer the people we were.

The first step was to recognise the connection between mood and thought, the book said. Whether sad, happy, or somewhere in between, there is a thought connected to our state that helps define the mood. The next chapters helped me

* By Dennis Greenberger PhD and Christine A. Padesky PhD (The Guildford Press, 1995).
** By the Greek philosopher Epictetus.

identify my feelings, and to rate how strongly I felt them. The four key feelings we can experience are: happiness, sadness, fear and anger.

Then I began to plot my 'automatic thoughts' as they occurred through my day in response to particular events or situations. The theory is that, over time, even disproportionate or out of place responses can become automatic and seemingly plausible. They become so ingrained that we don't even realise we are thinking them, like an old pair of glasses we've worn for so long we forget we're wearing them. But if we look more closely we may start to realise that our views are often distorted or unnecessarily negative.

I began to keep a 'thought record': there were columns for 'situation', 'mood', 'automatic thoughts', 'evidence that supports the thought', 'evidence that does not support the thought', 'alternative/balanced thoughts', and 'rate moods now'. In short, this was a method for looking at things differently and challenging my negative ways of thinking.

Once you successfully adopt such changes and start to recognise your own distorted perceptions, returning to your old ways 'violates' your new identity and the new mental muscle you have developed. It feels perverse and unnatural, like deliberately putting your hand in a flame.

I set out to become my own private detective. My notebook revealed when my negative thoughts were at their strongest. Unsurprisingly, they tended to be worse in the middle of the night, but also first thing in the morning when my inclination to slip into negative thinking was at its height.

My notebook also revealed exactly what I was worrying about. I'm embarrassed to say the worries were not about saving the world or preventing global warming. They were mainly about the minutiae of my interactions with other people, and coping with multiple demands and relationships. This had been true both when I worked full-time and when I was a full-time mother. I worried about managing all I set myself to do and getting through the notorious to-do list, with little sense of proportion: I might wake at three fretting about forgetting Edward's swimming kit. Fixating on seemingly small worries and failing to make the most of the present are exactly the pattern of the depressive.

These were typical of the automatic thoughts recorded in my notebook: 'I've offended her'; 'I've said something wrong'; 'I can't cope'; 'I may be ill again'; 'I need to sort it out'; 'I must try harder'; 'I must always try to do my best and I am failing.' Often the automatic thoughts developed in a sequence CBT calls 'catastrophising'. So I could move in a nanosecond from 'she doesn't like me' to 'I've done something terrible', then from there to 'I've got no friends', 'I'm a worthless person' and 'I might as well give up.' This is a typical 'catastrophising' sequence, whereby someone turns a worst-case scenario into a matter of fact in their mind. 'Sebastian's late home from work . . . he's probably dead' would be another example.

In a randomly chosen entry from my thought record, the situation was that I hadn't received the usual email from a parenting group to which I belonged. My automatic thoughts were: 'I must have affronted somebody'; 'I am not clever or good enough to be in the group'; 'I have been rejected.' Under 'alternative/balanced thoughts' I have speculated that it might have been a simple muddle rather than a conspiracy against me. No, I hadn't the slightest shred of proof that anyone had rejected me. Yes, there might be another technical explanation. Yes, the email might have gone into my junk-mail folder by mistake. No, there was nothing to suggest I had been a bad friend.

This all sounds easy. Filling in the situation and automatic-thoughts columns *was* easy. But the third stage was devilish: trying to look at the situation differently. The truth was that my automatic thoughts were just that: automatic, well-entrenched and polished with practice over time. For all that there might be evidence to question the automatic thought, the emotions the events provoked were so strongly embedded, and I was so used to feeling and believing them, that they were hard to gainsay. Moreover, I liked to be right, and changing the automatic thoughts meant considering that I could be wrong. A challenge!

In the battle to think differently, the book advised constantly sticking with the facts, rather than the strong emotions in which they were bathed. Over time, I realised how, while the facts were usually undramatic, my emotions were quite the opposite. I had melded facts and emotions together and needed to disentangle them. While it was futile to attempt to exert control over the facts, I could do something about my internal responses.

It helped that, as time went on, I began to realise just how often my automatic thoughts were wrong. I felt nicely silly when I realised there hadn't been a meeting of the parenting group at all. I even laughed at myself – often a sign of being on the path to good mental health.

I also began to be aware of how much time was taken up by negative thoughts. I could ruminate for hours. The parenting-group episode, for example, required me to continuously check my emails, to lie awake discussing tactics in my head about how to proceed, whether to dare to ask another member if they had all been talking about my behaviour or views on raising children, whether it would be better to email them casually to find out, or call instead so that there would be nothing in print that could be forwarded to some unknown enemy and used against me. More hours were consumed on which of all the members I should approach – the unofficial group leader, who would be bound to know what was really going on, though she might not care, or a more approachable figure, but then they might not be in the loop, and perhaps even the mousiest of the group had rejected me, too. Recalling these wasted hours was exhausting in itself.

I persevered with trying to alter my automatic thoughts. After two breakdowns, I had got to the point when I knew I had to. I also decided to believe in the possibility of change. Embracing the faith that things can shift is a huge challenge for those who can't imagine seeing things differently. It becomes much easier once you start therapy: even the faintest progress allows you to believe you may be changing for the better. It felt like opening the window in an airless room.

The sheer amount of work that CBT involved was a help, too. Keeping a proper thought record was hard and time-consuming but the effort of writing things down not only made me more aware of my behavioural patterns but also meant I had invested in the process of changing them.

Perhaps the final spur to change was that writing down my worries also revealed some of my own little secrets. So many of my concerns were narcissistic: they were all about my efforts to win approval and get people to like me. Often, in the pursuit of approval, I misleadingly said yes when really I meant no, and was left in a jam of misunderstanding later on.

And – this was hard to admit – it wasn't even clear that I was pleasing anyone, anyway. It was time to consider that maybe all these people didn't want or need me to please them. Pleasing others might even be a form of arrogance: superficially my concern seemed to be for others, but actually I was really concerned about my own constant need for reassurance. Such self-centeredness sat uncomfortably with my goal of trying to help others, or practise any kind of Christian faith.

I considered my 'present drawer', stocked in readiness for future birthdays and other occasions: in theory, it was all about others. But presents, I realised, were sometimes not just about pleasing the recipient. They could also be about the giver's need to feel good about themselves, because naturally they felt loving and generous if they dispensed gifts. If properly appreciated, presents could also feed the giver's need for reassurance and approval.

While busy disbanding my present drawer and trying to check my present-giving impulse and other habits of thought, I also had to find the courage to say yes to what had previously been too daunting to contemplate: actually working with a therapist.

While I was making some progress on ditching the automatic thoughts, I knew I was shying away from a crucial aspect that a good CBT therapist, as opposed to a self-help book, would have addressed. Where were these thoughts coming from and what were the feelings that underpinned them? In therapeutic terms, what were the 'core beliefs' that underpinned such thoughts? How did all this worrying fit with the fact that I enjoyed an outwardly enviable life? Why did I mind to such a degree that I might have offended people? Why did I believe I had to keep striving to be simultaneously a good wife, mother, friend, hostess and employee, to the point that it made me ill? The challenge was to establish how my past was constantly intruding on my present. These were frightening areas to venture into. I preferred the safety of books and private study to therapists.

I delayed signing up with a therapist through 2006. Partly it was because my physical symptoms were diminishing. Partly I felt I had made strides forward thanks to CBT. Partly I had less time on my hands, as I had signed up to a year-long foundation course in psychotherapy and counselling. I was unsure about whether this would be the first step to becoming a therapist with the huge commitment in time and training that such a decision would imply. But studying the work of Freud and Jung and the history of all the different therapeutic approaches was of huge intellectual interest to me. I felt privileged that I could indulge my curiousity and, I hoped, grow in understanding.

Studying felt like enough of a commitment to therapy, though I conveniently ignored the fact that undergoing therapy myself was supposed to be part of the course I had undertaken. If anyone asked, I would say I was just about to sign up. Partly I was busy with the children: Edward was now twelve, George ten, Katherine seven, and the twins four.

Ultimately, I think I didn't really believe what I know now to be true: that working with a therapist is completely different from following a book. Therapy is about a relationship between two people, in a room, in the moment. We gain our sense of self from our interaction with others. In theory, one plus one does and should equal more than the sum of the parts in a therapeutic alliance.

It doesn't mean that the therapist tells you the answers. The old joke still resonates: how many therapists does it take to change a lightbulb? It depends if the lightbulb wants to change. Since the 1960s, the prevailing trend in psychotherapy has been to try to empower patients. The therapist is constantly trying to probe the patient's view of the world by using phrases such as 'It sounds like . . .' or 'I wonder if . . .' If I began therapy, it meant accepting that the answers to my problems lay within.

January 2007

Come January 2007 there was no longer any doubt in my mind: I needed therapy. We had gone ahead and thrown another Christmas party. There were Christmas presents to buy, end-of-term plays and concerts to attend and the family to host for Christmas meals. My mother noticed an edge to my voice and a familiar, frightened look in my eye. I became busier and busier. I began waking routinely at three and failing to get back to sleep.

Hugging me in bed in the early hours of the morning, Sebastian assured me there was no need to buy anyone a present or host a single meal. I was the only person forcing myself on with this crusade, imagining the family needed some kind of perfect Christmas. I was officially to take the next few days off. I suspect I might have had a third depressive episode had Sebastian not intervened.

The more I studied the history of therapy at arm's length in an over-heated meeting room with thirty others, the more I realised I was avoiding confronting my own difficult feelings by shying away from therapy. The lecturers were one step ahead of me in their view that all those following the course needed to undergo therapy, too.

A friend recommended a therapist as we chatted over a cup of tea. I rang as instructed and agreed to see her, drawn to her warm voice and the straightforward way she dealt with my queries. She trained people wishing to be therapists as well as being a therapist herself. That sounded good. I didn't bother to ask which model she used.

The problem was that she lived about an hour away. By the time I arrived at her treatment room, I was flustered and annoyed. She had told me to go through a side entrance of her semi-detached house, but I couldn't establish which was the right door and rang the front doorbell instead.

She was equally flustered as she led me through her hall. The point of the side entrance was to preserve some professional distance and privacy. As she rightly feared, the former journalist in me was busy hunting for any clues about her. She looked like a retired teacher: grey-haired, with a sensible long waistcoat. I justified my nosiness by thinking it was natural to want to know something about the person in whom I was about to confide. I would later realise this is to misunderstand therapy. Your therapist is the one person who is entirely focused on you; you needn't know anything about them. From the accumulation of books and clutter, I gathered she had lived in the house a long time and enjoyed reading, and there were signs she had raised a family, all of which reassured me.

'So, then,' she began, and asked in a reassuringly normal way the reassuringly normal question 'How are you?'

Off I went. As I talked, I cried. Perhaps it was the sudden discovery of feelings I didn't know I had. The subject matter was seemingly straightforward: my childhood, parents, siblings, husband, work, children. In fact, the tangled emotions they gave rise to were anything but. I felt sad, angry, happy, surprised and confused by turn. But there was no logic or order or pattern to what I said, and she let me ramble on, with only the odd prompt.

At the end of the session I thanked her, even though I wasn't very sure what she had done. She replied, 'You are the one who has done all the work.'

As I travelled home, I didn't feel I had done any 'work' – only that I had wasted nearly three hours. I already knew I was in a terrible muddle. I didn't want to be left alone with my thoughts; I wanted her insights into why I was such a worrier. I wanted a sense from her that she could help and therapy could help. I had just spent fifty minutes with a complete stranger in a neighbourhood to which I had never been before and to which I didn't want to return. I was now literally lost at the very moment I had supposedly begun the journey to find myself.

The problem was simple: she lived too far away. The effort of getting to see her every week was too much. I should have told her straight away but I was in people-pleasing mode. So I was late for my second appointment, which she noted. She suggested it was symptomatic of an entrenched pattern whereby I ignored my own needs. Maybe – but the traffic had been terrible.

The strain of Christmas receded, I seemed to be righting myself. I shelved the idea of therapy. After all, my first encounter had been so unrewarding that I wasn't in a hurry to carry on. Been there, done therapy, I thought. Maybe I should try sex, (non-prescription) drugs and rock 'n' roll next time.

Spring 2007

By March of 2007 I had no choice but to reconsider. My tutors confirmed that I wouldn't be eligible to complete the course if I didn't begin therapy. This time, I found someone who lived a few streets away, which was a good start. However, I discovered that the trouble with seeing someone local is that you will bump into them. It can be dangerous swerving in traffic when surprised by a chance encounter with your former therapist.

I made no real progress with this second therapist, either. Again, I focused on her rather than myself: on her room off the half-landing with its statue of the Buddha in the corner, a throw on the chair and the box of tissues on the table, on the layout of her house and the shoes in the hall. It wasn't her fault, but it was a tell-tale sign that the therapy wasn't working.

I mainly chatted, she mainly nodded, and every now and then she would give me big marker pens to 'draw' my feelings on creamy sheets of paper. My mind was elsewhere and I was tempted to write a shopping list instead. Practically the only thing she said was 'Go well' at the end of the session; it seemed an awfully expensive going-home present.

I kept going intermittently for several months through the summer, sometimes using the family as an excuse for not showing up. As she was my first regular therapist, I didn't have anyone else with whom to compare her. Partly I hung around because I hoped she might be just about to give me the answers; perhaps this would be the week she would weigh in and say, 'Right: here's what you need to do . . .' Or, 'In my experience, this is what's going on. It's all about getting stuck up a tree when you were six.'

Partly, I wanted to find out more about her: whether she was a parent, married, divorced or single. The stark white bathroom upstairs yielded no clues at all apart from her brand of toothpaste. I wondered if she had experienced some trauma in her own life.

Only now did a friend put me straight. It is a particular approach for a therapist to keep so quiet. It can work for some people. The therapist wasn't going to change. Her approach had been consistent from the first session. It just wasn't working for me.

In a final clue that our relationship was going nowhere, we never talked about bringing our sessions to an end. That is standard practice in therapy, and necessary. My desire to please and sense of good manners meant I found it hard to say I was off. But she should have been handling the structure of the therapy, not me.

September 2007

I did eventually say goodbye, once I had completed my course. I think probably the only worthwhile session we had was one of the final ones: often the most interesting conversations in therapy happen at the beginning and the end of the process, when the relationship with the therapist necessarily comes to the fore, thereby revealing a lot about how the client relates to others. Actually, what the therapist did at our last meeting was to give me a passage by a writer called Marianne Williamson, often quoted by Nelson Mandela and other inspirational figures.

> *Our deepest fear is not that we are inadequate. Our deepest fear is that we are powerful beyond measure. It is our light, not our darkness that most frightens us. We ask ourselves, 'Who am I to be brilliant, gorgeous, talented, fabulous?' Actually, who are you not to be? You are a child of God. Your playing small does not serve the world. There is nothing*

enlightened about shrinking so that other people won't feel insecure around you. We are all meant to shine, as children do. We were born to make manifest the glory of God that is within us. It's not just in some of us; it's in everyone. And as we let our own light shine, we unconsciously give other people permission to do the same. As we are liberated from our own fear, our presence automatically liberates others.

She didn't explain how the words related to me in particular. I took it to mean that she felt I too was meant to shine, perhaps in a new, undomestic sphere. That seemed awfully little to take away from six months of therapy. I never managed to ask her about it, as it was the last time we met.

October 2007

Since therapy, I found my own forthrightness was a catalyst for others to reveal their problems. I kept finding women at the school gates, or at parents' evenings, who confessed to many of the same problems I had experienced. At one coffee morning, the entire group of six mothers admitted to being on antidepressants, for all that they seemed outwardly fabulous: well-groomed, well-dressed, many of them former lawyers and bankers, others still working. Whatever path they had chosen, they were finding the multiple demands on them hard to bear. One with a particularly stellar career said she longed to leave her job to care for her children. 'But I worry that if I don't work and keep achieving, no one will love me.' Many said they had a natural predisposition to worry about things, but it was the combination of this with overly busy lives and handling multiple relationships and roles that had led them to consult their GPs.

I had increasingly come to believe that women are the stressed sex: that the responsibilities of freedom and choice together with the responsibilities of motherhood can stretch us too far. (Later, reading around the subject would confirm my impressions: in the UK, rates for depression and anxiety are nearly 50 per cent higher for women than men and the odds that women will develop psychological problems are 1.2 times those for men.*)

More and more I realised that, far from struggling to make my way alone across some private desert, there were plenty of others among the sand dunes trying to find their own way out of depression. We began to gather other members of the tribe and started to meet regularly. The power of groups has been shown to help those fighting addiction: a sense of shared purpose and solidarity is the great strength of Alcoholics Anonymous and Weight Watchers.

We decided to start a book club, as seemed compulsory at the time in our neighbourhood, but ours had a twist: we would read self-help books. Once you have suffered, you become adept at spotting others who have been through the same thing. We naturally gravitate towards those who have shared our experience. I found others who, like me, had worries circling round them like birds of prey, plucking at their nerves and shredding their energies.

At various times I had been a member of a prayer group, a

* Professor Daniel Freeman and Jason Freeman, *The Stressed Sex: Uncovering the Truth about Men, Women and Mental Health* (Oxford University Press, 2013).

parenting group and a dance group. This group was different: we were trying to beat depression. Instead of reading novels, we would choose books that someone in the group had already read and found helpful, such as *The Artist's Way* or *The Secret Life of the Grown-up Brain*.* We would spend the six weeks between meetings road-testing its approach. Then we would gather at each other's houses and flats to discuss what had worked for us and what hadn't. I always served my best fish pie and frozen peas; the others came up with similarly nourishing meals, which added to the sense of being looked after and nurtured.

The only problem was that we didn't always manage to meet up: given the make-up of the group, crises, unsurprisingly, would often intervene. But when we did get together, it usually helped us feel better.

I had to resist the constant sneaky voice in my head that struggled to connect the more egregious platitudes of self-help with the horror of the breakdowns ('One day at a time!', 'Take a hike!' and so on). I usually felt more centred and supported afterwards, often more because of the people than anything we had read. The sessions could be heated, though, and inevitably there were tensions and differences between us. I took months to realise that just because someone disagreed with me, that didn't mean they didn't like me. We were – in the group, as we were in life – a nicely neurotic bunch, all capable of reverting to our childlike selves, albeit in grown-up bodies.

The group, at its best, provided safe respite and a wonderful

---

* Julia Cameron, *The Artist's Way* (Penguin, 1992) and Barbara Straunch, *The Secret Life of the Grown-Up Brain* (Viking, 2010).

sense that we weren't alone. Everyone was living proof that performing on multiple fronts was hard, and had contributed to our troubles, but also that recovery could happen. Our low spirits were always the worse for concealment. One woman was particularly impressive, the spiritual core of the group. She set the tone for the rest of us. Despite having suffered an abusive marriage for years, she embodied the kind of calm and mindfulness we all aspired to.

Often one person would dominate a session if they were going through an especially hard time. But the fact that there were six others there to help meant that pressure was never put on any one of us in particular, as can happen in one-on-one exchanges. Our leader, as I saw her, enforced good behaviour in the rest of us.

Feedback from a group is much harder to ignore. For example, if one person says that you are an approval addict, you can deny it. But if six others make the same point, you're likely to conclude they may be on to something. The collective voice was particularly strong when dispensing advice: if everyone thought the same, perhaps it was time to listen.

The group also helped me to get over my prejudices. I had previously stigmatised the self-help genre as something for the impressionable and weak-minded. The very fact that there were so many self-help books out there suggested they weren't working. Now I saw that though there are books full of platitudes, there are also others that contain tools for creating change. Even so, I still preferred a finely-worded prayer or a poem. This little prayer cropped up in church that month and I pinned it on my noticeboard.

Lord, help to me to notice all the signs of goodness
    around me and give thanks for them.
Lord, we are each other's gifts: help me to be thankful for
    every life-giving encounter and to see that your gifts
    are all around me if only I would look.
In gratitude I will find healing.

I persuaded the group that we should each bring along our favourite poem to the next session. I brought my faithful Herbert poem 'The Flower', with its message of rebirth. A friend brought this poem entitled 'Instants', its author unknown:

If I could live my life again,
In the next I would try to make more mistakes,
I wouldn't try to be so perfect, I would be more relaxed,
I'd be sillier than I have been this time around,
In fact, I'd take very few things seriously.
I would be less hygienic,
I would take more risks,
I would take more trips,
I would watch more sunsets,
I would climb more mountains,
I would swim more rivers,
I would go to more places that I've never been,
I would eat more ice creams and fewer lima beans,
I would have more real problems and fewer imaginary
    ones.
I was one of those people who lived prudent and prolific
    lives –
each minute of his life.
Of course I had moments of joy, but

if I could go back I would try to have only good
    moments.
After all, moments are what life is made of,
Don't miss out on the now!
I was one of those people who never goes anywhere
without a thermometer,
without a hot-water bottle,
without an umbrella and a parachute.
If I could live my life again I would travel light.
If I could live my life again I would walk bare foot
from the beginning of spring till
the end of autumn.
I would take more rides on merry-go-rounds,
I'd watch more sunrises and play with more children,
If I had the life to live. But now, as you see, I am
    eighty-five,
– and I know that I am dying.

We weren't eighty-five and we weren't dying. The time had come to watch more sunrises and play with more children, to shout with joy and swim more rivers.

We spent time at the group making our own lists inspired by 'Instants'. The idea was to disentangle the elements of our lives that were joyful from those that were destructive. One member of the group put it well, saying, 'Let's boost our sense of delight.' We made logs of the past year and recorded what we had most enjoyed doing, and what we hadn't enjoyed, too. This was my list:

1. *Being outside – find even the rain seems to rinse my*
   mind of worry.
2. *Climbing hills. Feel huge sense of solid achievement at*

the top. Didn't enjoy going to the seaside: dislike
expanses of open ocean, especially when the weather
stormy. However high up the beach we were pitched,
found myself worrying that the children would drown.
3. Walking on rough ground that echoes the countryside.
Like the feel of the earth coming up through the soles of
my shoes.
4. Work. Outside focus is good. 'Be not idle' is the advice
given at the end of Burton's Anatomy of Melancholy.
Find the pursuit that allows you to be your most
creative self. Go with the flow.*

A friend sent me the more comprehensive list Sir Sydney
Smith wrote nearly two hundred years ago in a letter to Lady
Georgiana Morpeth, on 16 February 1820, later entitled 'Advice
Concerning Low Spirits'. Much of his advice dovetailed with
my own guidelines for dealing with low spirits, notwithstand-
ing his advice to avoid poetry.

*Dear Lady Georgiana, – Nobody has suffered more from low
spirits than I have done — so I feel for you. 1st. Live as well as
you dare. 2nd. Go into the shower-bath with a small quantity
of water at a temperature low enough to give you a slight
sensation of cold, 75° or 80°. 3rd. Amusing books. 4th. Short
views of human life — not further than dinner or tea. 5th. Be*

---

* The idea of flow was first posited in the 1970s by the Croatian-born
psychologist Mihaly Csikszentmihalyi in *Flow: The Psychology of Optimal
Experience* by Mihaly Csikszentmihalyi (Harper & Row, 1990). For me, a
sense of flow happens when time flies and I am utterly absorbed in activity,
which can be anything from trying to compose a sentence to trying to
comfort a crying child.

as busy as you can. 6th. See as much as you can of those friends who respect and like you. 7th. And of those acquaintances who amuse you. 8th. Make no secret of low spirits to your friends, but talk of them freely — they are always worse for dignified concealment. 9th. Attend to the effects tea and coffee produce upon you. 10th. Compare your lot with that of other people. 11th. Don't expect too much from human life — a sorry business at the best. 12th. Avoid poetry, dramatic representations (except comedy), music, serious novels, melancholy, sentimental people, and everything likely to excite feeling or emotion, not ending in active benevolence. 13th. Do good, and endeavour to please everybody of every degree. 14th. Be as much as you can in the open air without fatigue. 15th. Make the room where you commonly sit, gay and pleasant. 16th. Struggle by little and little against idleness. 17th. Don't be too severe upon yourself, or underrate yourself, but do yourself justice. 18th. Keep good blazing fires. 19th. Be firm and constant in the exercise of rational religion. 20th. Believe me, dear Lady Georgiana,

Very truly yours,
Sydney Smith

Chapter Sixteen

Some Definite Service

2008 TO 2009

January 2008

An image from our Self-Help Book Club has stayed with me. One member had picked up her car from the garage that morning and discovered the radio had been set to a different station. She fiddled with the dial till she returned to her preferred choice. It occurred to her that this was a useful image: when the toxic thoughts came, she could imagine herself tuned to the wrong station. With some adjustment, I too could switch channels to a different frequency in my brain. Then I could start the car of my life and drive off.

One regular expedition we tried to make was to go to church on Sunday. Both Sebastian and I found that weekends could quickly descend into chaos without rituals to cement our family life. We would all walk to the Catholic church a few streets away. The older ones had received their first Holy Communion there and knew plenty of other children in the congregation, while the younger ones enjoyed playing among the pews and trying to open the doors of the confessionals.

Any dislike of sitting through the service was mitigated by the knowledge that there would be a treat afterwards for them, and a take-away cappuccino for me and Sebastian. Somehow as long as we went to Church, the rest of Sunday would proceed relatively smoothly and I would manage to stop the anxiety from rolling in. The day would culminate in tea at my mother's house with my brother and sister and their children.

One Sunday at church, the priest read out a passage by Cardinal Newman. It was only on looking it up later that I discovered it was the beginning of my favourite passage by him.

> *God has created me to do some definite service; He has committed some work to me which He has not committed to another. I have my mission – I may never know it in this life, but I shall be told it in the next. Somehow I am necessary for His purposes, as necessary in my place as an Archangel in His – if indeed, I fail, He can raise another as He could make the stones children of Abraham. Yet I have a part in His great work; I am a link in a chain, a bond of connection between persons. He has not made me for naught. I shall do good, I shall do His work; I shall be an angel of peace, a preacher of truth in my own place, while not intending it, if I do but keep His commandments and serve Him in my calling. Therefore I will trust Him. Whatever, wherever I am, I can never be thrown away.*

Newman's words seem to splash like healing drops of water to the base of the dry well of my being. The passage gave me a sense that I must never give up, even in the darkest moments of the depression. There was a reason for my existence, as indeed there was to everyone's: we were all 'links in a chain', the 'bond of connection between persons'. It was not for me to question what had befallen me, or what would befall me in the future, or to know the reason why. I had to trust in a power higher than me.

I also took from Newman's words a sense that we all have a service to others to perform. I was no 'angel of peace' but I resolved I would try to practise, in the old saying, 'random acts of kindness'. I would do it for myself, because it made me feel better. As I sat in the pew, I considered that the service I could best perform was that of listening to others. It had a selfish dimension: it would allow me to slow down, which might help me avoid depression.

Once again, I discovered later that my own experience was entirely consonant with wider research, which has found that helping others contributes to our health. Such intentional activities, as psychologists call them, are proven to aid mental wellbeing. Research recently uncovered just how powerful good deeds can be. In a study of elderly couples, researchers found that mortality was greatly delayed in individuals who reported giving help or emotional support to others compared to those who did not.*

Philosophers have long known that wellbeing is hard to obtain directly. It is much more likely to be the result of dedication to something outside oneself. As the Holocaust survivor Viktor Frankl put it, 'Happiness cannot be pursued; it must ensue, and it only does so as the unintended side effect of one's personal dedication to a cause greater than

---

* 'In Sickness and Health: Caring for an Ailing Spouse May Prolong Your Life', University of Michigan research paper published in *Psychological Science* (December 2008).

oneself or as the by-product of one's surrender to a person other than oneself.'*

A natural starting point for me was to try to help other mothers who were depressed. 'What I spent I had, What I saved I lost, What I gave I have' as the old adage goes, or as Emily Dickinson writes in her poem:

> *If I can stop one heart from breaking,*
> *I shall not live in vain;*
> *If I can ease one life the aching,*
> *Or cool one pain,*
> *Or help one fainting robin*
> *Unto his nest again,*
> *I shall not live in vain.*

Mid-November 2008

The first person I tried to help was Emma. She felt like a younger version of me: she was in her twenties and suffering a depressive illness after the birth of her second child, just as I had. It was her mother who rang me in the search for help. She was a health professional who I had seen about with one of the children years earlier and with whom I had talked to about my own depression.

I began by discussing the help Emma was receiving, starting with her GP. I suggested that at her next appointment, the mother should go with Emma armed with a list of questions, remembering how often I had realised on

* Viktor Frankl, *Man's Search for Meaning: An Introduction to Logotherapy* (Washington Square Press, 1963).

the journey home that I had forgotten crucial queries myself.

She then asked if I would talk to Emma. I was initially nervous. All I could offer, I said, were suggestions based on my own experience. But I warned her that I might not be the right person to talk to, especially if her daughter was really ill. Thanks to my psychotherapy course, I knew how little I knew. I was not a trained therapist, nor had I undergone much therapy myself. My role, if there was one, was perhaps to help those at a less extreme stage of the illness. I also stressed that everyone's demons are different and so is the care they need.

Emma's mother pressed on. She felt it would be helpful. So talk to Emma I did, having established the limitations of my role and after being assured that her main care was in the hands of professionals. We talked two or three times a week for several months.

The sense of responsibility was terrifying at first. She was at the point when the only voices that had any clarity in her head were those of destruction and obliteration. I thought about Dr Fischer and all my doctors and therapists in a new light: the daunting task they take upon themselves, with people's lives in their hands.

The least dangerous path was to listen. It was easy to resist leaping in to fill the silence as the stakes were so high: I didn't want to say anything that might tip Emma further into desperation. So my old habit of people-pleasing with lots of cheerful chatter was easy to set aside. It was good to find that the less I said, the more Emma talked. My approach was the basic one I had learnt on my counselling course: to act as a mirror to Emma, reflecting what she said back to her so as to try to help her re-evaluate her perspective.

It was almost surreal to hear her story. There was so much

that was familiar, as if my own experience were being played back to me. She too was torn between the conflicting demands of home and work; she too felt almost permanently anxious whatever course of action she embarked on, as well as worrying about the paths she hadn't taken.

My main value to Emma, it emerged, was that I was someone who had suffered depression and was getting better. It wasn't just about listening. The greatest salve I seemed to be able to deliver was this sense that I had recovered. Emma was reassured by hearing, again and again, that this too would pass, just I had been reassured by hearing the same mantra.

I was electrified when I found that sometimes I could provide exactly the mundane detail or particular approach that could make a small difference to Emma. She liked the prayers and poems I sent her, a particular favourite being Christina Rossetti's 'Up-Hill', with its promise of eventual rest. She was finding the experience of unremitting anxiety utterly exhausting, just as I had.

> *Does the road wind up-hill all the way?*
> *Yes, to the very end.*
> *Will the day's journey take the whole long day?*
> *From morn to night, my friend.*
>
> *But is there for the night a resting-place?*
> *A roof for when the slow dark hours begin.*
> *May not the darkness hide it from my face?*
> *You cannot miss that inn.*
>
> *Shall I meet other wayfarers at night?*
> *Those who have gone before.*

Then must I knock, or call when just in sight?
They will not keep you standing at that door.

Shall I find comfort, travel-sore and weak?
Of labour you shall find the sum.
Will there be beds for me and all who seek?
Yea, beds for all who come.

Much of what I said was very practical and would apply to anyone who was seriously ill, whatever the cause, just as many of the poems might comfort the unwell, whatever they were suffering from. Emma was finding it hard to eat solid food, as I had. We talked about the kind of soups that might help her rebuild herself, the kind of stretching exercises that could unwind her knotted body.

When she called to say she wouldn't be ringing any more because she felt so much better, my face was wet with tears, this time of joy. She began to thank me, but it was for me to thank her, I said. She had given me the confidence to believe that I might be of some use to others. That was her gift to me, and I was grateful. Somehow the air tasted different when I put down the phone.

Late November 2008

Gradually, I talked on the phone to more women who had fallen ill under the stress of looking after children. But I also began to speak to all sorts of other people who had been felled by depression, men included. I began sending letters to friends sharing my experience, with a copy of the poems that helped. The letters became the starting point for this memoir.

Typically, I would first get a call from someone close to a person who was suffering, asking if I could possibly talk to them. It was impossible to know whether I made a difference, since calling me was just one of several other steps they were courageously taking. But the calls kept coming.

There was one certain benefit for me. I knew that when I was listening I was totally absorbed, back in the flow, just as a return to the office had been a refreshing dive into another life away from my own chattering mind after I had first been ill. I felt suspended in a web of the significance of others. It was my acupuncturist's mantra: to live in the present. I was always astonished at the end of a conversation how quickly the time had flown.

The downside was the long calls. As I wasn't working in the classic therapeutic context of a timed fifty-minute slot, these conversations could run for ages. There was a particularly challenging period when I was away on holiday, but I didn't want those calling me to know.

I had to be careful to balance the benefits of helping without trying too hard to please: the work might prove both the panacea, but also the problem. Reaching out to others shouldn't lead me back into the despair I was trying to help them overcome.

January 2009

At times I knew I was out of my depth. I felt uneasy that I wasn't trained and I was aware that a prerequisite of training was to have had therapy yourself. Trying to understand someone else is impossible if you don't fully understand yourself. But I had tried therapy and it hadn't made any difference.

Only now did I realise the obvious: it wasn't therapy in itself that was at fault; I just hadn't found the right person. Sebastian encouraged me to keep trying. It had never been the case that I didn't need help: I was still prone to searing anxiety with its attendant physical symptoms. But I'd had bad luck with my first two therapists. It was partly their approach, and partly because I'd wanted to avoid confronting the difficult feelings that I feared might surface. Now I was ready to try again, partly to ease my worry about the ambiguity of my position as I tried to help others but chiefly because my ongoing troubles meant I felt I had no choice.

Once again, January was a particular low point after yet another exhausting Christmas. Despite Sebastian's entreaties, I seemed incapable of scaling back the festivities, the lists of people to please and the presents to be dispensed. Perhaps it was due to my competitive side, or because part of me wanted to be considered the queen of good cheer.

The result was the return of my early waking and gnawing anxiety in the pit of my stomach. I lost my car keys so often I took to wearing them on a string around my neck. I had fits of rage over my scattiness, chiefly directed at myself.

Once again I embarked on trying to find the right therapist. This time I knew it was no good going to see someone who lived far away. And I didn't want someone who didn't talk but just listened – a 'yes' therapist, as they are known. I needed proper feedback.

I found therapist number three thanks to another recommendation, this time from a friend whose symptoms and behaviour were astonishingly similar to mine. She had been transformed in the time she had been seeing her therapist, 'reborn and given a second chance at being and behaving differently', as she put it. This is my most heartfelt advice to anyone embarking on therapy: get a recommendation from a friend who is like you, who has been helped, and see whoever they have seen.

February 2009

My first encounter with Sarah instantly felt different from any previous experiences with therapists. She practised with three other therapists in the anonymous basement flat of a large brick house in a pleasant town square. There was nothing personal in her consulting room; indeed, we moved between two rooms depending on availability. Both had white walls, fitted beige carpets and a pair of grey armchairs.

Her timekeeping was punctilious. If I was a few minutes early, I waited in the hall even if Sarah was pottering around making herself a cup of herbal tea in the miniature kitchen under the front steps, and I was careful not to chat. We would start bang on the hour and end five minutes before the next. The whole set-up felt businesslike in a way that seeing someone in their own home had not. Psychiatrists referred clients to Sarah. She had had a long career and was clearly in demand. Within a few weeks she was able to estimate how long we would need to work together: for around thirty sessions.

The natural starting point was to flash a light back on my childhood: our adult behaviour has deep taproots in our earliest years, notwithstanding the importance of challenges we meet in adult life. Sarah's brand of therapy was known as Cognitive Analytical Therapy. It combined CBT techniques with an analytical approach, which very broadly meant tracing emotional issues back to childhood in a way developed by Freud.

The first step was for me to become more aware of my feelings. Humans are icebergs, she told me: the part you can see is greatly outweighed by the part you can't. This vast subconscious is an altogether murkier realm than the sunnier side on display. Jung, who developed Freud's ideas further, believed in a vast unconscious world of dreams and myths shared by the whole of mankind. So often we are not consciously aware of what we are feeling or desiring. And the starting point for developing more awareness is childhood.

As we talked I began to realise that I had felt easily rejected as a child, despite the constant, relentless encouragement and reassurance of my parents. I always seemed to need more. Possibly my parents had fostered anxiety by being so supportive: I was never left to cry on my own or to pull myself together. Unwittingly, by scooping me up and trying to soothe my worries, they had deprived me of the chance to discover that I could handle my fears myself. Avoidance actually made the anxiety worse.

I was reminded of one of our own children, who at times felt to me like a kettle with a perforated base. However much love and boosting I poured in, all my efforts seemed to drain straight through. It now occurred to me that perhaps I would be a better mother by trying to coax the children to confront their fears themselves.

My early anxiety had translated into being something of a striver, always trying hard to please and to do well: I was polite, non-confrontational, hard-working and dutiful. I always used to read my essays and stories to my mother for approval: so does one of my daughters.

I was sensitive to the point that I could easily become unwell. I relived one particular episode when as an eleven-year-old I had watched *Black Beauty*, which culminates in the brutal clubbing of a pet otter. While other children might have been momentarily upset, I took to my bed for an entire day and night. My mother ended up summoning a doctor. Highly sensitive children who seem to feel things more deeply than their peers may prove more vulnerable to depression as adults, Sarah explained. This was especially true if during adolescence they retained that vivid sensitivity.

We paused in my account of my background and Sarah continued her more general explanation about the roots of depression. Some characteristics that predisposed people to suffer the condition were genetic, she said, some were prompted by the environment. It was impossible to completely disentangle them; rather there was a delicate dance between the two. This holds true for virtually any condition you can think of, mental or physical. Take obesity, for example: in an environment where food is plentiful, those with a genetic propensity to obesity will put on weight as that tendency is 'switched on'. Were the same population to be moved *en masse* to a country suffering a famine, those characteristics would stay 'switched off'.

There is no doubt that today's environment is challenging for all parents, but mothers in particular. We can make choices, but whatever we choose we are haunted by the options we foreclosed. If we work, we worry we are not there for our children, and if we don't, we worry about the professional road we didn't travel. We often end up trying to compete on all fronts, managing badly and suffering the low self-esteem that is fertile breeding ground for depression.

In this kind of dance, it is also unhelpful to 'blame' outside circumstances or the manner in which a child was brought up, Sarah continued. It is more a question of how each individual experiences these factors. To one child, they may be a stimulus to growth; to another, a trigger for anxiety. Whatever the external 'truth', it is the child's feelings and the child's construction of reality that matter. These feelings develop into their 'core beliefs'. Different children in the same family will experience their upbringing differently, and therefore grow up absorbing different sets of 'core beliefs'.

Uncovering and labelling these feelings and investigating how they had solidified into beliefs was the central process of the therapy. I would often begin to explain in detail the events of a particular day, but Sarah would swiftly lead me on to try to identify the feelings that underpinned what had happened. The events themselves were unimportant. Indeed, I began to realise that although the events were seemingly diverse – a party we hadn't been asked to, a phone call that wasn't returned, the criticism of a friend, an article that had been rejected – the feelings they provoked in me were very similar. Nor was it a case of trying to change those feelings; rather, the aim was to accept them. Again and again Sarah explained: it is what you feel, both then and now, that matters, how you experience events rather than the events themselves. There is no external meaning: no one's reality is identical to anyone else's.

The first few sessions were dominated by actually working out what my feelings were. It helped to begin by sitting quietly and spending a few minutes paying attention to my breathing before we began. When Sarah first asked me how I was feeling, I would answer 'tired' or 'stressed'. But, as she explained, these are thoughts, not feelings. A thought may bear no connection to truth. After a few months, I learnt to identify and say out loud, 'I'm feeling angry/happy/sad/frightened' – the four core feelings. She helped me make the transition from saying 'I am sad' to 'I feel sad', thereby identifying a transient state rather than defining my whole self. By learning to be aware of this stream of feelings, we can identify less with each one and choose our response in a more autonomous, less automatic way.

April 2010

As the sessions continued, we turned to my adolescence. I had enjoyed my time at school but it was a highly competitive environment and at times short on praise. It increased my hunger for reassurance. I typically felt I was not good enough, however well I might supposedly have done.

Being fearful of rejection and needing constant reassurance translated into trying to garner more and more outward measures of success as a bulwark to such uncomfortable feelings. It meant applying high standards – at times ridiculously high – and being constantly busy, thereby avoiding any examination of the feelings that might lurk beneath.

Then, as an adult, the faster I moved, the more meetings and dates and appointments that filled my diary, the more I numbed myself to those uncomfortable feelings. Others might turn to alcohol or drugs to insulate themselves from the question of who they really are. I kept busy – probably the most socially acceptable form of addictive behaviour.

As we emerged into the world, in 1983, my generation of eighteen-year-olds had plenty of different lodestars of success to aspire to. We wanted not only to be career girls but great mothers and to fit into our skinny jeans, too. There were a lot of boxes to tick and I, like so many others, was trying to tick them all.

Tick them I did through my twenties, working hard, getting married and having a family. Outwardly, I might have seemed to be bursting with the self-confidence born of all these supposed achievements. This was probably why the depression had surprised many of my acquaintances. To those who didn't know me well, there seemed a mismatch between the outward show of competence and chutzpah and the inner life of a person with a depressive illness. I was like the swimmer in Stevie Smith's famous poem, 'Not Waving but Drowning': apparently swimming along fine, but actually struggling to stay afloat.

> *Nobody heard him, the dead man,*
> *But still he lay moaning:*
> *I was much further out than you thought*
> *And not waving but drowning.*
>
> *Poor chap, he always loved larking*
> *And now he's dead*
> *It must have been too cold for him his heart gave way,*
> *They said.*
>
> *Oh, no no no, it was too cold always*
> *(Still the dead one lay moaning)*
> *I was much too far out all my life*
> *And not waving but drowning.*

As Sarah explained, outward self-confidence is not the same as self-esteem. The latter is born of an inner self-acceptance rather than reliance on external measures of success, be they exam results, career success or material markers such as cars or houses.

Often, those who seem the most self-confident may actually suffer the lowest self-esteem: they have spent their lives achieving according to the standards of others, instead of accepting themselves as they are. Thus the reports of brilliant

A-grade students who are captains of the hockey team but have also tried to kill themselves.

The box-ticking had become increasingly hard to pull off as my life progressed and the demands grew. I was on an achievement treadmill and the speed setting was too high. One explanation of the illness was that trying to be simultaneously a perfect wife, friend, colleague, employee and mother was exhausting. The result for me was a breakdown. I had been driven mad attempting perfection, skewered on my generation's desire to excel at doing it all.

I learnt that trying to please on multiple fronts was particularly common both in women and in those who suffer from depression. Sarah told me that some psychologists believe more women than men get depressed because they set themselves unattainable targets. Hearing this, I was suffused with relief. It felt wonderful to hear an expert confirm that I was not alone and many other women felt the same way as me.

Unsurprisingly, I badly wanted to please Sarah, too. I often started sessions by saying how much better I was doing, that I had noticed I was less anxious. 'What does this remind you of?' she would ask. 'Trying to pass exams at school,' I realised. Luckily, she would stop me before I could launch into an impassioned outburst. 'What I really wanted to say is that everything feels different now and it's all thanks to YOU, and you are MARVELLOUS, and here's a present that has your name on it.' When I confessed this niggling need, we both laughed. Sometimes that was the only way to cope with the intensity of the sessions, the experience of several realisations all at once, cascading into each other and demanding to be understood.

Another revelation was noticing how everybody creates illusions of who we are, shoring up our sense of self. My self-image was based on trying to combine all my different roles as perfectly as I could, to win as much reassurance as possible that I was acceptable. When I could no longer sustain all these roles, my very identity was called into question. I fell apart as the curtain of my own delusion was ripped away.

More and more, I began to see how my personality made me a target for depression. Now I could see where all the automatic thoughts – 'I'm not good enough', 'They don't like me', 'I've done something wrong' – were coming from. In turn, it was these thoughts that compelled me to take on too much: I was constantly telling myself I had to try harder.

I also realised how many of my automatic thoughts had to do with fear. There had been more than an undercurrent of fear beneath all that trying to please and being seen to be perfect. There was a fear of not being liked, of not being good enough, not holding everything together, a fear of failure and my own vulnerability. Fear is a prime characteristic of depression.

If being fearful had contributed to the onset of depression, once I had been ill I was naturally fearful that the illness would come back. This can become a self-fulfilling prophecy, just as it had in my own second breakdown. I am frightened of becoming ill; fear feeds the depressive state; as a result I become ill.

Psychologists who lead so-called 'happiness courses' know this. One begins his five-day course by asking whether it will make anyone content.* His answer to his own question is no. But that need not matter, he adds, if you can learn not to be frightened. You will never be happy as long as you are afraid of your sadness. You don't have to like your unhappiness, but you do have to learn not to be afraid of it.

* Dr Robert Holden, founder of the Happiness Project.

Chapter Seventeen

Joy Illimited

2010 TO 2012

June 2010

As spring turned to summer, Sarah and I moved from examining what lay behind the depression and the automatic thoughts to trying to do something about them. She took a sheet of paper and began to plot a map of all the different Rachels that coexisted, how I moved between these different selves and the rules of behaviour I had created around my different identities. Here, in this place, is anger; here is sadness; here is joy; here is fear.*

Unlike my previous therapists, she was both guide and instructor. She didn't believe in therapists who kept quiet, she said. Their patients were often in distress and in need of help; it would be irresponsible to leave them alone. Yet the process was delicate. Her aim was to make herself redundant by teaching the patient to become their own guide.

---

* A mind map is a diagram used to visually outline information, often around a single word placed in the centre of the page to which associated ideas and concepts are added. The term was first popularised by the British author and psychologist Tony Buzan, Such maps are often used as a speedy way of taking notes or explaining a complicated idea. Their use has since been developed in many areas, including psychotherapy.

I had a particular pattern of recruiting others to my cause rather than relying on myself: I had leant on Sebastian and my mother, recruiting Felicity, Lucy and now Sarah for support and validation, rather than looking inwards and asking myself what I needed. Turning to others had also been a way of avoiding unpleasant feelings, particularly fear and anger, rather than confronting them and acknowledging what I was feeling. 'What are you thinking? What are you feeling?' was Sarah's mantra. Her challenge as we sat opposite each other on our grey armchairs was to avoid telling me what to think or feel and to help me work it out for myself. Then I needed to be compassionate to myself as I identified painful feelings of fear or shame, rather than trying to avoid them by rushing to confide in others.

Sarah's stress on the need to be compassionate and gentle with myself was the key difference between our sessions and my previous work on my own with the CBT book. Then, I had tended to belittle the reasons for my worries as trivial and narcissistic. Yet, as Sarah explained, worrying about whether I had upset a friend, for example, made perfect sense if my self-esteem and wellbeing were inextricably linked to the approval of others, which is often the case for women.* 'You have placed an awful lot of power over your happiness in the hands of others,' she explained. 'No wonder it feels frightening to have offended someone.'

She was practical. Every time I felt like ringing Sebastian when I felt angry or sad or in need, I should try to wait for a few minutes, then a few more, till I could withstand those

---

* Close female friendships are identified as a possible cause of anxiety in women by Daniel Freeman in *The Stressed Sex: Uncovering the Truth About Men, Women and Mental Health* (Oxford University Press, 2013).

feelings without ringing him at all. If I was finding the wait unbearable, a good trick was to concentrate on my breathing. It was about practising new habits, just as if I were learning tennis, but in this instance, the habit was of connecting my mind with sensations in my body. This in turn would bring my anxiety levels down.

It was as if she had ignited a pilot light, but it was for me to keep the flame alight. Throughout the process, she encouraged me to keep acknowledging feelings that hitherto I had denied or avoided, especially anger, which I had always found too frightening to acknowledge. Simultaneously, she counselled me to be gentle with myself as I did so.

One common explanation of depression is that it is rage turned in on itself, she explained. It had never occurred to me that I might be angry as well as frightened. Our family's culture was one of consensus, and rarely did anyone raise his or her voice. But though it might not have been obvious at the time, I realised that beneath all the trying to please was a complicated fury that I began to unpick: a fury with myself that I was unable to say no and that I kept on striving to manage and be a conduit for other people's supposed pleasure to the point where I became unwell. I had not realised it at the time, but I was angry about trying to look after George as a baby and also support Sebastian's political career. The truth was that I was often angry, but because the feeling was so frightening I would do anything to avoid it. Then in turn I would be even more angry with myself for denying my feelings in the first place.

There was a kick of anger, too, that I had been denied my time with my children when I had been so unwell. And of course, I realised that sometimes I was angry with Sarah. Please, I sometimes wanted to scream, don't ask me how I feel.

The difference was that with Sarah, as I told her, I was beginning to be less frightened of the anger.

As Sarah explained, repressing such anger is exhausting because essentially you are not being true to yourself in relation to others. I was good at maintaining comfortable relationships by giving up on genuine ones. By acknowledging my angry self, I would be less weary. It could actually be a healing anger, and could be expressed safely and in an adult way, by learning to say no. Rather than being frightened that saying no would lead to rejection, I should focus instead on what I was saying yes to: I was affirming the truth of my real feelings.

Other 'selves' I had constructed to deal with challenges in the past could be unhelpful: the pleasing self, for example, which had so often led in the past to exhaustion and feeling overwhelmed. Again, Sarah explained, this was a very common character trait among those susceptible to depression.

Our unconscious mind has a design fault: it has no sense of time and can keep on harking back to an event or person from long ago, sometimes to traumatic effect. Increasingly, when strong feelings came up, I became adept at spotting whether my past was hijacking my present: was I feeling like a frightened six-year-old, for example? The ultimate aim of the therapy was to emerge more psychologically integrated, to knit these different aspects of myself together.

These 'selves' were all variations on the 'trying to please' Rachel, the self that dispensed thank-you letters and presents, the self that needed constant reassurance and approval and was fearful of rejection. It was hardly surprising that I had become overwhelmed, given my propensity to try to please too many people and do too much.

Confusingly, in the eyes of myself and others, there was

also another Rachel, a more party-loving, adult, self-confident Rachel who coexisted with the at times anguish-ridden, child-like, anxious Rachel who wished for the regard of others and lacked a strong sense of herself. It became clear that if I wanted to guard against depression, I needed to take better care of my more anxious self and in turn nurture the adult person I could also be.

It was easy enough in theory to abandon my people-pleasing self and develop my resilience, but of course actual change was far harder. These were long-ingrained patterns going back decades. In his book *Buddha's Brain*, Rick Hanson compares toxic feelings to Velcro: they stick. Meanwhile, positive feelings are more like Teflon: they slide off easily.*

Sarah's response was hugely helpful: I should stop seeing the process as some sort of examination that I would pass by beating the bad feelings. Rather, I should learn to be gentle on myself and accept what I felt in a non-judgemental way: beware of 'shouldas, oughtas, couldas and musts'**, she would say. You feel what you feel. Life has its night and day. I had to learn to be comfortable with my own shadows and those cast by others, to live with my mind's chatter and accept it with kindness and curiosity – the word derives from the Latin for

---

* Rick Hanson with Richard Meadows, *Buddha's Brain: The Practical Neuroscience of Happiness, Love, and Wisdom* (New Harbinger Publications, 2009).

** The danger of 'shoulds' and 'musts' was highlighted by Albert Ellis, who invented Rational Emotive Behaviour Therapy (REBT), a precursor of CBT. Ellis's ideas and key teachings are incorporated in some (but sadly not all) of the many types of CBT. I found the best introduction to his work was *How to Stubbornly Refuse to Make Yourself Miserable about Anything – Yes, Anything!* by Albert Ellis (Carol Publishing Group, 1999).

'to care for'. The less harsh I was on myself, the less harsh I would be in judging others.

The challenge was how to behave differently when the familiar feelings came up; how to look after the frightened child, for example, if that was where the feelings led. I drew on imagining how I would behave, as a mother, if I were comforting that child. Sarah likened the process to creating an internal map: over time I would become more adept at navigating between the different Rachels that populated my internal psychodrama, as if they were familiar roads on which I was used to travelling. I would be able to recognise the road, without necessarily having to take it.

'Imagine you are a king sitting at a table surrounded by his knights, all telling different stories. Over time you will become more and more adept at identifying the different voices and the familiar feelings they evoke. You can even label them. Oh yes: "Here comes the need for reassurance." Or: "Here is that inability to be criticised"; or: "Here is that feeling of rejection"; or: "Here is that Rachel who seeks the approval of others." Or: "There is that voice telling you to keep on striving." Become a curious observer of yourself, develop a third eye. Give yourself space and distance to recognise your own self as someone worthy of the compassion and empathy you hope to give to others.'

You can no more stop these voices than stop a river flowing but you can learn that they are neither good nor bad, and that you don't need to judge yourself one way or another for having such feelings. Sarah taught me to say 'judging, judging' to myself whenever I did so – which was often. Perhaps viewing the destructive thoughts as a temporary weather pattern could help, Sarah suggested. You wouldn't blame yourself for the fact that it was stormy outside. Equally, you can let the storm in your head pass, and make your own weather.

The more you can just accept fearful feelings, for example, the more their intensity will diminish. It was a bit like Dr Fischer's approach to beating insomnia: the more you resist, the more something persists. By pausing and recognising those various voices you may be able to decide which one you wish to believe, and give yourself time to hear a different one.

Good therapy allows patterns played out in previous relationships to become obvious. Sarah told me she was constantly aware that she mustn't become yet another person I relied on. The real breakthrough would be learning to face up to difficult feelings on my own and to rely on myself. 'Give your own reassuring voice time to assert itself,' she would say. Look after that nervous child: give yourself a hug.

'The different voice may be a voice that is more appropriate for the grown-up Rachel, a more compassionate and accepting voice that dovetails more closely with the facts of your life now,' Sarah said. 'Concerns will begin to settle in to their rightful place. Return yourself as a friend to yourself. Get alongside yourself in a kind, compassionate and curious way. Only by experiencing these strong feelings will you be able to change and free yourself from a life of anxious striving.'

I imagined myself as being rather like a demented hen that had been screeching around a farmyard, finally to find a comfortable patch of straw where I could sit quietly as the ruffling of my feathers ceased.

July 2010

At one session we discussed a nerve-racking party for a book launch coming up that very evening. Many of the people who would be there had in the past triggered huge anxiety and plenty of automatic thoughts: they were contemporaries who were ambitious and successful. I told Sarah that even thinking about the event felt like entering the lion's den, the sort of dread you feel when you narrowly miss being hit by a car and your stomach lurches. My typical automatic thought in this situation was 'I'm not good enough.' In my self-centred way – another characteristic of the depressive – I imagined the company judging me and finding me wanting.

'It is only the lion's den of your own mind,' Sarah replied. The other guests weren't going to be judging me. In fact, they almost certainly wouldn't be thinking about me at all. As one saying has it, at twenty you worry what people think. At forty, you no longer worry what they think. At sixty, you realise they are not thinking about you at all. If there was any judging going on, I was the one doing it. I was judging myself. It was one of those pesky inner voices again: judging, judging.

Sarah made me get up, close my eyes and imagine I was walking around the room arm in arm with the person of whom I was most scared. At first I felt like a frightened child. But the slower I breathed, and the slower I walked, the more I realised that I wasn't actually that six-year-old anymore, and had no need to be so. The fear diminished as I allowed a new voice to be heard. This Rachel was trying to live in the present rather than worrying about the past or future, and to identify exactly what I felt right now and whether those feelings were appropriate.

I now knew that I had a choice. Instead of running away from that fearful voice or seeking to drown it out by getting reassurance from others, I could accept and manage it. I sat down, elated.

Later, at the door of the party, I stopped, breathed, remembered my rehearsal with Sarah, heard her voice in my head, and gave a metaphorical hug to the frightened Rachel. Then, I turned to greet a different Rachel. The fearful Rachel momentarily returned when I couldn't see anyone I knew. But she disappeared again when another guest confided in me that she found the event daunting as well. An inkling of lightness in the air grew. Anxious as I may have been, it was also a matter of fact that I enjoyed enormous blessings, the more confident Rachel reminded me: healthy children, a devoted husband, a home and financial security. Fear turned to shared laughter with my fellow guest – the easiest way to be utterly in the present.

August 2010

Having therapy also began to change my relationship with Sebastian. It was he who, over the years, had borne the brunt of my need for reassurance, along with my mother. My therapist prompted me to consider what that must be like for him, and how it had locked us into a particular pattern. How much less exhausting it might be for him if I became aware of, and reduced, my demands.

Though I was loath to admit it, my neediness meant I tried to grip life tightly around me. I looked back on the breakdowns and realised that during both episodes I had desperately tried to control myself and others, starting with my forlorn attempt to force myself to keep going as the perfect mother when I had first stayed awake all night.

Mental health, like physical health, was about being more flexible. The more relaxed and accepting I could be of myself, the less fearful I became, the less I imposed unreasonable expectations on myself, the more relaxed and accepting I could be of others. I was not just liberating myself but liberating others, too. Perhaps that was what the Marianne Williamson quotation I had been given was really about.

As I began to dismantle the scaffolding that I had previously created around me and Sebastian, I was able to see him more clearly as a person independent of me and my needs. I was humbled as I realised the extent of my demands, never more so than when I had been unwell and required continuous reassurance. I was shocked to realise the extent to which life had revolved around me. It was time for me to consider the family's needs. It gave me an extra incentive to change.

September 2010

One autumn morning I was chatting with my mother, telling her a little about therapy. I explained the patterns that Sarah and I had identified, especially how much reassurance I always seemed to need. I had been very needy as a little girl, my mother confirmed, and then reflected that she herself wasn't a very 'huggy' person, or one who verbalised her undoubted devotion and approval. Her own parents, bringing up their five children in the 1940s and 1950s, were steeped in a culture of stiff upper lips and a wariness of verbal emotional outbursts, even positive ones. It hadn't bothered her. She had always been certain of their silent love for her, and I should be certain of hers for me, too.

The exchange provided a piece of evidence to help explain something of my neediness and I was immensely grateful to my mother for volunteering it. She sent me a bunch of flowers later that day, with a note attached saying 'Fresh start time, All love M'. I felt, if that were possible, even more love for her than I had before.

My relationship with my own children changed, too. Sarah had said this was why she particularly liked working with mothers: if you help a mother, you also help her children; there is a chance of preventing damaging patterns being handed down. I learnt to become more attuned to perfection-ist and people-pleasing tendencies in the children. I endeavoured to strengthen their ability to say no, to allow themselves to explore what it felt like to be angry and to process difficult feelings. I wanted them to learn to be happy to be alone with themselves and not to always recruit others to help them in difficult times, as I had done. My constant mantra was that they should be kind to themselves. The kinder they were to themselves, the kinder they could be to others.

My habit had always been to say 'Love you' when I tucked the children up in bed. I would wait for them to say 'Love you' back. If they didn't, I would say 'Where's my "Love you"?' and chide them if it was not forthcoming. Now I realised that in doing so I was asking them to reassure me, reversing the roles of mother and child. I stopped prompting them to tell me I was loved. I had to develop my own inner voice to deliver those shots of reassurance.

In some ways, having so many children proved a blessing when it came to trying to ease up on my efforts to please everyone. It was impossible to meet all their needs at all times, so I had to develop a more reasonable, realistic voice about what I could and could not offer them.

October 2010

One night Charlotte was furious because I had been absorbed in doing a puzzle with Arthur. Blotchy-faced and quivering like a bird with puffed-up feathers, she lay with her head down on the pillow, avoiding my gaze. I lay next to her and stroked her back. Instead of telling her that I would make it up to her the next day and instead of trying to rescue her from her hateful feelings, I waited silently. Very gently, I asked her to talk about how angry she felt, how hard it could be at times to be part of a big family. Just as I was learning to explore the contours of my fear, anger and grief, so was she. The more she felt listened to and that it was safe to express her feelings, the more her anger visibly dissolved as she felt her true self was acceptable. The problem was not the anger itself, but denying its existence.

Sometimes it wasn't possible for me to spend time with her, we agreed. She volunteered that she could play with Katherine instead. It was a revelation: freed of my attempts to answer all her needs, she had found her own solution. Perhaps she would avoid some of my troubles; with luck, I might now be able to help her do so. We as a family were all growing up together.

November 2010

After nearly a year of talking to Sarah, something magical began to happen that winter. The intensity of my anxious feelings began to diminish. A certain spontaneity broke out in the house: there would be the odd burst of what the children called my 'jazzy dancing', even as Christmas, always a harbinger of worry, approached. I developed a habit of bursting into song, an enthusiasm that dovetailed with an ever-increasing love of birdsong and a desire to encourage it with endless bird feeders.

My mother nudged me towards another poem, knowing my love of birds as symbols of hope: Thomas Hardy's 'The Darkling Thrush'. How could I not have discovered it before? I loved the contrast between the first two verses evoking deathly winter and the joy heralded in the third verse with the burst of the thrush's song: 'At once a voice arose among/The bleak twigs overhead/In a full-hearted evensong/Of joy illimited.'

'Joy illimited', with its suggestion of uncircumscribed abundance and love, fitted my new mood perfectly. Here is the full poem, as the sense of joy is only fully experienced by reading of the bleakness that precedes it.

> *I leant upon a coppice gate*
> *When Frost was spectre-grey,*
> *And Winter's dregs made desolate*
> *The weakening eye of day.*
> *The tangled bine-stems scored the sky*
> *Like strings of broken lyres,*
> *And all mankind that haunted nigh*
> *Had sought their household fires.*
>
> *The land's sharp features seemed to be*
> *The Century's corpse outleant,*
> *His crypt the cloudy canopy,*

Joy Illimited

The wind his death-lament.
The ancient pulse of germ and birth
Was shrunken hard and dry,
And every spirit upon earth
Seemed fervourless as I.

At once a voice arose among
The bleak twigs overhead
In a full-hearted evensong
Of joy illimited;
An aged thrush, frail, gaunt and small,
In blast-beruffled plume,
Had chosen thus to fling his soul
Upon the growing gloom.

So little cause for carolings
Of such ecstatic sound
Was written on terrestrial things
Afar or nigh around,
That I could think there trembled through
His happy good-night air
Some blessed Hope, whereof he knew
And I was unaware.

I rushed to tell Sarah of my new-found love of singing, both the warbling of what Sebastian called my feathered friends in the garden and my own. My enthusiasm proved no surprise to her: spontaneity and authenticity are close bedfellows, she said.

From our first session, Sarah had focused on how our emotions take bodily expression. Unlike some psychotherapists, who only concentrate on the 'psyche' part of the illness, she was attuned to the effects of sleep, diet, exercise and breathing as weapons in the battle against anxiety. She would ask me to describe the precise feelings in my body evoked by fear or anger, and to use breathing to slow my heart rate and regain a sense of calm. One particular trick I already used was simply to close one nostril with a finger to slow down my breathing. We also practised standing against a wall to create a sense of security, sending my breath through my body, right down to my feet, rooting myself in the earth, thereby creating a sense of stability as if I were a well-rooted tree.

As we worked on changing the feelings in my body, I learnt how neurological patterns were shifting, too. As I learnt to think and feel differently, and allow myself to hear different voices, I would no longer be reinforcing those negative neural pathways and experiencing the same feelings over and over again. The more often you practise different connections, the speedier they in turn become, bypassing the slow, deliberate circuits of the brain in favour of more immediate, intuitive responses. It's the same mechanism that permits us, after years of driving, not to think about gear changes as we did when we were still learners. It was as if I were learning to drive a different car.

Very slowly, given the strength of my old negative thoughts, I began to withdraw from identifying with my fearful, anxious self and create new thought patterns born of different feelings. Incredibly, I could feel that the process was actually changing my brain chemistry: happy thoughts were reinforcing happy neural pathways, reconfiguring my brain.* I might enjoy a

* Ruby Wax's book *Sane New World: Taming the Mind* (Hodder & Stoughton< 2013) is among the best explanations I've read of how our brains work, how we can rewire our thinking and how we can become the master rather than the slave of negative thoughts.

different relationship with myself, a new sense of untrammelled freedom. I might welcome a different Rachel, who had existed all along but had hitherto been hidden.

December 2010

A letter arrived in the post from a friend who also had depression. It contained the poem 'Love After Love' by Derek Walcott, which imagines this sense of having a new relationship with yourself – an uncanny echo of George Herbert's 'Love', a poem I had long enjoyed. It seemed heaven-sent and perfectly summed up my new awareness.

> *The time will come*
> *when, with elation*
> *you will greet yourself arriving*
> *at your own door, in your own mirror*
> *and each will smile at the other's welcome,*
>
> *and say, sit here. Eat.*
> *You will love again the stranger who was your self.*
> *Give wine. Give bread. Give back your heart*
> *to itself, to the stranger who has loved you*
>
> *all your life, whom you ignored*
> *for another, who knows you by heart.*
> *Take down the love letters from the bookshelf,*
>
> *the photographs, the desperate notes,*
> *peel your own image from the mirror.*
> *Sit. Feast on your life.*

I took the poem's message to be that the only way to live comfortably was to start getting along with yourself, ignoring the need to be acceptable to others. Along the way I could ditch being perfect for being realistic, and give up trying hard for being good enough.

All this requires courage. The word courage derives from *coeur*, the French for heart. I needed to find that courage to be wholehearted, in spite of my imperfections, and to know myself, to unbreak my heart. The more you know and accept every last bit of good and bad in yourself, the less you are vulnerable to outside snipers or inner voices attacking you: you already know and accept your own shortcomings.

Maybe the difficulty of the process was part of the point and could in itself be rewarding. If we could feel better without effort, then it probably wouldn't feel as good. The search for meaning could itself be meaningful: it was about the happiness of pursuit, not the pursuit of happiness.

Chapter Eighteen

Ordinary Human Unhappiness

2012 TO THE PRESENT DAY

I continued to have therapy until the summer of 2012. By then I had begun to be annoyed by the way the therapy appointments cut into my day, even if it was only once a week. I began to skip the odd session and make excuses for lengthening the gaps between them. All of which were good signs, Sarah said, that I wanted to rely on myself and move on from my old patterns of being soothed and reassured by others. So we stopped. I hugged Sarah goodbye and we both cried a bit. There would be more struggles ahead, she said, and my battle to soothe and reassure myself and others would continue.

Thanks to therapy, though, I now have a new voice inside my head, alongside the other voices that I internalised as a child and through my life. Whenever I feel troubled or on the verge of trouble, I know to consult my internal map and that it is up to me to choose which road I take. Yes, I may still get lost from time to time, but I have the tools I can use to get me back on the right track.

Sarah was as professional and skilful at ending therapy as she had been throughout. She had established from the outset that the therapy needed to be limited in time as it was particularly important that I grew to rely on myself. I had also been struck by a friend's comment that long-term therapy is not the answer to mental health problems: a life that works is. I was lucky. I was beginning to reclaim a life that worked by aiming to be good enough.

A second stroke of good fortune was to find part-time work that boosted my confidence. A friend who had embraced the digital world, in particular her iPad and iPhone, had spotted the potential of this new technology and envisaged creating an app of children's poetry. The app would consist of around 270 children's poems, divided into sections by category and age, with recordings of famous actors reading the poems. Knowing that I was a poetry fan, she asked me to help her select the poems for inclusion. We decided to give 10 per cent of sales to Save the Children.

Though I loved the work, this was a considerable leap into the world of new technology for me, schooled as I was in newspapers and 'old' media. Developing an app was not in my natural orbit at all. But I was drawn to being involved with a poetry project. Not only had healing words been at the heart of my recovery; throughout the illness I felt grateful that I had been introduced to poetry at a young age by my mother. It was she who had laid down the foundations of knowledge and enjoyment that were to prove so crucial when the trapdoor opened and I plunged into illness as an adult. I had already tried to do the same for my children, reciting them short prayers from when they were babies and later tempting them with humorous verse to foster their instinctive delight in words and rhythm. If my own offspring's love of fiddling with my phone was anything to go by, creating an app might help introduce more children to poetry by embracing their technology-centred worlds.

I already had a rich collection of poems on which to draw. I had followed in my mother's footsteps and carefully written out by hand all the poems she and other friends had shared over the sixteen years since my first illness, as well as snippets of prose that had consoled or inspired me and some favourite poems from my childhood. I found it therapeutic to write each poem by hand into my red A4 students' notebook. This was something positive and tangible that had emerged from the sadness. Sometimes I mused about which objects I would grab were the house to burn down (assuming all the family were safe). It would be my notebook of poems, as well as the diaries in which I had recorded the lives of each child from their births.

We named our app 'iF Poems', after the Kipling poem. It did well: the day we launched in Apple's app store in October 2011, we raced up the charts, beating many well-known games. A leading publisher asked us to create a print anthology of the poems, and co-editing this collection returned me to working with words in a way that I knew and loved. I took particular pride in the section at the back of the book, entitled 'If you need help', of poems that might provide consolation.

Even more fulfilling were some of the opportunities that began to arise to introduce others who found life hard, in prisons, to the healing power of poetry. Working with other people made me less frightened and more confident, as I became determined to try to share the benefits of poetry with others.

These projects mean I have plenty to talk about other than how old the children are. But somehow I no longer mind: I'm happy to talk about my children. I no longer see a rigid division between 'work' and 'home', or believe that one path can ever be more valid or worthwhile than the other. I am as respectful of mothers who work as I am of mothers who stay at home with their children, though the latter are unlikely to enjoy much worldly recognition; inevitably their voices are not heard as often as those of the politicians, journalists and captains of industry who tend to command the platform in public debate.

On difficult days, the timeless ending of George Eliot's novel *Middlemarch* still consoles me. I would quote it to any mother who feels daunted about stepping off the career ladder, or indeed anyone afflicted with a tendency to perfectionism or suffering from depression, who is questioning their personal worth.

For the growing good of the world is partly dependent on unhistoric acts; and that things are not so ill with you and me as they might have been is half owing to the number who have lived faithfully a hidden life and rest in unvisited tombs.

Reflections

More than sixteen years after my first serious depressive episode, and thanks to the many people who have helped me, I seem to be managing. Perhaps I should say 'we' seem to be managing, as Sebastian is, as he has always been, by my side. A friend made me contemplate his steadfastness when she pointed out that many relationships would have crumbled in the face of the demands I had placed upon him. It is a mark of how I much I take his strength and support for granted that such a thought hadn't occurred to me.

The children I described at the start at the book are now teenagers: Edward is eighteen and more than a head taller than me. Our ten-year-old twins take the school bus on their own. Poetry is now at the heart of my own working life, as I try to continue to use the power of words as one approach to helping those with depression. I have embarked on creating an app of inspiring, consoling poetry to try to provide greater access to the balm to hurt minds from which I benefited so much.

Attitudes to depression and mental illness have changed radically since I first experienced the illness. Some of the stigma associated with the illness has gone. Having experienced a depressive illness is almost in danger of being a badge of honour. It is no longer true that people are afraid of talk about mental health in the way that they once were fearful of talking about cancer. But for all these advances, mental health charities confirm that there is still much work to be done in making mental illness acceptable, especially in the workplace.

The role of therapy in recovery is now considered much more important, while the limitations of some drug-based approaches have been realised. There are new challenges for the anxious with the twenty-four-hour call of smartphones, and information overload. We bring our own selves to our smartphone and computer screens: unsurprisingly, I struggle with being addicted to the screen rather than being present in the moment. I am also an expert at deconstructing sign-offs on texts and emails, analysing what is meant by one, two or three xxxs. Technology has also brought with it huge opportunities for helping those with mental-health problems. Crucially, online help is available twenty-four hours a day, when it may take weeks or even months to see a therapist or psychiatrist in the flesh. The suicidal can't wait. It has also allowed the mapping of mood to be far more accurate than when I was first ill: there are apps and websites which allow you to track your ups and downs, and share the information with others.*

More research is being done on the pressures facing women in particular as they try to achieve a calmer balance between work and home life. There is still no obvious path for how we should handle the multiple choices that rightly now exist.

---

* www.moodscope.com as per earlier footnote (page 85).

Levels of anxiety and depression continue to rise, and our society seems to make women more anxious than men.*

But at least the true cost of choice is now more widely appreciated. For me, the answer has been to find work about which I am passionate and which I dare to think might help others, but to value just as much my other roles as mother, wife and friend. This may not be what others define as having it all, but I certainly feel blessed by a new sense of balance in my life.

When I feel fragile, I no longer try to attend a film and a drinks party in one evening as I once did; I stay at home. If our picnic ends in chaos, it doesn't matter. Sarah has taught me to be more of a friend to myself and to be compassionate when I find life daunting. Poetry remains my companion and solace. I do my best to eat well and exercise, and have turned to antidepressants off and on over the years, as and when my doctors have felt I need help. I see my depression as something I must manage, and on the whole, I do.

For all the changes in treatment and attitudes to depression, the experience of actually having the illness hasn't altered. The fear that the depression might return constantly haunts me. It always remains, like the little rock pools on the shoreline after a tide has gone out.

Unlike the moment I fell ill, I can't pinpoint the exact moment I got better. This is a relative term. Depression has changed everything for me. I will never *not* need to manage this illness. The severity of the symptoms comes and goes. The

* Daniel Freeman and Jason Freeman, *The Stressed Sex: Uncovering the Truth About Men, Women, and Mental Health* (Oxford University Press, 2013).

illness is not me; I'm just someone managing its symptoms, in the way that many people manage many conditions.

Sometimes I can start the day with a racing heart and sweaty palms. I can feel breathless and I still occasionally throw up. When this happens, there's nothing for it but to force myself up, to let go finger by finger of the pillow I am hugging with its faint reassuring scent of Sebastian.

The very action of rising helps reverse the negative thoughts willing me to get back under the duvet. It's important that I get out of bed instantly. Even a second's delay could mean that I end up staying in bed for hours. Drinking water helps. I force myself to eat breakfast and help the children get ready for school. By about nine o'clock, the worst of the anxiety has ebbed away.

My days are filled with reminders of my illness. I still feel uneasy sitting in the centre of a café and prefer to sit by the wall. The illness has left its mark on the rest of the family too; if I get a cold, the younger children still ask if I'm going to be in bed for months and will I die? The day has the same pattern of improving as it goes on, albeit in a much less dramatic way. My bed is still an object of dread in daylight; it reminds me of all those months spent lying in it, and I avoid going anywhere near our room until bedtime. If I need a nap, I decamp to a child's room. Then I am disciplined about not resting for too long, for fear it might trigger insomnia.

On occasion I have had to return to Dr Fischer. I see my wonderful GP regularly. There have been two periods since my second major episode when I had to see him more frequently because I sensed that the depression might be returning. But I've moved from hysterical misery into 'ordinary human unhappiness', as Freud called it, and by this one measure at least, I am better.

Everyone who has suffered depression has their own way of judging the extent of their recovery. Mine is air travel. When I was ill I was tormented by the sense of being stuck inside a crashing plane. So the clearest sign that I am fully recovered is being able to fly again. The physical fear I experience on a turbulent flight is the nearest I have come to being back in my sickbed. But I have managed to get back on a plane.

I have made my peace with the idea that yes, the plane could crash, for as Montaigne put it, to philosophise is to learn how to die.* I recite my favourite prayers and poetry, breathe slowly, take care of what I eat and drink on the flight and absorb myself in a boxed set of DVDs. In some ways, flying is the moment when I marshal all the resources I have gathered over the past decade to manage the depression.

As for the future, like many who have suffered from depression, I'm always afraid the hidden rocks of a bereavement, a family drama or some other challenging event may tip me once again into anxiety and illness. Or that I will succumb for no obvious reason and all pleasure in beauty, in being loved, in friendship, and in making a home will once again be toppled and uprooted. I no longer believe I must always have an explanation for suffering.

I live in a state of constant alertness to the possibility of relapse and am ever vigilant to the bat squeaks that might hint at a return: sudden crying, or feeling that fizzy head, that feeling of death by a thousand cuts. Then all my techniques come into play with a vengeance. I try to avoid high

---

* Michel de Montaigne, *To Study Philosophy Is to Learn to Die* (1580).

levels of stress or excitement. I follow my own prescriptions on diet and exercise. I now look after myself as if I were looking after a rather nervous pet. The difference is now I know what is at stake. If I don't calm myself down, I'll get sick. A younger me didn't realise the risks I was taking. Now I have a sense of the need for self-preservation, whereas previously I had few limits. On the two occasions when I felt close to the abyss more recently, my own homespun strategies initially seemed laughable, a waste of time. And yet I haven't succumbed.

Once I came very close. Terror returned with its familiar symptoms. I identified two main sources of anxiety: first, one of the children was unhappy at school; and second, I was worried about writing this book. Was I 'over-sharing' – was it 'too much information'? Would it be any good? When a friend read a very early draft of this book, she told me that my story and the way I had told it were both insufficiently dramatic. I stopped the car to take her call. Even now I can't go down that particular street without feeling sick with nerves. I seemed to have learned nothing, still trapped in a need for approval and acceptance from others, rather than myself. There was a nice irony about getting depressed about trying to write a book about depression.

Another friend Eliza proved a saviour. No, she said, I must perservere and keep writing. I did have something to say. Without her excellent editorial advice over several years, this book would not have happened.

Some describe having depression as living with a permanent dark cloud that might descend on top of them. To me, the image of a black rainbow is more helpful. I try and remember that when the darkness descends, it only temporarily blocking the light and colour that lies behind. As Edward said, rainbows are never black in truth. And only by the blackness had I learnt to more properly appreciate the joyful colour in my life.

For there are positive changes that depression has wrought in my life. The cliché is that we are sent what we need to know, and only the most painful of experiences will effect deep change. When you are in the grip of depression, you cannot learn anything. The idea that something positive could come from such agony is as offensive as the idea that cancer could be good for you.

When you recover, it is possible to try to be grateful for the immense humanising force of depression. The illness forced me to change; it didn't make me stronger, just different. Mostly I am grateful for the bits of self-knowledge I have gained. I am attuned to the pressures that need to be resisted, both from the outside world and my own inner judging voice.

It took me two breakdowns to realise I needed to change. The first time I was sick, I was instinctively conservative, seeking to return to the familiar. Quite naturally, the life I had previously experienced seemed so much better than the horror of the illness. I wanted to recover it, and quickly. It was what I knew, what my generation had been trained to do. So I dutifully went back to work, back to tailored suits and time-tables, back to the life and roles I knew. I wished for the certainty of my previous routines.

The second time, I was so ill that I was forced to recognise I needed to change fundamentally. I had been spat out as a different person. The harshness of the second episode meant that it was no good trying to hang tightly onto my previous assumptions. Our own brokenness is a fact of life, and with it comes an appreciation of our flawed natures. I was going to have to tolerate sadness, anger, failure and uncertainty. Indeed, one definition of anxiety is an intolerance of uncertainty, which leads to a disabling caution and self-doubt.

I learnt to try to become more compassionate towards myself, as well as others who suffer – and there are many of us. Nothing humbled me more than one discussion with Dr Fischer. Yes, he agreed, I had been very ill. But many of his patients were far worse off. 'If I had to judge, you would be about in the middle in terms of the seriousness of your mental illness,' he said. I found it breathtaking that people could be more seriously ill than I had been. But now I know that others battle far worse depression with courage and bravery, often with little or no hope of recovery. It is easy to forget that your own experience is no finer or deeper or more painful than anyone else's: it is just your experience. I enjoy no special dispensation or immunity from humanity's lot.

I learnt to reassess my notions of success and failure. Being supposedly successful in a worldly sense neither spared me from illness nor made any difference in recovering from it. There are other, quieter ways of achieving, which are just as valid. Life is uncertain: sometimes dark, at other times lit up. There is a randomness to it all. I no longer make any assumptions about the future of even my most competent friends (or my own), but try to live in the present. Nor do I assume that anyone's achievements matter as much as their inner contentment. It doesn't matter how satisfactory your life appears to be or how comfortable your mattress is; you still lie there just as terrified if depression takes hold. Whatever the differences in people's backgrounds, they become alike in their experience of the horror of depression.

I've learnt to appreciate everyday moments of transcendent joy. For me these are now all the sweeter for having lived through hell. As Psalm 84 says, 'Who going through the vale of misery, use it for a well.'*

Life must be grabbed. Being ill inevitably leaves you with a sense of life's impermanence. I learnt to try to become braver, more adventurous: writing this memoir, for example, and learning to manage the fearful voice inside. The way we live, bold or not, will have been our life.

When I list it like this, it sounds as though I've learnt a lot. Some days I feel I have. Other days I don't. Knowledge and experience haven't set me free; they have only given me a sense of the limits of my understanding. The conclusion I have written sounds far more conclusive than the messy muddle of my life. On the very good days, I have moments when I glimpse the person I could be. On the less good days, at least I know the qualities of fortitude and resilience I need to find within myself. Other days, any certainties slip away.

On bad days, much as I try to remind myself of the positives of knowing what it is to suffer depression, there is no denying the sadness and suffering that it has also brought, and the sense of wasted months and years, particularly with my children when they were young. Although thankfully I now seem to be able to manage the condition, and pray I will never

* Psalm 84, verse 6, sometimes translated as 'Who passing through the valley of Baca make it a well.'

suffer another major episode, I see myself as recovered rather than fully healed.

Sadly, this prognosis is very true of mental illness generally. The outcomes are poor and sufferers must learn to manage their condition and not necessarily expect to be cured. This clearly affects the families of those who suffer, who will have to support them in the long-term.

As a mother, one obvious implication for me is how important it is to try to bring up our children to enjoy good mental health. One approach might be to teach children the rudiments of CBT so they are equipped to handle anxious situations. Another might be to try to equip parents with more skills to improve their children's emotional wellbeing, and to spot depressive tendencies early on. (Perhaps in my case, my perfectionism and the way in which I demanded too much of myself.)*

Meanwhile, even at the worst of times, I never forget Dr Fischer's card, with his firm capitals inked in blue saying 'YOU WILL GET BETTER'. It still gives me hope. In the words of Derek Mahon, 'Everything is going to be all right'.

> *How should I not be glad to contemplate*
> *the clouds clearing beyond the dormer window*
> *and a high tide reflected on the ceiling?*
> *There will be dying, there will be dying,*
> *but there is no need to go into that.*
> *The poems flow from the hand unbidden*
> *and the hidden source is the watchful heart.*

* There are free computerised CBT programmes such as moodgym.anu. edu.au, and www.llttf.com for those in their early teens,

Reflections

The sun rises in spite of everything
and the far cities are beautiful and bright.
I lie here in a riot of sunlight
watching the day break and the clouds flying.
Everything is going to be all right.

Afterword

When I finished writing this story, I asked Sebastian to read it and add his own words.

This book is about many things, but for me it's about the choices we made in our careers and about what we both learned.

I was astonished when you became ill. We both had a lot on and the usual pressures of young children. But you became very ill very quickly. Nothing prepared me for the sight of you lying on the floor screaming in pain and saying over and over 'we are going to crash we are going to crash'. You were unable to sit up or stand up. You couldn't make any sense. It seemed as though you had lost your mind. You were extraordinarily unwell when we moved you to hospital.

It happened so fast it was like a car crash in our lives. You would be hysterical for a period and that would be followed by massive sedation which knocked you out and then things would be quiet. The pattern would repeat itself. It was just so extreme that it was tiring but not emotionally draining. You had no real involvement with me or your mother. We were not able to connect with you. You were no longer Rachel.

It seemed obvious that you might not recover. I had never

seen someone so ill. I was strangely calm although I realised that our lives would change. The thing that did rattle me was your mother. I was definitely shaken that she had not seen anything like this before. We thought that the older generation had seen everything. I felt astonished that it was happening to me. It seemed rather extreme that I would be left with two small children to look after if I lost you. But I didn't really have time to think. I do remember thinking that if we came through it I would have lots of time to reflect in the future. I just tried to focus on the situation.

I don't think you really noticed the psychiatric hospital much. You were strangely pleased to be going there, you like that sort of thing. But I thought the hospital looked really alarming. There were padded doors and secured windows.

The second episode was different. I knew that things would be challenging but that you were not going to die. Dr Fischer said you would get better, and I was impressed by him. He tried to get his mitts on me at one point which I thought was going it a bit. You began to be better for a period each day, though only a very brief period at first. You started reading poetry. You began to express yourself. You were good at expressing yourself. You could be quite theatrical. You would talk about how ill you were and then you would be really ill again and in enormous pain and you would stop talking. Then you would be knocked out by the drugs. This was a much more emotionally involving stage.

On both occasions we worried that you were a suicide risk, and this was a real concern for the doctors. You kept making references to wanting to die, which I found unhelpful. I thought you would be sufficiently incompetent not to manage it. Still, it was definitely better not to leave anything lying around. Then there was a later period when you decided you did not want to die after all and became quite affectionate. This was especially true in the evenings when you would be at your best. The next morning you would be ill again.

I did wonder about the circumstances of our lives and how we came to be in this situation. We had had a tough couple of years. We worked long hours. You worked very long hours. You often worked late at the office and then worked when you came home and then worked at the weekend. We had two children who hardly saw us in the week. We had a nanny who worked long hours. I stood for Parliament. We were really stretched. Maybe it was the children but maybe not, it happened some time after childbirth and then only on the second and fourth. Maybe it was nothing to do with the children.

Maybe the stress of it all, what you call the stressed sex, tipped you over the edge but even then you still wanted to go back to work! The arrival of our third child finally stopped you working. You then moved from being a working mother to a non-working mother and BANG you got sick as a non-working mother. So we tried that and it didn't work too well either.

This is the story of how we muddled through together. We tried to combine a career at Goldman Sachs with a career at *The Times*. We tried working mother. We tried stay-at-home mother. We tried the choices. We found that there is no road map, no safe harbour, no safe roles. But we also found extraordinary joy, extraordinary friendships and the blessing of children.

When you were first ill we had your family doctor visit. He recalled a lovely memory of you as a child. You cried and cried after *Tarka the Otter*. I think we all cried. But you cried all night and you were still crying next day and your mother was so concerned that she took you off to see the doctor. So maybe you were always pretty sensitive. But nothing could have prepared us for the real thing when we tried to do it all.

Still, I wouldn't have it any other way and it's nice to have you back.

December 2013

APPENDICES

More information about strategies I used other than poetry and prayer, and how I got the most out of them.

Exercise

Having worked on my mental health, I knew I also had to improve my physical health through diet and exercise. I was aware that the two are indissolubly linked.

The first big physical step was literally that: to take exercise. I'd love not to bother keeping fit, but I now recognise that I can't afford not to.

Exercising can be a challenge to someone with depression and during the acute phase, when you are very ill, it is laughable to suggest that going for a run might help. As you recover, though, it gets easier. My answer has been to try to find whatever makes it at once more palatable and more possible.

Everyone's body chemistry is different: one friend who suffers from depression has found that if her heart pumps hard for forty minutes a day with a vigorous jog, her anxiety is kept at bay. Another can only cope with the day ahead thanks to a leisurely walk in the park first thing in the morning, when she renews an otherwise weary spirit.

For me, teaming up with others helps. So does getting outside. Being outdoors exposes you to natural daylight, the lack of which can cause the depressive condition Seasonal Affective Disorder. There is now proof that outdoor activity provides more of a boost than going to the gym. Light triggers messages to the hypothalamus, which controls sleep, sex drive, appetite and mood. More natural light equals a better mood. It was a bad day for me when the children started taking the bus to school and I had to build in another walk to compensate.

I already knew how much I liked being in the countryside. I am soothed by the connection to something bigger and grander than myself. My head tingles with clarity after a proper four-hour walk in the Lake District; at these times I can't believe I could ever feel depressed. Jung believed our neuroses are far worse when we are removed from nature.

But mostly I live in the city and there are no such grand walks on offer. There are parks, though, and going with a friend can compensate. One friend has become my unofficial outdoor counsellor. She is also a worrier. We live near to one another and walk fast round our local park when we can, taking turns to talk about our concerns. One psychiatrist friend does the same with his patients. This is a practice with an impeccable pedigree: Freud conducted a 'walking analysis' of Max Eitingon on their regular forays round the Ringstrasse Park in Vienna.

I also took up Pilates, an exercise system of stretches similar to yoga. The essence of Pilates is core stability allied to body awareness. There are eight basic principles: relaxation, concentration, coordination, being centred, alignment, breathing, stamina and flowing movements. When I was recovering, committing to a regular class seemed a huge step. But it gave my day its first hint of structure and provided company.

Pilates is literally grounding because it involves doing exercises lying flat on a mat. The requirement for total concentration calms and declutters the mind, while the focus on breathing rhythmically allows the mind to calm itself by paying attention to the rhythm of the breath and little else. Physical relaxation brings mental relaxation.

But I still have a need for that endorphin high of something more intensive than Pilates or walking. The answer for me is dancing. I set up a class with like-minded friends. Once again, being part of a group was helpful. We like dancing to tracks with a survival theme: Diana Ross's 'I Will Survive' and Elton John's 'I'm Still Standing' are particular favourites.

Activity leads to equilibrium. As you might imagine, 71 per cent of people suffering from depression reported a lifting of their mood after a walk through a park or the countryside, 22 per cent felt worse after a stroll through an indoor shopping centre. According to the mental health charity Mind, three to six weeks of walking therapy are needed before levels of depression lift, and three bursts of walking for ten minutes is the minimum recommended to increase happiness.

Successive research papers show that exercise can be as effective as some drugs in the treatment of mild to moderate depression. One in five GPs now prescribe exercise to treat depression as an alternative to drugs, a survey from the Mental Health Foundation (www.mentalhealth.org.uk) found.

There are around 1,300 exercise referral schemes in Britain, whereby after assessment patients are given discounted access to swimming pools, gym sessions, yoga or dance classes. As the Mental Health Foundation's chief executive says, exercise is just one approach to a complicated illness, but typically we over-think and under-exercise.

'The purging process that comes from exercise is perfect,' says Philip Hodson, a fellow of the British Association of Counselling and Psychotherapy (www.bacp.org.uk). 'The muscles feel rested and the body floods with relaxing hormones.'

Diet

I never considered myself a bad eater. It wasn't as though I ate poorly before I became ill. At the height of the illness, I couldn't eat at all but as I recovered, instinctively I felt I could no longer take food for granted. If food is fuel, depressives need the nutritional pump to deliver premium-grade help.

This was an area I knew little about and much of the evidence seems contradictory. Alice Mackintosh, a nutritionist who works at The Food Doctor Clinic, kindly shared her expertise and gave me the following advice. Naturally it would be best to take independent professional advice as appropriate.

There are two main strategies. The first is to try generally to eat healthily, which must underpin any approach to treating illness. The second is to adopt a more rigorous overhaul of one's diet, targeting depression in particular, including taking supplements. I found that, for me, the best approach was the first.

Neither strategy was something I could even have thought about when very ill. It is nonsense to tell someone suffering from acute depression to choose the fruit, vegetables and fish that might actually help them to feel better. When you're that ill you are in no position to decide what you eat, let alone to seek out the right shops to buy the right ingredients. You are no different to someone suffering any other serious illness who struggles to eat anything at all; your best hope is to be fed soups, smoothies or soft foods that can be eaten easily.

Even as you get better, it is still hard to change your diet if you are suffering from depression. There seem to be few enough pleasures in life when you are feeling low. Our emotional brains can associate eating sweet food with reward, reminding us of being comforted as a child. If eating a chocolate biscuit cheers you up, finding a healthier substitute when life is bleak is going to be difficult. Anxiety can affect digestion, too. Our stomachs are often referred to as our second brain. When I was especially nervous, I found it hard to digest anything solid, just as I had when I was first ill.

I also needed to find a diet that fitted into a busy family life. I knew I wouldn't have the time to prepare any special dishes just for me.

So these are the general principles that I adopted. The changes were small, but they did make a difference. What follows is not the kind of detailed advice you need if you wish to maximise the chances of beating depression through diet; there are excellent guidelines on how to do this in far more comprehensive books than mine.*

My approach was to try to eat healthily, but I didn't take any extra supplements, apart from fish oil. I switched to a Mediterranean-style diet. Studies suggest that our brains are

* One of the best guides to diet is included in *Beating Stress, Anxiety and Depression: Groundbreaking Ways to Help You Feel Better* by Professor Jane Plant and Janet Stephenson (Piatkus, 2008).

developed for a diet many of us no longer eat, but which sustained us for about 99 per cent of human history and 30 million years. The Mediterranean-style diet balances healthy sources of protein with complex carbohydrates. In practice, this means lots of pulses, fruits, fish, nuts, cereals and olive oil. Sweetened desserts, fried foods, processed meats, refined grains and high-fat dairy products are to be avoided.

This helps in two ways. The nutritional needs of your brain cells are satisfied by the antioxidants, vitamins, minerals, enzymes and phytochemicals that a Mediterranean-style diet provides. Secondly, this diet helps increase the amount of tryptophan in your system, the molecule from which serotonin, the brain's chemical messenger, is synthesised. Serotonin helps improve your mood.

I gave up Diet Coke. The chemical sweetener aspartame has the opposite effect of the Mediterranean-style diet. Aspartame is found in diet drinks and used to sweeten everything from yoghurt to processed foods. It has been linked with feeling anxious, jittery and hyperactive.

I cut out alcohol. It can appear to help with anxiety in the short term by raising the levels of certain neurotransmitters in the brain (though the research is inconclusive). On a day-to-day basis, we need those chemical messengers to be busy sending messages to each other saying 'I feel happy' from brain cell to brain cell. But after drinking, these neurotransmitters are broken down and excreted from the body, which may make people feel low afterwards. It is especially dangerous for those like me who feel most anxious in the mornings, since hangovers create a cycle of waking up feeling even more nervous and ill. I hardly drank before and certainly had not done so when ill; now I have stopped altogether.

I increased my iron intake. Chemical messages in the brain and their receptors can also be affected by low iron levels. It's worth getting tested by your GP to see if you are anaemic: it turned out that I was. Anaemia has many of the same symptoms as depression, notably a sapping tiredness that quickly leads to feeling low. The lack of iron means inadequate blood supply to the brain, as well as all the other organs, which in turn decreases those chemical messages and changes in their receptors.

I reviewed the kinds of fats I was consuming. There is strong evidence linking depression with good and bad fats. Fat is essential to the brain, which is itself 60 per cent fat. We want our brains to be made up of the good, unsaturated fats known as omega-6 and omega-3 essential fatty acids, rather than animal-based fats. We also need the correct ratio of omega-6 to omega-3 oils: most of us eat too little of the omega-3s.

I found the easiest way to put my research into practice was to make lists of what to eat more of and what to avoid, meal by meal. At breakfast, this translates into eating sugar-free muesli with berries, porridge or wholegrain or sourdough toast spread with peanut butter, oatcakes with goat's cheese, eggs or other protein. Breakfasting well, combining protein and complex carbohydrates, has proved the best way for me to balance my brain chemistry for the rest of the day.

At lunch, protein-rich food such as chicken, turkey, fish or pulses with vegetables and salad are good. I avoid sandwiches, instead sprinkling nuts and sesame seeds on to salads to better combat anxiety.

In the afternoons, I've found the best snacks are fruit and

nuts, Brazil nuts in particular. If you can't resist chocolate (and I can't), at least make sure it is dark chocolate. It's never worth going hungry, as the brain needs that steady supply of nutrients to keep your mood on an even keel.

At supper, I find that a meal rich in carbohydrates with the addition of some protein helps me to sleep better and improves my mood. Protein is important to help balance blood sugar before bed. Wholegrain pasta with a tomato and prawn sauce, a stir-fry with brown rice and chicken, or a baked or sweet potato with some cheese, even porridge sprinkled with nuts, are all good choices. And I try to drink plenty of water, as I had already learnt its beneficial effects.

I found the easiest approach was to adapt slowly, rather than to enforce wholesale change overnight. I might now ask for a pizza without the mozzarella and add extra olives, capers, mushrooms, peppers and aubergines. I may have a cooked breakfast, but will have tomatoes alongside the bacon. I haven't abandoned salad dressings, but I do use different oils: wheat-germ or flax, sesame or sunflower oil, as well as the more usual olive oil. I add almonds, pecans, cashews, walnuts and pine nuts to salads. I might have an omelette but I will add vegetables on the side.

Even if you know what you should eat, it is still hard to break old habits. It's a case of mind over platter. It's not what you are eating, but what's eating you. For me, and I suspect it is the same for most people, our attitude to food is as much about emotion as it is about satisfying hunger.

All the therapeutic techniques I had learnt were as relevant to the dinner table as any other aspect of life. CBT helped. Instead of allowing a rush of emotion to drive me towards comfort food, I tried to stop and judge instead what my body, or more particularly my brain, needed. It deserved better. It might be as simple as getting a boost from somewhere else rather than from a pudding.

I was interested to read about the experience of the tennis player Monica Seles, who battled with binge-eating for ten years but was cured when she began to focus on food properly for the first time. 'Every time I sat down to a meal, I could make a decision,' Seles writes. 'Was I going to treat myself with love and respect, or was I going to sabotage my own happiness and health for a short-term rush. The decision was an easy one: I chose nourishment over destruction every time. Eating wholesome food left me satisfied much more quickly than mounds of processed fake food ever did.'

The other psychological shift is to move from feeling deprived to feeling you are gaining something extra. It is not about suppressing all pleasure in food. I tried not to focus on what I couldn't eat but on all the delicious dishes I could enjoy: what I could add rather than what I had to take away (literally).

Seles writes of how important it was for her not to feel she was on a 'diet'. As she rightly says, that implies there is a danger you could fail to keep to your diet. And nothing is more tempting than something that is forbidden.

Once you start to eat well, the process gets easier. You begin to feel better. By taking charge of your life, you enter a virtuous circle of looking after yourself. One of the most terrifying feelings about being depressed is the utter lack of control; you feel like a piece of flotsam, blown by icy winds to terrifying places.

Gradually I became more attuned to the connections between mood and food. The science was there to be experienced if I stopped to think about it; the sugar-rush I felt after those refined carbohydrates and the crash in mood that followed; the steady and calming effect of an oatcake mid-morning; how much more effective my day would be if I ate a good breakfast; how much better I would sleep after a bowl of porridge at night.

As I found I was able to achieve more, I realised I couldn't afford not to eat well. I had commitments I wouldn't be able to fulfil if I stopped being properly nourished.

Supplements

Although new research is being published in this area all the time, the doctors I consulted were reluctant to endorse taking supplements as a way to help reduce depression. Nonetheless, I have included this section as I personally found it empowering to follow the research and to try supplements to see if they helped me. It was something I could do without a prescription. Once again I was lucky enough to be able to draw advice from Alice Mackintosh, nutritionist at The Food Doctor Clinic, and once again the ideal would be to get independent professional advice.

The latest research suggests that those susceptible to depression may be low in vitamin D, explaining the tendency of those in northern climes to be more likely to suffer depression than those in sunnier parts of the world.

Many depressives have been found to be low in vitamin B, specifically vitamin B1 (thiamine), B3 (niacin), B6 (pyridoxine) and B12, as well as folic acid. Vitamin B1 is essential for the metabolism of glucose, the brain's main food. The best natural sources of folic acid include green leafy vegetables, beetroot, pulses, mushrooms, nuts and whole grains. Tuna and lentils are good sources of B1; eggs, pulses, wholegrain cereals such as brown rice, quinoa, barley and oats, nuts, meat and fish are good sources of B3; wholegrain cereals, leafy green vegetables, pulses, fruit, eggs, meat and fish are also good sources of B6.

Vitamin E is the major fat-soluble antioxidant in the body, and depression has been shown to be accompanied by low levels of vitamin E in the blood. It is particularly important in maintaining the brain's fats in a healthy state, and can be found in nuts, seeds, wholegrain unrefined cereals, plant oils and leafy green vegetables.

If you take only one supplement, the single most important one to take is omega-3, or essential fatty acids (EFAs). Psychiatrists report that levels of serotonin increase as more omega-3s are introduced into the diet. This is an area of really conclusive scientific research; moreover, EFAs have no side effects. Professor Basant Puri of the Imaging Sciences Department at Hammersmith Hospital has produced evidence about the 'fat profile' of an individual's diet being crucial to mental health; studies in Israel show improvements in patients with mental health problems within two weeks of their taking fish oil high in EFAs; in another study at Sheffield University large doses of omega-3s were given to seventy depressed patients who had failed to respond to Prozac. After twelve weeks, 60 per cent of the patients showed a marked improvement, compared with 25 per cent of the control group.

Good sources of EFAs are wheatgerm, walnuts, flax, hemp oil, and oily fish. But beware: do not stuff yourself with oily fish. It can contain high levels of pollutants, which badly affect brain function. Hence the advice from the Food and Drug Administration in the USA and the Food Standards Agency in the UK is to limit fish to two portions a week, of which only one should be oily fish. Fish obtain their omega-3 fatty acids from the marine algae and plankton they feed on: one option is to cut out the fish altogether and buy ultra-pure fish oils, which have been processed to remove pollutants.

Getting help

The most obvious first step is to go to your GP for a correct diagnosis of your low mood. You may be suffering from depression, but the cause of your symptoms could be some other ailment, such as a thyroid problem or anaemia.

If you are diagnosed with depression, a GP may refer you to a psychiatrist or help you find a therapist. The government is in the process of regulating counselling and psychotherapy, and aims to create a statutory register of all therapists. Until this process is completed, referral by your GP or a personal recommendation are the best ways to find a therapist.

I would have loved to make Dr Fischer my therapist. However, in general, psychiatrists are doctors specialising in mood disorders and mental health, who tend not to focus on the day-to-day managing of the illness. Essentially, psychiatrists are experts in drugs and believe they can be used effectively to manage most mental health conditions, sometimes in combination with therapy. While some psychiatrists will provide weekly sessions of therapy and advice, many will not be available for regular appointments in the same way as a therapist. Furthermore, the help offered by therapists is of a different nature; some studies suggest patients may benefit from a separation between the prescribing of drugs and the receiving of therapy.

Given the depressive episodes I had suffered and the degree of help I sought, psychotherapy was a better option to manage the illness long-term. As I recount in my text, finding a good therapist is incredibly hard. A therapist needs to be more than the sum of their training. They must be intuitive on a profound level, and intuition is a gift and cannot be taught.

The practical first steps to finding a therapist are easy enough: there are several professional bodies for counselling and psychotherapy in the UK, including the BACP, UKCP and BABCP, which can provide lists of counsellors in your area (see below for details). The BABCP specialises in CBT therapists.*

But I wasn't comfortable signing up to a stranger without a personal recommendation. A straw poll of my friends revealed that they had found their therapists through friends, relations or sometimes their GPs. Most of them hadn't bothered to check their therapist was accredited. Instead, they judged their efficacy by finding out how long they had been practising and how many clients they had. This unscientific method did not always have good results. One friend told me of a therapist who employed family members to act as clients, to give the impression of a busy practice. But the therapist who can fit you in at short notice is not necessarily short of patients. They may have a slot if, for instance, a client of many years' standing has just ended therapy.

* An excellent new website, welldoing.org, helps match up patients with therapists by allowing therapists to set out their particular ways of practicing on the site. The website has recently been launched by Louise Chunn, former editor of *Psychologies Magazine*.

It's also worth remembering that even if a counsellor comes recommended, there is no substitute for judging by your experience during an initial assessment. An approach that suits a friend may not suit you. In some ways, a personal recommendation can be a disadvantage: you may feel obliged to sign up to a therapist out of social pressure. It is important to bear in mind that you may have to try a couple of therapists before you find one that suits you; so it proved for me.

The timing of when you start therapy can also have an impact on how easy it is to find the right person to work with. I embarked on the process when I was well enough to do so but I might have been better off if I had seen a therapist sooner, when I was more unwell. Had I done so, though, I would have needed help. You too may not be well enough to engage in multiple interviews or to hunt for different candidates. More than likely, you will have to rely on friends or relatives to help you. Someone in better health than you may have to take the step of interviewing a therapist on your behalf and judging whether they would suit. Realistically, this may take the form of a telephone interview. My rule of thumb is to try to find someone who has treated someone whose experience of depression was similar to yours, and for whom the therapy has worked. The most important thing is just to start. Almost any therapist is better than none (though this assumes that you are robust enough to walk away if someone is hindering rather than helping, and it may take several months to work this out).

The question then is how to establish a good relationship with this new person in your life. First, treat your therapist as an equal. Don't expect a teacher-pupil dynamic: therapy is about two people working together.

You are likely to have to pay for therapy, especially if you wish to start immediately, or if you want flexible time slots. Despite the obvious need for free counselling, NHS waiting lists can often be longer than six months and counselling resources are often the first victims of cutbacks. It's estimated that the National Health Service needs another 10,000 therapists to meet demand. In recognition of this, the government announced in March 2008 that it was going to spend nearly £200 million on training therapists for the NHS over the next three years, but progress is still slow and funding unforthcoming.

The two main counselling organisations are the British Association of Counselling and Psychotherapy (BACP), www.bacp.co.uk, and the United Kingdom Council for Psychotherapy (UKCP), www.ukcp.org.uk. Both organisations will send you a list of therapists in your area with details of the therapeutic approach they adopt. They also provide accreditation for private therapists. The BACP has details of members on its website for the public to access free of charge.

Some employers, colleges and schools provide counselling, and some counsellors advertise in magazines and newspapers. Your local council social services department, Citizen Advice Bureaux and the Yellow Pages may have details of counsellors in your area.

Fees for private therapists vary: between £40 and £80 per session of approximately fifty minutes, higher for therapists who work near Harley Street, the centre of private medicine in London. (The last ten minutes of the hour are normally used by the therapist to take notes on the session before the next client, who will arrive for their appointment on the hour.)

Some therapists take on a limited number of low-fee

patients or offer a sliding scale depending on your ability to pay. Some voluntary organisations provide free counselling.

How long you should see a counsellor for and how much you should pay will depend on you, the counsellor and the nature of your illness, according to BACP. A spokesman says, 'Often half a dozen sessions will resolve the problem; sometimes you may see a counsellor for several months.'

The Hoffman Process (www.hoffmaninstitute.co.uk) is an eight-day residential course that explores how early experiences may still be controlling your adult life. You are given a name that encapsulates your issues: mine was 'Good Girl'. I would thoroughly recommend the course; but it would be inappropriate to reveal more details about how it works, as much of its effectiveness depends on an element of surprise.

Mental health charities

Given the pressures on the National Health Service and the growth of mental health problems, the services that charities provide for those who suffer poor mental health are crucial. This book has been written in aid of two charities that do outstanding work in this field and are close to my heart: SANE and United Response.

SANE was established in 1986 to improve the quality of life for people affected by mental illness, following the overwhelming public response to a series of articles published in *The Times* entitled 'The Forgotten Illness'. As a former *Times* journalist, I have felt particularly drawn to trying to support SANE's work. Written by the charity's founder and chief executive, Marjorie Wallace CBE, the articles exposed the neglect of people suffering from mental illness and the poverty of services and information available for individuals and families. SANE's vision is of a society where mental illness is free from stigma, and where each individual can receive the care and attention they require at any stage of their life.

SANE has been at the forefront of mental-health innovation for over twenty-five years. Examples include its Helpline service and Black Dog campaign, which aims to reduce the stigma that still surrounds mental illness. SANE provides confidential help and expert information on all aspects of mental health. Anyone can receive emotional support, free of charge, at any time of the day or night, 365 days a year. SANE employs an expert team of mental-health professionals who train and manage a skilled volunteer force of 150 people. SANE Services represents the combined activity of these people and offers the following specialist resources: SANEline (telephone helpline); SANEmail (email advice) and askTheSite (email advice for young people); Support Forum (peer-to-peer support via SANE's website, moderated by their professional team); Caller Care (call-back service for people in crisis and/or with long-term needs); and Textcare (personalised therapeutic text messages).

SANE also directly supports fundamental neuroscience research alongside studies into treatments and therapies. The charity shares its Prince of Wales International Centre for SANE Research with the Oxford Mindfulness Centre, which provides Mindfulness-based cognitive therapy training, integrating brain research with meditation techniques.

For more information, please visit the SANE website: www.sane.org.uk.

The second charity of which I am a passionate supporter is United Response. Founded in 1973, the charity began by supporting disabled adults who had spent much of their lives in dehumanising long-term institutions, as a result of which many of them struggled with mental-health difficulties such as depression. Building on this expertise, United Response now employs over 3,000 staff and supports around 2,000 people at any one time. Among those 2,000 are hundreds of people with mental-health needs, including people with depression and long-term conditions such as schizophrenia and psychosis. The organisation's emphasis is on helping people to manage their mental health, recover where possible and live more independently in the future.

Partnership is the key to success. This means working closely with other agencies such as local authorities, community nurses and psychiatrists, so that nobody feels lost in a system where communication has broken down. Even more importantly, it means creating services in close collaboration with the person receiving them. Some people may need help on hand twenty-four hours a day; others may only need a little support from time to time; and others' needs will fluctuate. The support people receive therefore needs to be responsive. It includes outreach programmes, drop-in centres, community services or support in the home as well as creative workshops. For more information, please visit the United Response website: www.unitedresponse.org.uk.

Other useful places to find help include Mind, which offers a helpline, drop-in centres and supported housing and counselling: www.mind.co.uk; and Rethink, which offers support and advice for those affected by mental illness: www.rethink. org.

Rachel Kelly was a journalist for many years, and spent ten years on *The Times*, where she was variously a reporter, feature writer and columnist, writing the paper's 'Alternatively Speaking' health column. Her interest in health and therapy led to her completing the first year of training as a counsellor. Her long-standing passion for poetry led to her becoming the co-founder of the iF poetry app (2011) and co-editor of *iF: A Treasury of Poem for Almost Every Possibility* (Canongate, 2012).

Rachel lives in London with her husband, Sebastian, and their five children.

NOTE

Some names have been changed.

Permission Acknowledgements

With thanks to the copyright holders for their kind permission to use the following poems and copyright material:

'The Sickness unto Death' by Anne Sexton
'i thank You God' by e.e. cummings
'Apple Blossom' by Louis MacNeice
'You'll Never Walk Alone' by Oscar Hammerstein
'The Guest House' by Jalal al-Din Rumi
'Everyone Sang' by Siegfried Sassoon
'Underneath an Abject Willow' by W.H. Auden
'The Seed-Shop' by Muriel Stuart
'Résumé' by Dorothy Parker
'The Bright Field' by R.S. Thomas
'A Poem Just For Me' by Roger McGough
'Musée des Beaux Arts' by W.H. Auden
'Cure Me With Quietness' by Ruth Pitter
'Happiness' by Raymond Carver
'A Return to Love' by Marianne Williamson
'Not Waving but Drowning' by Stevie Smith
'Love After Love' by Derek Walcott
'Everything is Going to Be All Right' Derek Mahon

List of Poems and Extracts

List of Poems and Extracts

yellow kite

books to help you live a good life

Join the conversation and tell us how you live a #goodlife

@yellowkitebooks

YellowKiteBooks

Yellow Kite Books

YellowKiteBooks